CONTROL SHIFT

HOW TECHNOLOGY AFFECTS YOU AND YOUR RIGHTS

by

David Meyer

For Paul

INTRODUCTION

True balance has always been hard to find, particularly in times of great upheaval. When change brings new opportunities, there's usually one group of people that gets to seize them first. That's how they gain advantages over others, upsetting the balance of power. Where equilibrium exists, it's after the storm, when things have settled down.

We are currently in the middle of a storm that shows no signs of abating. The internet is changing so many things, and at such speed, that it's difficult to figure out what's happening, let alone what the implications are. No-one can divine the future – reality is far too chaotic for that – but some have a better idea than others as to how this tumult might give them the edge they desire. And so, we see control shifting all around us. The traditionally powerful are losing their grip, while others are finding new sources of power over us.

Where we once got our information through a limited number of traditional media outlets, we're now influenced by a flood of information from a variety of good and dubious sources, funnelled through services that know us in minute detail and try to shape our realities accordingly. These online platforms use their detailed knowledge to sell us things, but the ways in which we expose ourselves online have also provided a gift to governments and spies, making the internet an ideal tool for tyrants and troublemakers. Our attempts to maintain control over our digital selves are undermined by a mix of slack regulation and poor security, made even weaker by those claiming to protect us. In trying to reconcile law and order with the realities of a borderless internet, and freedom from abuse with freedom of expression, our lawmakers are devising half-baked rules that are far more heavy-handed than they realise. Companies are gaining extreme power over us as consumers by eroding our property rights and devouring whole markets. Everything is in flux, and power is concentrating at a dangerous pace.

For better and for worse, we can't turn back the clock. However, we still have the opportunity to take control of what's happening, through a series of actions that range from the political to the personal. Technologically and as societies, we're at an inflection point. A generation has now grown up with the internet and is intimately familiar with its potential and pitfalls, but connectivity has not yet been fully embedded into our environments – we're mostly used to computers and smartphones by now, but it's still a relative novelty to have internet-connected sensors built into everyday items, our homes and our streets. Meanwhile, we're conceptually familiar with the algorithms that make our increasingly automated world tick, but we still have control over them in a way that we soon won't.

Our future needn't be scary, but if we want it to be fair and free – if we want to retain the rights and personal power that we enjoy as citizens in democratic societies – then we need to take action now. We can tell our technologists what we want to see and what we won't tolerate. We can demand that our politicians grapple with the implications of what's happening and what's around the corner, and vote out those who don't offer us the control we deserve. If we're going to ensure that power doesn't end up in the wrong hands, to a degree that seems difficult to contemplate today, then we need to think about these issues and take action, and we need to do it now.

It's not too late for us to make sure that our technology works for rather than against us. But first, we must figure out how we got here. And to do that, there's no better place to start than with the subject at the core of this chaos: information, and how we get it.

CHAPTER 1: SORTING THROUGH THE NOISE

In 1996, the venerable *New York Times* launched its website with the hope that it would become "a primary information provider in the computer age". The site was designed to be more-or-less a straight digital version of the *Times*' paper product: it included most of the articles from the printed version, along with classified advertising and an interactive crossword puzzle. Access was free, as the *Times* intended to make its money from online advertising. "We see our role on the Web as being similar to our traditional print role – to act as a thoughtful, unbiased filter and to provide our customers with information they need and can trust," said *Times* publisher Arthur Sulzberger Jr. at the time.[1]

But times changed for the *Times*, as for everyone else in the media industry. And then they changed again. Nine years after its launch, the *Times* started trying to charge readers for accessing the articles of its most popular opinion writers. The experiment lasted two years before the newspaper went all-free again in 2007 – there weren't enough paying customers to outweigh the advertising revenue that would be gained by making the articles free to access.[2] "Readers increasingly find news through search, as well as through social networks, blogs and other online sources. In light of this shift, we believe offering unfettered access to *New York Times* reporting and analysis best serves the interest of our readers, our brand and the long-term vitality of our journalism," the paper admitted in a letter to its readers.[3] Four years later, the *Times* again started charging people for access, giving readers only a few free articles each month.[4] Over those preceding four years, advertising revenues at The New York Times Company – publisher of

---

[1] http://www.nytimes.com/1996/01/22/business/the-new-york-times-introduces-a-web-site.html
[2] http://www.reuters.com/article/us-newyorktimes-idUSWEN101120070918
[3] http://www.nytimes.com/ref/membercenter/lettertoreaders.html
[4] http://www.nytimes.com/2011/03/21/business/media/21times.html

one of the three biggest American papers and one of the best-known outlets in the world – had fallen by 40 percent.

The publisher's strategic swerving was entirely characteristic of the wider journalistic industry. The field has been turned upside-down by the internet. The media is far from alone in that respect, but journalism's turmoil has a particularly profound impact on us all. The way in which we get our information is changing, and with that change comes a massive shift in power. And to understand how the balance of online power is tilting these days, we must first focus on the fuel of that change: our valuable attention.

The mechanisms of power can be coercive, as with law enforcement and brute force, but they can also be discursive. We can change people's minds by convincing them that we are right, or by framing reality in the way that suits us. Philosophers, politicians, propagandists and salespeople have always understood that communication is a powerful tool. If you can get someone listening to what you have to say, you have the opportunity to influence what they think and do. And the internet, to which many of us are constantly connected throughout the day, is the most effective conduit for this power that we've ever seen. Many processes and developments led us to this point. Speech, paper, the printed word, phone and fax, radio and television, the roads and bridges that allowed people to get to places that were previously inaccessible, the railways that got them there faster, and the planes that made the global village a reality – all these things made communication progressively more powerful and more efficient. Now we have a growing internet infrastructure that allows us to communicate with one another as pairs or groups or overlapping, transient communities.

What's particularly groundbreaking about this connectedness is the fact that we can, as ordinary individuals, easily reach a mass audience. First came simple message boards, where we could insert our views and knowledge into discussions involving people from around the world. Then came the web, along with the ability to write personal or professional blogs that anyone, anywhere could read. Then came social networking. Our communication abilities have now developed to the point where we can express a thought through a service like Twitter and

4

have it resonate across the world in seconds, reaching people who've never heard of us, but to whom we are connected through chains of unlikely links. That means, in theory, that more people can get their messages through to us.

However, there's only so much we can take in. Our time is a limited resource, and we're developing new ways to choose how to spend it. Gone are the days where most people would be watching or reading the same news and entertainment. Now we have a seemingly infinite list of information sources on tap – too many, indeed, to easily organise or prioritise. Those who help us sort through the noise are the ones gathering unprecedented amounts of power over us. And it's a kind of power that other players are able to hijack.

Opening Up The Field

In a democracy, the media is traditionally supposed to keep an eye on governments and other powerful people and organisations, by exposing what they do and telling citizens about what they're trying to achieve. Journalists have long been seen (by some) as an unofficial part of a nation's governance. Writing in the 1830s, Thomas Carlyle quoted the politician Edmund Burke as saying there were three "estates" in the British Parliament: a reference to the clergy, the aristocracy and commoners. "But, in the Reporters' Gallery yonder, there sat a Fourth Estate more important far than they all," wrote Carlyle.[5] "Whoever can speak, speaking now to the whole nation, becomes a power, a branch of government, with inalienable weight in law-making, in all acts of authority."

However, for all their power, journalists have never really been able to just tell people what they think they ought to hear. The media must also entertain in order to first get the public's attention. That makes the job a constant balancing act – trying to keep people usefully informed while also showing them what they want to see. At least, that's the job of a responsible media that's trying to fulfil its civic function. It would

---

[5] https://www.gutenberg.org/files/20585/20585-h/20585-h.htm

be naïve to suggest the media is always sober and fair-minded, but the idea of this function has always been the driving force for "serious" newspapers, broadcast outlets and websites. Many journalists are in the game because it *matters*. To be sure, it's an insecure and demanding business that the public often treats with contempt, so it is not entered into lightly. In that sense, journalism is rather like politics, another profession where instruction and prioritisation must usually be balanced with an element of telling people what they want to hear. Both jobs give power to those who hold them: a politician gets to draw up and promote policies that shape lives; a journalist gets to describe reality and, in that sense, shape it. Journalists prioritise all the time and, by covering one thing rather than another or emphasising the views of some sources over those of others, they have traditionally moulded their readers and listeners' ideas of what is important.

However, this formula is in flux. Journalists are at their most influential when they can rely on readers, viewers or listeners regularly returning for more. But that power is waning as the public gets a greater choice of news outlets and starts to consume news in different ways. Relatively few people access articles on a news website by visiting the site's homepage – the modern equivalent of picking up the day's paper and starting on the front page. Instead, most find their stories through search engines and social media, where every media outlet is competing against everything else that's out there.

Once upon a time, the range of options available to a news consumer was limited by production and distribution costs. You'd usually only read a publication if it was on the rack at your local newsagent, or if it was delivered to your door. Either way, someone would have also had to stump up a significant amount of money to buy or hire printing presses, and to have the product physically delivered to homes and shops. Before the days of cable TV, there weren't many broadcast channels, either. The number of radio stations was limited to the number that could be crammed into the airwaves without interference problems, and the production of high-quality broadcast video was prohibitively expensive for all but a few. Thanks to the internet, distribution is now much less of a challenge, to the extent that pretty much anyone can get their views out there in the form of text, video, audio or a mix of these different media, using consumer-grade laptops and smartphones. Regional publications can reach people around the world and, conversely, people can consume news written anywhere in the world, as long as they can understand the language in which it is written.

However, production and distribution problems have not been entirely solved by the possibilities of online publication. Particularly where video and high-quality graphics are concerned, and where there a lot of readers and viewers are trying access the same material, it still costs a fair amount of money to host a publication on a web server and deliver it reliably through the networks that make up the internet. And, as has always been the case, a serious publication will also need to pay editorial and production staff to generate informed and slick "content" (to use the mercenary language of media executives).

This creates something of a dilemma. The costs of production and distribution have fallen enough to allow many more competitors onto the scene, but that makes it harder for any one publication to get the kind of hold on its audience that was once possible. Meanwhile, significant costs still remain. Together, these factors make it very hard to guarantee the returns that are needed to produce the news in the first place, and to satisfy those who have invested in the publication.

There are essentially three ways to make money as a news publication. You can get people to pay for what they read, you can carry advertising, and you can run side-businesses, such as conferences, that attract custom by being connected with your reputable journalistic brand. By far the most straightforward of these three options is to carry advertising. And indeed, this has been a core part of the news model since the 18th century.[6] Without advertising, newspapers and magazines would have always been more expensive to buy, limiting their distribution and therefore their civic role in democracies. Because most websites don't charge anything to view their output, and because

---

[6] http://adage.com/article/special-report-the-advertising-century/ad-age-advertising-century-timeline/143661/

conferences and the like are costly and hard to scale, advertising remains the central pillar of today's media.

Advertising presents its own challenges, though. Firstly, people tend to mentally block it out. Online advertising does not earn much money for the publisher purely by virtue of being there – to maximise the revenue, lots of people need to actively click on the ads, which takes them through to the advertiser's own website or special offer. That doesn't happen if people aren't really paying heed to the ads. In many cases, publishers and advertisers have tried to overcome this problem by making the ads harder to ignore: they pop out, they dance around, they auto-play sound and video. In short, they are deliberately distracting and almost always annoying. At their worst, they make it impossible to actually see the article or video you're trying to view.

The other big problem with today's online advertising is that it looks back at you. When you see an ad in a newspaper or magazine, you are seeing the same ad as everyone else who bought the same edition. The online equivalent is essentially an empty frame, waiting to be filled with something that is tailored specifically to you. The ad you see is based on what giant but hidden profiling systems know about you – knowledge that they have because they constantly track you. Online ads don't just show you the results of this tracking; they often also do the tracking. Among the pictures and links that make up the ad, there are also little fragments of hidden code that quietly connect to those profiling systems in order to trigger a two-way exchange of information. The code will try to identify who you are by checking your browser for "cookies" – bite-sized chunks of unique code that websites have left in your browser to help build a more detailed picture of you. Once it has identified you, the profiling system will use that description of you to fill the frame with an ad that it thinks is likely to draw your focus. It will also add a new detail to its profile of you: the fact that you were reading that particular page, and are therefore probably interested in its subject material.

Once, advertisers would have placed their ads in certain publications because they knew that these newspapers or magazines were likely to be read by a certain audience – say, reasonably affluent men with an

8

interest in home improvement. This was relatively inefficient, because the ads were still being shown to a lot of people who were unlikely to buy the advertised item. Advertisers were paying to reach every reader, so this inefficiency meant they were wasting a lot of money. Now, advertisers can target their ads much more narrowly, making advertising more cost-efficient for them. As those giant profiling systems also take in information from other sources, from social networks to store loyalty schemes, advertisers linking to those systems can rest assured that they will be addressing very tightly defined groups of people. For example, advertisers can target men of a certain age, living in a certain area, who the profiling system *knows* have already expressed an interest in something like the advertised product. This targeted approach means the advertisers waste less money than before, allowing even businesses with very small budgets to find likely customers.

This is what is meant when people talk about paying for things with your data. You may not be paying money to read an article, or play a game, or use an email or social networking service, but what that page or app learns about you will add detail to those remote profiles. The producers of that article or app then get to make a living by showing you the resulting ads, and advertisers don't waste as much of their budgets addressing the wrong people.

Although there are clear benefits to this way of doing things, a lot of people are uncomfortable with the implications. Firstly, the invasion of privacy is rarely clear on the surface. Secondly, many people couldn't care less whether the ads they're shown are more or less relevant; they're trying to ignore them anyway. Thirdly, it's incredibly difficult to escape this surveillance-based economy. Even if a publication tries to make money by charging people for subscriptions in order to read it – a risky strategy in this era of free-to-access online publications – it's often the case that the publication *still* carries privacy-busting ads.

Advertising isn't a safe bet for the publishers, either. In the old, offline world, it was straightforward for publishers to go to an advertiser and say they had a certain number of regular readers that fit a certain broad profile, and negotiate how much they charge accordingly.

To a certain extent, niche publications can still play this game if they are willing to invest in an ad sales team. For example, a technology publication can still strike a deal with a company like IBM or Samsung to carry those companies' big banner ads. But many if not most of the ads on a typical webpage are "programmatic" – automatically generated – and in this realm, the brokers run the show. They run highly automated bidding processes that determine how much advertisers are willing to pay to fill that ad space, each and every time it's filled. Because there are so many publications out there competing to sell ad space on their sites, and because automated bidding processes always seek out the cheapest space, the competition will usually drive publishers' advertising prices lower.[7] So even if publishers treat advertising as a volume game, trying to pull in as many readers as possible in order to generate as many clicks as possible, they are likely to struggle unless their reader numbers are constantly growing at a high rate. This click-centric approach may be the main model for online publishing today, but it's a losing game.

So who's winning? In 2017, almost two-thirds of the revenues of the US digital ad market is expected to go to two companies: Google and Facebook.[8] The previous year, 99 percent of growth in US digital ad revenues was attributable to the same twosome.[9] Why? These are the firms that are the most successful at attracting our online attention. You may think of Google and Facebook as the suppliers of handy online services, but they really built their fortunes as titans of the advertising world, using those services as bait. In the first quarter of 2017, ads accounted for 87 percent of the total revenues of Google parent Alphabet, and 98 percent of Facebook's total revenues.[10] Neither company acquired its powerful position by accident, and the stories of

---

[7] http://www.ibtimes.com/alphabet-inc-goog-q1-earnings-falling-ad-rates-google-hit-revenue-profits-while-2357770

[8] https://www.emarketer.com/Article/Google-Facebook-Tighten-Grip-on-US-Digital-Ad-Market/1016494

[9] http://www.businessinsider.de/facebook-and-google-dominate-ad-industry-with-a-combined-99-of-growth-2017-4

[10] https://www.wired.com/story/google-facebook-online-ad-kings/

their ascent are tightly bound up with two giant technological waves: the web and the smartphone.

Google and the Web

In the early days of the mass-market web, it seemed that a single "portal" might be able to satisfy a consumer's needs. For a time, the providers of the internet connection itself, such as AOL and the big telecoms firms, tried to grab that role. The idea was that, because you use a particular company to go online, that company would get to hold your hand throughout your online experience, mediating the experience through its own curated menus of sites and services – here's the sports site you need to give you the latest scores, here's our online dating service and here's our messaging service. However, that's not how the web evolved; there was too much choice to make such structured confinement an attractive option. Without the production and distribution constraints of the old media system, why would people settle for the same hand-holding in new media?

After all, the web is perfect for niche interests. All that's needed to produce and consume information is a connection to the internet and a computer with a browser on it. Of course, in the early days of the web, relatively few people had such equipment and connectivity – only 1.3 percent were using the internet in 1996, compared with 48 percent in 2017.[11] But apart from that significant obstacle to true egalitarianism, the network tended towards neutrality, promoting competition and rewarding diversity. The web lets people compile their own experiences, according to their own particular tastes, drawing on many sources. No journalistic outlet can claim to be a "primary information provider", as *The New York Times* once hoped it would become.

It's important to remember just how big a change this was. Before the web appeared in the 1990s, the mass media was a relatively homogenous affair. Sure, some countries had a profusion of amateur

---

[11] http://www.itu.int/en/ITU-D/Statistics/Documents/facts/ICTFactsFigures2017.pdf

channels on cable TV, and people had long been able to publish magazines for niche audiences, but when it came to the best-known channels and publications, certain voices were over-represented – in the West, these were typically white men. If you were looking for alternative perspectives, particularly in less urban areas, you'd have to look hard. This uniform voice was largely down to the media traditionally operating like a club, with new members getting in by virtue of who they know. Nepotism plays a role, with people filling posts with children of friends, or people who went to the same universities, rather than looking outside their circles for fresh blood. Mainstream publications also tend to hew to the ideological centre, where advertisers feel most comfortable spending their money, so radical viewpoints limit how far a writer can progress in their career. And the path towards greater racial, social and ideological diversity in traditional media is long. According to the American Society of News Editors, just 16.6 percent of US journalists in 2017 were from ethnic minorities, compared with 23.1 percent of the wider population.[12] In the UK, where around 13 percent of the population are from ethnic minorities, just 6 percent of journalists in 2016 were non-white.[13] However, the internet provides shortcuts to change.

The internet's diversity, and its appeal to niche interests and subcultures, is not just down to its lack of space or distribution constraints. It's also a result of interactivity. The internet makes it easy for people, who may be scattered across the world but who share common interests, to form virtual communities. Whether they're mushroom enthusiasts or Turkish diaspora Kurds, there's somewhere online where they can get together, no matter where they're physically located.[14] However, first they need to find one another. In the early days of the web this required a widely-used system for organising and searching through all the information that was out there. So, as power

---

[12] http://asne.org/diversity-survey-2017
[13] https://www.theguardian.com/media-network/2016/mar/24/british-journalism-diversity-white-female-male-survey
[14] http://rudaw.net/english/middleeast/26032014

slipped out of the hands of the early portals, it was gathered up and consolidated by the first real titan of the online world.

Google was by no means the first search engine, but over time it became the most successful, for a variety of reasons. Importantly, it provided a clean, minimalist interface with a front page that was free of advertising. The idea was to send people to their destination as quickly as possible, in order to keep them coming back. Internet access was slow in those days and, unlike rival services, which blasted users with ads from the first glance, Google's search page loaded quickly.[15] Google's underlying technology was a system called PageRank, which essentially made a copy of everything on the web in order to figure out which pages had the most other pages linking to them. Because the most-cited pages were the ones that were likely to have the most useful information, Google ranked them higher in its search results. When Google decided to start making money through ads and sponsored results, it did so through a bidding system that let anyone get their results to the top of the list, as long as they could pay. This was good for small businesses trying to develop an online presence, and it was good for Google's users too, because it helped them find useful services, although it did begin to warp the neutrality of the ranking.

Google's explicit mission to "organise the world's information and make it universally accessible and useful" made it a *de facto* portal, but one that did not explicitly try to exert power over its users by limiting what they could access.[16] Indeed, the company didn't bother with producing content itself, instead relying on the fact that people would come to it in search of what everyone else was producing. Its biggest investment, at least in the early days, was in its search algorithm, which made it the best at ranking information and helping people to quickly find what they were looking for. Crucially, Google's search algorithm thrived on feedback: the more people used it, the more it could analyse how they used it, and the better its systems became at serving them. In

---

[15] https://www.amazon.com/Digital-Wars-Google-Microsoft-Internet/dp/0749464135/

[16] https://www.google.com/about/company/

13

doing this, Google was exploiting the potential of "usage data" – information about how people use its service, that ultimately helps it continuously refine and retrain that service. This iterative, constantly analytical approach is a recurring theme in modern, internet-connected technology.

The secret to Google's success did not only lie in its data-derived quality. It also thrived because it was everywhere. Commercial deals made Google the default search engine in browsers, starting with Mozilla's Firefox in 2004. Later on, Google became the default search provider on mobile devices, through agreements with mobile operators and through the roll-out of its Android operating system. People could generally choose to use another search engine if they wanted to, but real power lies in being the option that's already in operation – most people never bother to change the default settings in their programs or on their devices. Eventually, people started searching through the address bars in their browsers, rather than using them to type in web addresses, because tools like autocomplete and autosuggest would get them where they were going more quickly. And Google, whose Chrome browser became the world's most popular in recent years, was again best-placed to take advantage of that phenomenon.[17] Today, according to the market-share-tracking service StatCounter, more than 90 percent of the world's internet users search through Google.[18]

There are other reasons why Google beat rivals such as Yahoo – it had more efficient internal technical operations, for one thing – but the result of its tactical and strategic victories was that it became the go-to gatekeeper for online information.[19] Google would give people an easy route to almost everything they wanted, with the exception of highly illegal content like child pornography, and, thanks to copyright-holders applying a lot of pressure, services that help people "pirate"

---

[17] https://gizmodo.com/google-chrome-is-now-the-most-popular-web-browser-1774266161

[18] http://gs.statcounter.com/search-engine-market-share

[19] https://techcrunch.com/2016/05/22/why-google-beat-yahoo-in-the-war-for-the-internet/

entertainment.[20] The search engine would provide this route to knowledge for free, but it would make a lot of money out of its position. As the conduit for its users' curiosity, Google could see everything they were searching for and track where they were going. This vantage point didn't only help the company improve its own systems; it allowed Google to build up a detailed and highly valuable profile of each user.

Particularly after Google released its Android mobile operating system in 2007 and acquired the DoubleClick online ad network the following year, it gained unprecedented profiling capabilities. People were pouring details of their interests and desires into its homepage and the search bars in their browsers. They were feeding information into Google's systems through the company's phones. Many publishers also included Google's search technology in their own websites, rather than building their own search tech or buying in other, less widely-used services. Again, these "Custom Search" bars dropped Google's cookies into users' browsers, making it easier to track them.

The media's influence diminished as Google's increased. Online publishers became dependent on Google in many ways; some voluntary, some not. For example, no-one held a gun to publishers' heads and told them to hand over their advertising space to Google, but many did. It's a much simpler and cheaper mechanism than running expensive ad-sales departments, particularly if you're a smaller publication, and the ads could well end up being more relevant to the reader. Since publishers get paid when people click on the ads they carry, relevance is useful to them as well as to the advertisers. Unfortunately, by handing over their ad operations, publications were now feeding their readers into Google's big surveillance machine. But if it meant survival in an increasingly cut-throat media environment, then so be it.

---

[20] https://publicpolicy.googleblog.com/2010/12/making-copyright-work-better-online.html

It's hard to overstate just how pervasive Google's tracking has become. When Princeton University researchers Steven Englehardt and Arvind Narayanan studied a million websites in 2016, they found 81,000 third-party trackers – pieces of code, hidden in webpages, that provide tracking information to companies that aren't the website's publisher.[21] Truly pervasive tracking capabilities are concentrated in the hands of a select few companies, though. Of the 81,000 trackers, only 123 were present on more than 1 percent of the sites – and only Google, Facebook and Twitter's trackers were present on more than 10 percent of sites. "All of the top five third parties, as well as 12 of the top 20, are Google-owned sites," the researchers wrote. The sites infested with the most trackers, they noted, were news sites.

So far, so voluntary. But publishers also found themselves unavoidably at the mercy of Google's ever-changing algorithms for ranking search results. Google is so effective as an advertising company because it is everywhere. That's partly down to Google being the default search mechanism most places, but it's also because Google is a good search engine – it excels at serving up the results people are looking for. And Google is a good search engine not only because of the astounding amount of data it holds, but also because it keeps changing its algorithms to stop people from playing the system in order to boost their rankings in the results.

There's a vast industry out there that's dedicated to performing "search engine optimisation" (SEO), which essentially means making one's site as easy-to-find as possible. This can be a perfectly legitimate pursuit, but sometimes "SEO experts" go too far. For example, they might load pages with keywords that aren't actually part of the article, in an attempt to trick Google's algorithms into ranking the page highly on the basis of relevance. Many sites out there also straight-up copy articles from legitimate websites, in order to show lucrative ads next to the text. Google constantly tries to fight these scammy practices with new algorithms that try to figure out whether websites are "high-quality" and genuinely useful, before giving them a good position in the

---

[21] https://webtransparency.cs.princeton.edu/webcensus/

search results.[22] However, these updates to Google's ranking logic can sometimes punish legitimate sites for not meeting various criteria. For example, a Google algorithm update in 2014 lowered the ranking of the *Christian Science Monitor* in a way that cut a third of the news site's traffic. The same update eliminated a whopping three-quarters of *GlobalPost*'s traffic.[23]

As a result, publishers are in thrall to what sometimes feels like Google's whims. After all, if you're not on the first page of results, you're nowhere – "I hate feeling desperate enough to visit the second page of Google results," ran the caption to one memorable instalment of the web comic XKCD.[24] Google keeps its ranking algorithms secret and claims that this is necessary to stop hucksters from cheating the system, but this opacity sometimes makes the all-powerful gatekeeper seem capricious.

On top of that, publishers that want to carry Google's lucrative ads find themselves with certain limitations on what they can publish. For example, in 2014 Google demanded that the UK-based music website *Drowned In Sound* censor some of the album covers that it displayed next to its music reviews (specifically, the covers of albums by Lambchop and Sigur Rós), on the basis that the covers showed naked people. Google told *Drowned In Sound* that it could not display any images containing nudity next to Google ads. The website, which said it earned a fifth of its revenue through Google Ads, had little choice but to do what it was told. "Google said if we didn't comply by Friday they'd pull all of their advertising," *Drowned In Sound* founder Sean Adams told the BBC. "As a small music magazine we can't lose that revenue." [25]

---

[22] http://searchengineland.com/google-panda-is-now-part-of-googles-core-ranking-signals-240069

[23] http://blog.searchmetrics.com/us/2014/05/21/panda-update-4-0-winners-and-losers-google-usa/

[24] https://xkcd.com/1334/

[25] http://www.bbc.co.uk/newsbeat/article/28225712/google-tells-music-website-to-censor-album-covers

In early 2017, the South African news site GroundUp announced it was removing Google Ads from its website, partly because of the low-quality, scam-like nature of many of the ads, but also because of censorship. When the site ran a non-pornographic photo of people protesting an art exhibit while partially clothed, Google warned GroundUp that it had violated the web giant's policies. "So Google accepts get-rich-quick ads featuring famous people without their permission, but will not let us run those adverts on a page with a photograph of nudity, even if it depicts news in the public interest," spluttered editor Nathan Geffen. "The insane hypocrisy and irony of it!"[26]

With Google exerting such influence over the workings of the media, it's not surprising that certain media houses have tried to push back. The most dramatic example of this phenomenon is the push in Europe for something called "ancillary copyright" – a new power for news publishers that would allow them to enforce rights over the stories they publish. In Europe, the rights to a story automatically belong to the author, not the publisher. The author might sign away those rights to the publisher, but ancillary copyright is a right that's held directly by the publishers, making it easier for them to demand licensing fees from those who reproduce parts of their stories. What does that mean in practice? We can see from what happened in Germany and Spain, the two countries that have so far introduced ancillary copyright, following much pestering from large, influential local press publishers.

Although ancillary copyright allows publishers to try collecting licensing fees from anyone who reuses fragments of their content, the big target has always been Google and its Google News aggregation service, which uses bits of their articles' text and thumbnails of their pictures in its search results. Germany went first: once an ancillary copyright law had been passed there, major media houses such as Axel Springer and Burda co-opted a royalty-collection organisation called

---

[26] http://www.groundup.org.za/article/why-were-dropping-google-ads/

VG Media to collect fees from Google and others.[27] Google's reaction was to simply stop using the publishers' text snippets and picture thumbnails in its results. Traffic to Axel Springer's articles from Google quickly fell by 40 percent, and referrals from the Google News page fell by 80 percent. It turns out that people are more likely to click through to article pages when they have an idea of what they're going to find there.

So, in late 2014, the German publishers backed down, giving Google a free (and supposedly temporary) license to use their snippets and thumbnails without paying.[28] However, in Spain the publishers had managed to get an ancillary copyright law that was so tightly drawn up that it didn't even give them the option of backing down. Publishers there had to demand licensing fees from news aggregators whether they wanted to or not, and, when the law came into effect in late 2014, Google simply shut down Google News in Spain. A study the next year, commissioned by a publishers' association, found that traffic to Spanish websites fell by 16 percent on average. This hit advertising revenues in a way that disproportionately harmed small publications, according to the association.[29] Of course, it also made it more difficult for Spanish news consumers to find the information they were looking for. Ancillary copyright laws reduce competition in the news sector, because the larger media houses, which pushed for these laws, have better brand recognition thanks to larger marketing budgets and their presence on traditional news racks. Their smaller rivals need the web, and by implication Google's search and aggregation facilities, to get their names and articles out there. Closing local versions of Google News may also hurt domestic media by steering news-seekers towards foreign versions of Google, which will more likely promote their own territories' media.

---

[27] http://searchengineland.com/german-ancillary-copyright-to-go-into-effect-imposes-limits-on-search-results-159843

[28] http://www.reuters.com/article/us-google-axel-sprngr-idUSKBN0IP1YT20141105

[29] http://www.aeepp.com/noticia/2272/actividades/informe-economico-del-impacto-del-nuevo-articulo-32.2-de-la-lpi-nera-para-la-aeepp.html

The thing is, Google was never going to pay up. It can't – if Google were to start paying organisations to link out to their webpages, its entire business model would be undermined. That business model depends on a simple idea: linking to a webpage gives that page more visitors and therefore more revenue. Google gets to run ads next to its search results and build up its profile of the user, but in exchange the linked-to website gets the lifeblood of traffic. Adding massive new costs to that system would make no sense for Google, particularly when the company doesn't run ads next to Google News results anyway – if it were to pay for listing those results, it would actually be losing money.

Despite both the German and Spanish experiences having ended in catastrophe, the European Commission in late 2016 proposed extending ancillary copyright across the entire European Union.[30] Perhaps as a precaution, Google in mid-2017 tweaked Google News so that it no longer reproduces snippets of articles' text apart from the headlines.[31] But if the EU-level proposal were to go through in its proposed form – which could allow publishers to demand fees for reproducing the headline itself – it would probably lead to Google News shutting down across the EU. This would help the bigger news publishers fight back against the effects of the internet, which opened the sector up to floods of new competition. But it certainly wouldn't be good for free expression, nor for consumers.

There's clearly a huge power struggle going on between Google and the publishers, even though Google has not actually taken power directly from them. Yes, Google's revenues are rising while the publishers' are falling, but Google has been successful because of the rise of the web and the way in which the company cemented its role as the web's most successful directory service. At the same time, the publishers have suffered because of the rise of the web, and the way in which it has exposed them to much more competition, most of which is free to access. Google is not to blame here – the web is the culprit. But,

---

[30] http://fortune.com/2016/09/14/europe-copyright-google/
[31] https://www.blog.google/topics/journalism-news/redesigning-google-news-everyone/

that said, the publishers have a lot of lobbying power with politicians, and Google knows it. As a result, it has put tens of millions of euros into something called the Digital News Initiative Innovation Fund, which is supposed to help publishers develop new, viable business models, though its main impact is arguably to help Google's defensive lobbying efforts. Google has promised to distribute a whopping €150 million through this fund.[32] In October 2017, the company also started working with online publishers to help them set up paywalls, so they can start making money from subscriptions as well as advertising.[33] The early results of this program suggest people will be encouraged to buy a bundle of article-reading credits through Google, which can then be spent across websites that work with the web giant.

In the context of the web, publishers may largely be at Google's mercy, but at least people are visiting their websites, leaving them with a reasonable amount of control over what they do and how they present themselves. At least people are focused on their brands. That all changes as the web gives way to a different, mobile-app-based environment. Here, the focus shifts from the sites producing the content to the social networks, in particular Facebook, through which people access that content.

Facebook and Mobile

In 2011, global smartphone shipments overtook those of PCs for the first time.[34] Small screens were becoming people's primary way of connecting to the internet and consuming information – a trend that was already very pronounced in developing markets, where most people had never been able to afford a PC and were therefore going online for the first time with a handheld device.

---

[32] https://blog.google/topics/google-europe/digital-news-initiative-second-funding-24-million/

[33] https://www.blog.google/topics/journalism-news/driving-future-digital-subscriptions/

[34] https://www.canalys.com/newsroom/smart-phones-overtake-client-pcs-2011

Small screens require a drastic re-thinking of how you present information and create an interactive experience with the user. For a start, you're much more limited in the amount of information you can fit on there in a legible way. You can't bunch up links as much as you can on a big desktop screen, because it's harder to click the right link with your finger than it is with a more precise mouse cursor. Typing is harder on a screen than on a keyboard. Phones are great devices for consuming information, but not in the same way as on a laptop or desktop PC. Sure, you can search for stuff on a handset, but it's far easier to just have it come to you in the form of big – and therefore fewer – links that have already been selected for you. That's why social media and smartphones work so well together. If you have a spare moment, why search for something to read if you can just check Facebook and see a selection of what your friends are reading, organised by algorithms that study your behaviour and show you what they think will interest you most? Facebook is winning at this game because of its scale – it's increasingly likely that most of your friends are on it – but also because it takes so little effort to use. That makes it the biggest threat to Google, which has repeatedly tried and failed to be a major player in social networking with services such as Orkut, Buzz and Google+.[35]

Facebook's command of people's concentration makes it essential for online publications – it's the virtual town square where people share information that they find interesting and, crucially, where they discuss that information. Back in the days before social networking was as big as it is now, publishers tried to keep people on their sites, and therefore viewing their ads, by creating their own communities. They built comment sections and forums, where their specialised audiences could find likeminded people and hopefully start conversations that would keep them coming back for more. But running such communities is hard and resource-intensive. If you're going to do it properly and you care about the sort of environment you're creating, you have to

---

[35] http://www.adweek.com/news/technology/look-back-googles-history-social-media-failures-158700

moderate the conversation in order to stop fights. You constantly have to fight spam. With Facebook providing the platform for countless discussions of articles, it's more than tempting to allow the social network to handle all that bother – for most publishers, it's inevitable. Sure, Facebook has rules on things like nudity that amount to censorship, but it's where everyone is anyway, and the discussions help to attract more people to your story, so why fight it? Facebook's embedded "like" buttons provide a handy link between the publisher's story page and the social network (and, thanks to code hidden behind them, a handy way for Facebook to track the page's visitors). The web giant even makes it easy to embed its discussions at the bottom of your articles, so it feels the same when you're on the website as it does within the social network – again, these embedded comments sections track visitors.

This is how publishers have become as dependent on Facebook as they are on Google, again by effectively outsourcing core functionality to an advertising giant. And, ironically, the annoying nature of online advertising is helping to push publishers further into these companies' arms. Apart from ads being obnoxiously distracting, they also tend to use up a lot of data, not just because of their graphics but also because they are constantly communicating with many profiling services. This has a devastating effect on mobile, where loading speeds are typically slower than on the desktop. People have short attention spans, particularly when they're accessing articles through social media platforms that have many other stories and videos on offer. If a page takes more than a few seconds to load, most people are likely to just go back and try viewing something else, according to a 2016 study by Google's DoubleClick ad network.[36] Worse, they might start using ad-blockers to stop those ads from loading at all – a practice that is perfectly legal everywhere in the world except for China.[37] These tools started out as third-party plug-ins for browsers, but now some browsers

[36] https://www.doubleclickbygoogle.com/articles/mobile-speed-matters/
[37] http://www.tomshardware.com/news/china-reforms-internet-ad-blocking,32297.html

even come with ad-blockers built in. The Norwegian browser firm Opera claims that turning on this feature in its browser will cut page-load times by about 90 percent.[38]

Ad-blockers are also attractive because some online advertisements are booby-trapped – if you click on them, your PC may become infected with viruses or other malware. This doesn't just affect dodgy sites dealing in porn and copyright infringement. In early 2016, mainstream websites such the BBC, *The New York Times*, MSN and AOL unwittingly carried ads that attacked readers by downloading nasty software onto their computers.[39] That sort of danger makes people rightly suspicious of online ads.

What's a poor publisher to do? Unsurprisingly, both Google and Facebook are trying to solve the bulky-ads problem in their own ways, with their own aims in mind. Google is working with publishers to develop technology that makes webpages load more quickly on phones (a project called "Accelerated Mobile Pages" or AMP). [40] This is a variation of the HTML technical format in which most web content is written, only it's designed to be speedier. It works for articles but also, crucially, for ads. In other words, Google wants to maintain the web's dominance as an information delivery platform by making it work more smoothly.

Facebook, meanwhile, wants news and entertainment publishers to simply publish their articles within the social network itself, rather than outside on the web. Facebook has long had a browser built into its mobile apps, but its Instant Articles program takes the concept to the next level.[41] As the name suggests, stories published to the platform load almost instantly within Facebook. If publishers sell the ad space on those pages themselves, they get to keep all of the revenue; if they

---

[38] http://www.pcworld.com/article/3042172/browsers/operas-testing-a-browser-that-kills-ads-accelerating-webpage-loading-by-up-to-90-percent.html

[39] https://arstechnica.com/security/2016/03/big-name-sites-hit-by-rash-of-malicious-ads-spreading-crypto-ransomware/

[40] https://www.ampproject.org/

[41] https://instantarticles.fb.com/

leave it up to Facebook to fill the space with ads from its own network, then Facebook takes a cut. Either way, the publishers hand control of their audience over to Facebook, and make their own brand less relevant than ever before. But at least they're relatively safe from the effects of ad blockers, as Facebook puts a lot of effort into making sure they can't block ads inside its apps and website. In 2016, Facebook figured out a way to sneak its desktop site's ads past the blocking filter of Adblock Plus, a popular browser extension used by over 100 million people.[42] Adblock Plus updated the filter, effectively blocking Facebook's attempt to bypass the blockers.[43] However, Facebook successfully fought back by making it impossible for the automated blockers to tell that its ads were ads at all, meaning they couldn't block them without stopping users from seeing the whole page.[44] And that's just the desktop. Facebook gets most of its revenue from ads on its mobile app, and so far mobile ad-blockers haven't been able to reach inside that app.[45]

If publishers go with Facebook's well-maintained defences against the ad-blocking threat – not a sure thing, as publishers such as *The New York Times* and *Guardian* have already pulled out of the Instant Articles scheme – they make sure people see their ads, but in doing so they cede control over their readers and entrench the social network's walled garden.[46] In that sense, people using ad blockers are helping to erode the web, pushing the industry to depend ever more on a heavily centralised service. Google's alternative is at least better for maintaining a heterogeneous web that isn't under the control of one company, though of course Google, which makes its money off being the web's foremost search and surveillance player, stands to gain from this outcome.

---

[42] https://techcrunch.com/2016/08/11/facebooks-blocker-blocking-ads-blocked-by-blockers/
[43] http://fortune.com/2016/08/09/facebook-ads-adblock-war/
[44] https://techcrunch.com/2016/09/18/faceblock/
[45] http://fortune.com/2016/02/19/three-network-ad-blocking/
[46] https://digiday.com/media/facebook-faces-increased-publisher-resistance-instant-articles/

Either way, news publishers are by this point far from being in control of their own destinies. The more they lose control, the less relevant they become, making it harder for them to get people to spend time looking at their wares. And to make matters worse, their desperation is leading them to put their credibility on the line.

Cheapened Media

The war over ads isn't just making publishers more reliant on Facebook. In an effort to overcome people's subconscious and active blocking-out of online advertising, publishers have also been increasingly turning to what is blandly referred to in the trade as "native advertising" – that is, ads disguised as regular stories. Different publications choose to admit this to the reader to varying degrees: some label such stories as sponsored content; some clearly say they're advertisements; some give no signal that this isn't straight journalism. But at its heart, native advertising is an attempt to fool the reader's brain into focusing on something, or even believing what it says, because it looks and feels like a regular article. That resemblance is valuable because, for all but the most cynical reader, regular articles are associated with facts and at least some attempt at impartiality.

The tension between advertisers and journalists has always existed, but publishers have traditionally kept an internal wall between these two sides of the business. This separation tells readers and viewers that the editorial side has not been corrupted by business concerns – that stories are not warped or softened by a desire to make advertisers look good. That's how a newspaper could, for example, write about the misdeeds of the automotive industry while still carrying car ads. If the wall is in place, the journalism retains authority. Without it, the effect fades.

The Atlantic, a well-respected publication, learned this the hard way when it published a native ad about the Church of Scientology's expansion in 2013. It may have been labelled "sponsor content" but it looked just like *The Atlantic*'s regular posts, and earned the site a great deal of criticism from other journalists for its unquestioningly positive tone. "We now realise that as we explored new forms of digital advertising, we failed to update the policies that must govern the decisions we make along the way," *The Atlantic* said in a subsequent statement, after removing the article.[47] And in 2016, the UK's advertising standards watchdog reprimanded Buzzfeed for running a native advertising piece, called "14 Laundry Fails We've All Experienced", that was not properly labelled as advertising. The article was sponsored by a dye manufacturer called Dylon and even sang the company's praises.[48]

"Clickbait" headlines, which oversell articles in an attempt to get people to click through, also hurt journalistic brands. After all, you can't fool all the people all the time, and those who have been tricked and left dissatisfied a few times might end up viewing the publication negatively.

Native advertising and clickbait headlines feed off the authority of journalism. They may work for a while, but ultimately they are self-defeating. If power is currency, then using such tactics will in time mean devaluation. As in politics, the media becomes poisoned when trust is diluted or replaced with cynicism. When nothing is truly authoritative anymore, the risk is that unreliable sources of information will be taken more seriously, because people see little difference between them and more professional information sources. In much the same way as contempt for the political establishment provides a great opportunity for charlatans and demagogues, contempt for the mainstream media is a boost for fringe "news" outlets that are in many cases peddling utter nonsense, and for those charlatans and demagogues who feel they can dismiss articles exposing their falsehoods and corruption as "fake news". The survival of news publications may be at stake here, but so is the truth.

***

---

[47] https://mediadecoder.blogs.nytimes.com/2013/01/15/the-atlantic-apologizes-for-scientology-ad/
[48] http://fortune.com/2016/01/13/buzzfeed-native-advertising/

The maturation and spread of the internet was responsible for the amount of our focus that we've handed over to the Googles and Facebooks of this world. These companies acted smartly to get where they are, but they were also in the right place at the right time. The internet's democratisation of information led to information overload, and Google and Facebook provided the tools to help us cope. Now they have the power over the information we receive, while the actual producers of information are in crisis mode, slashing jobs and struggling to find viable business models. While the media burns, the great advertising companies thrive. They have your attention, and you have theirs.

We'll come to the profound implications for us, the information consumers, in a moment, but what's the way out of this mess for the media? Advertising rates are falling and billionaire benefactors aren't widely available. Clearly, to keep journalism afloat, more people need to start paying to read the news, much as used to be the case with print media. Old-school subscriptions are a simplest option, but they'll remain a tough sell for a lot of people (although a handful of US outlets, including *The New York Times*, have seen subscription numbers rise thanks to attacks by president Donald Trump).[49] We're now all used to reading from a wide variety of outlets, and few of us have the spare cash to subscribe to all of them.

Many in the industry have long dreamed of so-called micropayments, where people visit a platform that carries articles from a variety of outlets and pay tiny amounts of money to read each article – small enough to seem fair to the reader, but enough in aggregate to fund good old journalism. But despite the attempts of numerous startups to make this idea work, the success of micropayments remains elusive. To make it work, you still need to convince people to give up their payment details to some new platform, even though they can endlessly read stuff for free.

---

[49] https://www.cnbc.com/2016/11/29/new-york-times-subscriptions-soar-tenfold-after-donald-trump-wins-presidency.html

Ultimately, the power to get journalists paid may lie in the hands of big social media, Facebook in particular. If Facebook really dives into e-commerce, it would easily get millions of people to give it their credit card details. As the go-to destination for increasing numbers of people looking for news, it would also be in a great position to collect payments for reading those articles. And indeed, the company is working with several big news publishers to make this a reality.[50]

This is good news in a way, if it can help journalism survive. On the other hand, it would only increase publishers' reliance on Facebook, while further entrenching the company's status as the gatekeeper for people's online activities. It would be most fortuitous for Facebook if, having contributed to the media crisis, it could profit off the solution. Those who are less keen on feeding the surveillance machine, however, would be out of luck.

---

[50] https://digiday.com/media/facebooks-working-publishers-paid-subscriptions/

CHAPTER 2: THE SURVEILLANCE MACHINE

In late 2016, security contractors discovered that software found in many Android smartphones sold in the US was secretly sending sensitive information about the phones' users back to China. This personal data included the full contents of text messages, contacts lists and location information. The software, written by a Chinese company called Shanghai Adups Technology, also made it possible for someone to remotely install new apps on people's phones, without them knowing.[51]

Google was outraged, ordering Adups to remove the surveillance capabilities from phones that use Google's app store. The US authorities initially thought the surveillance was for the benefit of the Chinese intelligence services or some advertising scheme – it was reportedly hard for them to tell, given how similar the mechanisms are.[52] In the end, Adups said the contentious software was intended for phones sold in China, not in the US. It was only supposed to report back on Chinese users' behaviour, to make customer service in that country easier.

Ordinary users would never have been able to tell that their phones were infected with this spyware. Even if they could spot it, they wouldn't be able to find out what happened to all the texts and tracking information that was sucked into that mysterious hole. This case was particularly concerning because of the Chinese government's authoritarian nature and its habit of spying on all its citizens. But when it comes to losing control of our personal data, it should be a familiar tale to all of us.

51

http://economictimes.indiatimes.com/news/international/business/chinese-company-shanghai-adups-technology-admits-it-planted-spyware-in-mobile-phones/articleshow/55472239.cms
[52] http://www.nytimes.com/2016/11/16/us/politics/china-phones-software-security.html?_r=0

Even those of us not living in authoritarian states have reasons to be concerned about the rapid erosion of our privacy – however we choose to define the idea.

The Sliding Scale

Privacy is a concept that means different things to different people, largely depending on the context. For some, it means the ability to go about their lives without anyone watching them at all. For others, who might enjoy living most of their lives quite openly through social media, it means being able to pull down the shades at a time of their choosing.

It's also a concept that has meant different things at different times. Once upon a time, we mostly lived in small, dispersed communities where everyone in that community knew what everyone else there was up to, but perhaps not what those in other villages were doing. Now we live in cities where we may not know our neighbours or what they get up to, but we participate in multiple, overlapping online communities where we might expose only carefully crafted aspects of ourselves. For example, a keen guitarist may tell other members of a musicians' forum about their new instrument in great detail, discussing specialist things like pickup strength and tuner quality, but they probably wouldn't discuss non-guitar-related life events with them. They might tell their Facebook friends about those life events, and also about their new guitar, while avoiding detail on both subjects. On WhatsApp, speaking one-on-one to a close friend – who might be both a Facebook friend and a member of the same guitarists' forum – perhaps they will discuss their life events in greater detail, and save the guitar-geek talk for the forum.

Because our communities are so fluid and diverse yet interconnected, and because privacy levels very much depend on specific contexts, we need to recognise modern privacy as a complex, nuanced thing. But this complexity doesn't just come from our modern communities – it's also down to the fact that, once our data exists and is shared with someone, it's really hard to be sure what happens to it afterwards.

Wearable fitness trackers, like the Apple Watch or the Fitbit, provide a great example. The information they record about heart rates and calorie-burning can be helpful to us and our doctors. Some of us choose to wear these devices and transmit the resulting health data to the companies selling the devices, or their partners, so they can help us monitor and analyse our health. However, we do so on the understanding that our personal data will be kept private or, if it is publicised in any way, that it will first be mixed into a set of data about a wider group of people, that doesn't identify us personally. This aggregated, anonymised data can be really useful for medical research – it can help doctors study things like ageing or track the spread of diseases. But we need to be able to trust that everyone who handles our personal data respects the privacy settings that we've chosen, and it's unfortunately not easy to make sure that that's the case. When you visit the doctor and share intimate information about your health, you're probably confident that the person in front of you will keep that data confidential. When you're dealing with a faceless chain of tech companies that regularly pass data among themselves, that confidence may not be justified.

Privacy has always been bound up with power – to know all about someone is to know where their exploitable weaknesses lie, and to be able to predict their next moves, because we are creatures of habit. So, the more control we have over what people know about us, the more individual power we retain.

Privacy is essential for the development of individuals and societies – the person who never changes their mind is rare and probably quite dull. The richness of the evolved human personality is the product of trial and error, and if every mistake we make could always come back to haunt us, we're more likely to avoid experimentation and remain stunted. Meanwhile, societies rot if their elites and their assumptions remain unchallenged; there is always room for improvement and, if we do not evolve, we stagnate. The authoritarian in power, who wants to avoid being challenged, will always clamp down on privacy. If people can't communicate in private, they can't organise an effective opposition. If people know they are being watched, they won't experiment with forbidden ideas that are heresy in that place and at that time, even if a more enlightened society would see them as common-sense truth or merely an acceptable personal choice.

However, many current technological trends are based on the idea of people surrendering their privacy so they can get certain supposed benefits in return. If you allow Google to build a profile of you by recording and analysing your web searches, you get that service for free, and Google's systems will try to show you the things that most interest you. Google develops the most popular mobile operating system in the world, Android, largely because it allows the company to track its users' movements and desires everywhere they go. You use Facebook for free because it allows that company to map who you know, what you like, what you do and ultimately what kind of person you are – all in the service of making money.

Are you comfortable with that? You may decide it's a fair trade-off, and that's up to you. However, even if you think these profiling systems are secure, and that better-prioritised results and better-targeted advertising are useful to you, that doesn't necessarily mean you don't care about privacy. You still probably don't want the world to see you naked, or to know what you're thinking all the time, or to be able to see all your medical details. There may be things about you that you want only your family, or just that one special person, to know. Perhaps you're happy to tell your friends something about yourself at a certain time, but you'd prefer that piece of information wasn't permanently recorded and accessible to people you don't know.

Perhaps you're doing something that's illegal but not morally wrong, and that doesn't affect others; something that will, in time, rightly be legalised. As Moxie Marlinspike, the lead developer of encrypted-messaging app Signal, has pointed out, homosexuality was illegal in the US state of Minnesota until 2001, and Minnesota now allows same-sex marriage. If perfect surveillance and law enforcement had been a reality while the old sodomy laws applied, things may have turned out differently. "How could states decide that same sex marriage should be permitted, if nobody had ever seen or participated in a same sex relationship?" Marlinspike mused.[53]

Being able to choose who knows what about you – and when they know it – is a form of control that you need to keep for yourself. Privacy is not binary, like a switch that's either on or off. It's a sliding scale and, outside of exceptional circumstances, we should always retain the power to choose which point of that scale is best for us in any given situation. Without that ability to establish nuance, we've lost control. And unfortunately, few people really have that ability these days.

Ubiquitous Tracking

There are three big reasons why we're largely unable to calibrate our own privacy. The fundamental problem is that we don't always know when we are being tracked online, partly because the mechanisms are not obvious, but also because many services constantly change the terms of service that explain how users are followed around. Secondly, once our data has been collected, we have very little idea what happens to it. And thirdly, even if we do know we're being tracked and have an idea of what happens to our data, and if we don't like what we see, then we still can't do anything about it.

Many websites will deposit tracking cookies in your browser, or let profiling systems know what you're up to by hiding "tracking pixels" in their pages. This doesn't require you to be logged into any service. For example, if you visit a page that has an embedded Facebook "like" button in it, Facebook will put one of its tracking cookies in your browser. You don't need to be visiting a Facebook.com page to be followed around by the company, nor do you even need to be a registered Facebook user.[54] Google's advertising cookies will track you around any site that features Google's ads. Many of these "third-party"

---

[53] https://moxie.org/blog/we-should-all-have-something-to-hide/
[54] http://www.socialmedialawbulletin.com/2016/04/privacy-laws-violated-by-facebook-like-button/

cookies (as in, those not set by whoever runs the website in question) track users across multiple sites. And Google and Facebook are just the big names you'll recognise. There are many, many more.

Some of the most important players in the tracking game are unfamiliar to most people – companies like Acxiom, Quantium and eBureau, and several, including Datalogix and BlueKai, that were bought by the business software firm Oracle. These outfits describe themselves as "big data", "marketing technology" and "customer relationship" companies. All are data brokers and data mixers that traffic in information coming not just from online tracking, but also from more traditional marketing schemes such as store loyalty programmes and mailing lists. There are many of these companies, and it is perfectly common to be tracked by dozens of them at any given time.

Back in 2010, *The Wall Street Journal* examined 50 popular sites to see where they sent information about their users. Dictionary.com topped the list by exposing its users to a whopping 234 trackers. Even the *Journal* itself sent readers' personal data out to five dozen companies. Of the 50 websites studied, all but Wikipedia exposed their users to third parties, 37 sites sent data to more than 30 companies, and 22 included more than 60 trackers.[55]

And that's just the web. Tracking is also rife across the world of smartphone apps, which introduce a whole new level of surveillance. Your smartphone is itself a tracking device. Your mobile operator constantly knows where you are – it has to, in order to let you receive calls and use the internet. If you leave GPS turned on, many of the apps on your phone use the connection to GPS satellites (which are run by the US Air Force) to figure out where you are. If you carry your phone around with you all the time, some of those apps with access to your GPS location are passing on that information to third parties. This means you're being physically tracked around by organisations with whom you have no direct relationship.

---

[55] http://blogs.wsj.com/wtk/

A 2014 study by the US mobile security firm Appthority suggested that 82 percent of free Android apps and half of free iOS apps used location tracking. Of those, almost three-quarters of the free Android apps and a third of the free iOS apps were sharing data with ad networks. The figures for paid apps were lower, but not insubstantial: 38 percent of paid Android apps and 16 percent of paid iOS apps also shared data with ad networks.[56] In the same year, privacy regulators from around the world banded together to study the permissions that apps demand when people download them. They found that 31 percent asked to access more information than was necessary for the apps to function, and just 15 percent clearly explained to downloaders what data they would collect, how they would use it, and to whom they would pass it.[57]

Like smartphones, fitness trackers are loaded with sensors producing data that can be sent back to the providers' servers. They aren't as common as smartphones, but they're getting pretty popular – according to Forrester Research, 18 percent of US consumers owned such devices in 2015.[58] In late 2016, the Norwegian consumer watchdog made a formal complaint against four of the most popular fitness tracker firms: Fitbit, Garmin, Jawbone and Mio. It said these trackers all collected more data than they needed to provide their service, and none of the companies selling them fully explained where this data would go. That meant the companies were breaking European privacy laws on multiple counts. "It is important that we don't give up basic rights in order to use the products and services of the future," said Finn Myrstad, the regulator's director of digital services.[59]

---

[56] https://www.appthority.com/company/press/press-releases/appthority-exposes-security-and-privacy-risks-behind-top-400-mobile-apps/
[57] https://www.dataprotection.ie/docs/10-09-14-Global-Privacy-Sweep-raises-concerns-about-mobile-apps/i/1456.htm
[58]

https://www.forrester.com/Wearables+Will+Reach+CriticalMass+Adoption+By+2021/-/E-PRE9364
[59] http://www.forbrukerradet.no/siste-nytt/fitness-wristbands-violate-european-law

None of this happens by coincidence; app developers have many reasons to over-collect information about their users. For a start, the data they gather becomes a key asset when – as most developers hope will happen – the time comes to sell their company. Venture capitalist investors may be banking on massive data collection when they fund the developer in the first place, knowing that it will boost the company's value. But even before sale time, there are plenty of companies willing to pay good money for people's information.

For example, the navigation company Telenav has a mobile advertising division called Thinknear that sent out a pitch to developers in September 2016, offering them "the opportunity to partner with us to help monetise the exhaust data from their apps". According to the slides in the pitch presentation, here's how the system works. Developers install Thinknear's code in their apps, which consumers then download while giving the apps permission to track their location. Thinknear then aggregates the resulting location data, promising to strip out personally identifiable information, and sells it on. Thinknear said it would pay the developers 1 cent per user per month, and claimed the hidden code would only chew up 2-3 percent of a user's battery per day. The term "exhaust data" is interesting. It's accurate in that it refers to the trails people leave behind, but it implies that this data is mere waste, and that sucking it up is some kind of service. Strange, then, that so many people refer to data as "the new oil", a phrase apparently coined in 2006 by Clive Humby, one of the creators of the Clubcard profiling scheme for UK supermarket giant Tesco.[60] Like crude oil, data needs to be refined – through algorithms in this case – into profiles that can generate money. That's not exhaust; it's at the opposite end of the processing cycle. And we are the producers of that oil.

The telecoms operators that run our internet connections watch our data flow all day long, and are keen to cash in. Several operators have tried monitoring their customers' web traffic in order to find information that they could sell to profiling companies. In 2008, a tracking company called Phorm said it had signed up three of the UK's

---

[60] http://ana.blogs.com/maestros/2006/11/data_is_the_new.html

biggest internet service providers (BT, TalkTalk and Virgin Media) to use its "deep packet inspection" technology, which would closely monitor broadband customers' online activities. However, it then turned out that BT and Phorm had previously conducted secret trials of this technology on thousands of BT's customers without getting their consent – consent was essential if the surveillance service was to remain legal.[61] "Customers absolutely can trust BT, and I'm here to reassure them that, y'know, this is a service that is looking to provide them with an improved browsing experience," BT executive Emma Sanderson said when quizzed on breakfast TV.[62] However, telecoms regulator Ofcom criticised the firms for not getting customers' consent, and Tim Berners-Lee, the inventor of the web, said what they were doing amounted to "snooping". The police dropped an investigation into BT and Phorm because they could not find "criminal intent", but the media storm sunk Phorm's ambitions.[63] In 2009, BT dropped its plans to use the company's technology.[64]

The concept has taken off elsewhere, though. For example, the US telecoms firm Verizon modifies its customers' web traffic in order to track them and feed its advertising programs.[65] When people found out about the scheme and got upset, Verizon eventually let its customers opt out of being tracked in this way.[66] But real consent doesn't mean being able to tell someone to stop spying on you – it means demanding that they ask permission before they even start. And sometimes even this isn't enough to keep things fair, as AT&T demonstrated with its "Internet Preferences" programme. When AT&T rolled out its new

[61] http://www.telegraph.co.uk/technology/news/8438461/BT-and-Phorm-how-an-online-privacy-scandal-unfolded.html

[62] https://www.theregister.co.uk/2008/04/03/bt_phorm_interview/

[63] http://www.zdnet.com/article/police-drop-investigation-into-bts-phorm-trials/

[64] http://www.ft.com/cms/s/0/4090a9e0-6a8c-11de-ad04-00144feabdc0.html

[65] https://www.wired.com/2014/10/verizons-perma-cookie/

[66] http://www.pcworld.com/article/2878561/verizon-to-allow-opt-outs-of-dubious-perma-cookie-program-but-isnt-giving-up.html

fibre internet service in 2013, it only offered its lowest rates to people who allowed AT&T to spy on their online activities. This effectively meant that the operator was charging people extra to avoid being spied on. After a public outcry in 2015, AT&T ended the practice the following year.[67] In 2016, the US Federal Communications Commission banned internet service providers from profiling their users for targeted advertising, without getting their explicit consent first. But the next year, under Donald Trump's new administration, Congress blocked these internet privacy rules.[68] "I guarantee you there is not one person, not one voter of any political stripe anywhere in America, who asked for this," pointed out the comedian Stephen Colbert.[69]

Where does all this surveillance data go, once it's been collected? That's a good question with no easy answer, but what's certain is that it gets passed around an awful lot. In 2014, the US Federal Trade Commission examined nine of the biggest data brokers and concluded that it was "virtually impossible for a consumer to determine how a data broker obtained his or her data".[70] Why? Because seven of the nine brokers passed data to one another. As fragments of your data get distributed around, they are correlated with other fragments in order to paint a more detailed picture of you. Personal data that might seem unimportant on its own becomes more significant when part of a broader profile. All that's needed to join the dots is a link between the disparate pieces of data, such as a common email address or phone number.

---

[67] http://arstechnica.com/information-technology/2016/09/att-to-end-targeted-ads-program-give-all-users-lowest-available-price/
[68] http://thehill.com/policy/technology/326145-house-votes-to-send-bill-undoing-obama-internet-privacy-rule-to-trumps-desk
[69] https://www.washingtonpost.com/politics/how-congress-dismantled-federal-internet-privacy-rules/2017/05/29/7ad06e14-2f5b-11e7-8674-437ddb6e813e_story.html?utm_term=.13dc1974a2c5
[70] http://www.ftc.gov/system/files/documents/reports/data-brokers-call-transparency-accountability-report-federal-trade-commission-may-2014/140527databrokerreport.pdf

"Big data" is also correlated between the online and offline worlds, where possible, largely because marketers are desperate to know when an ad viewed online leads to a sale in a physical store. Google, an ad company that also happens to provide the popular Google Maps app, can see when Android and Apple users are visiting stores, as long as those people have Location History activated on their phones. This means Google can go to retailers that are running online ad campaigns and tell them when those campaigns appear to be sending more people to their shops. These analyses are only based on sampled and aggregated data, rather than directly linking specific clicks on ads to specific store visits – even Google is cautious about privacy sometimes. But the potential to establish those connections is there.

Retailers can also make links between people's online and physical presences by using little sensors called beacons. Installed around shops, beacons can recognise nearby mobile devices by picking up the Bluetooth and Wi-Fi signals that the phones are sending out. These sensors can be useful for helping you find your way around a covered space, such as a mall, where your phone won't be able to communicate with GPS satellites up in the sky – by judging its distance from nearby beacons, the phone can work out where it is. But the main purpose of beacons is for the retailer to know when a particular person is near the store who has been doing online searches for a product sold there. With this knowledge, the retailer can then send a targeted advertising message to that person's phone, to entice them to come in and buy that thing they were thinking of buying.

To really understand why all this profiling data is so valuable, we need to take the perspective of the entity that ultimately wants to use it: the advertiser. Let's say we're an app developer that's trying to get people to download its new app. The best way to do this is probably through Facebook, because the social network has the most powerful sets of data about its users. This is partly because of the amount of time those users spend there, and partly because of Facebook's extensive partnerships with data brokers. Either way, Facebook is the place where we want to put our ads.

First, we go to Facebook's online advertising toolkit and create an "audience" for our ad. This is a list of people that's drawn from data we already have, such as records of existing customers or lists of those people who did a particular thing in our apps. We can also hide Facebook's code on our website to track everyone who visits, see what they do on our site and then add them to the list. When we upload this audience list to Facebook, we can either just target our ads at the people on the list, or we can ask Facebook to analyse the list and create an extended "lookalike" audience of users who share characteristics with those people. The lookalike function lets advertisers target up to 10 percent of an entire country's Facebook users, though the more people we target, the less focused and more expensive the audience is likely to be. What we want is to target people as specifically, and therefore as cost-efficiently, as possible.

By tracking usage within our own apps and combining the data from multiple advertising platforms (such as Google, Facebook and Twitter), we can create quite detailed profiles of the people we want to target the most: those users who installed the app and then bought something through it. The more we keep track of all this, and the bigger and more detailed our database becomes, the more efficient our operations can become, because we can see what really works and what doesn't. It's important to note that, as advertisers, our big fat database does not include people's actual names, but rather their ID numbers on platforms such as Facebook. We don't know who these people are, as such, though we do have a lot of detail about them. Conversely, Facebook knows which ID number corresponds to which name, but it does not know everything we know about how these people use our app. Profiling systems are not yet completely interlinked, but all the fragments are there. With the right access to the various databases in this ecosystem, it would be possible to glue them together and paint very detailed portraits of identifiable individuals.

It wouldn't be quite right to say people have no control whatsoever over any of this. We can turn off Wi-Fi, Bluetooth and GPS on our mobile devices when we don't need them, though that means having to constantly remember to turn such functions back on when we want to use things that are connected to our phones, such as fitness trackers or home entertainment systems. We can set up different email accounts for each app we use, though that too can easily become difficult to manage. In some countries we can get a SIM card and a phone without registering our personal details, and we can make sure not to use services such as Google or Facebook on those handsets, in order to make it harder for the profiling systems to link our identities to those devices.

But all these things take a lot of effort and can be highly inconvenient, and we may not remember to do them all the time. The profiling systems only need to make connections between our various online and offline identities once, and the game is over. What's more, services' default settings tend to leave us exposed, and few people change defaults. We can tell Google to "pause" its recording of our web and app activities and our location histories – and if we look really hard, we can even find out how to tell Google to delete some of this data – but the firm will by default record these things. Most people won't know they *can* tell it to stop, let alone bother to do so.

This system of "surveillance capitalism", as Harvard professor Shoshana Zuboff calls it, is useful to advertisers and very lucrative for the companies that are tracking us.[71] However, to appreciate what it means for us as individuals, it's worth putting it into context by imagining what it would mean in a purely offline world.

Let's say you live in a town with a typical high street that has bars and shops and perhaps a library. If you go into a clothing shop, you may well ask a shop assistant to make recommendations based on looking at you – your build, complexion, age and so on. The shopkeeper makes those recommendations by just looking at you. After you've left the shop, having bought something appropriate, they'll probably forget you. The shopkeeper has made a sale, you have new clothes, and everyone's happy. However, in the online version of this scenario, the retailer is able to make good recommendations because it

---

[71] http://www.faz.net/aktuell/feuilleton/debatten/the-digital-debate/shoshana-zuboff-secrets-of-surveillance-capitalism-14103616.html

has paid someone to follow you around all the time, observe what you're doing, and remember that information. And the spies won't forget what they've seen.

Imagine you're having a conversation with your friends in a bar, only to have someone listen in so they can then make targeted recommendations ("I heard you mention you're thinking of having a baby – are you interested in vitamin supplements or perhaps some nappies?") That's not so far from having Google scan through emails in search of advertising keywords, as it did to Gmail users until late 2017.[72] An even creepier scenario might involve someone trying to sell you stuff based on the things you're merely thinking about. After all, web searches are often just expressions of curiosity.

On the plus side, the systems doing all this tracking are not actual people. While many will find creepiness and danger in the way that they're constantly monitored, there would be added problems if the monitoring systems had human traits such as sexual impulses and jealousy. They do not pose such immediate dangers. However, it's the issue of visibility that makes these online-offline comparisons particularly disturbing. People don't tend to follow others around and listen in on their conversations in the physical world, partly because they could be seen doing so – it's obvious, and obviously unacceptable. It's far easier to stay hidden while doing the same things online. And so, for the person being followed, it's much harder to be sure that you've achieved privacy online than it is in the offline layer. Yes, you can see if websites have set tracking cookies in your browser, but that takes a technical inclination that most people don't have, and even *then* it's hard to tell what the cookies are really for. Are they just there to build your valuable advertising profile, or do they actually help to improve the web services you use by monitoring how you and other people use those services? You have no idea.

There have been attempts to give people the power to fight back against this tracking, most notably the introduction of a new browser

---

[72] https://www.blog.google/products/gmail/g-suite-gains-traction-in-the-enterprise-g-suites-gmail-and-consumer-gmail-to-more-closely-align/

setting called "Do Not Track" (DNT). The idea here was to let people effectively put a notice in their browsers saying they do not want to be followed around by profiling systems. When standards-setters were defining how the system would work, representatives of the direct marketing (tracking) industry tried to argue that it shouldn't affect their profiling cookies.

As the whole point of DNT is to stop such tracking tools, some members of the standards-setting group expressed surprise. Here's what the marketing industry representatives replied: "Marketing fuels the world. It is as American as apple pie and delivers relevant advertising to consumers about products they will be interested [in] at a time they are interested. DNT should permit it as one of the most important values of civil society. Its by-product also furthers democracy, free speech, and – most importantly in these times – JOBS."[73]

In the end, the marketers didn't get their exception and DNT became a standard. However, its success relied on web services respecting people's wish not to be tracked. Less than two dozen websites (including Twitter and Pinterest) chose to respect the DNT setting, and everyone else, from Google to Facebook to LinkedIn, decided to ignore it. The US Consumer Watchdog organisation tried to get the Federal Communications Commission to force web firms to honour DNT, but the regulator denied having the authority to do so.[74] Without muscle to back it up, the privacy standard was a failure. By mid-2017, even Twitter stopped supporting it.[75]

Our lack of control over the spread of our personal data is bad enough in itself, because of how, well, *personal* that information is. It's not nice to have others watching you constantly and to be powerless to stop it. But the modern surveillance machine isn't just creepy. Although the profiling giants are keen to extol the benefits of more relevant

---

[73] http://www.zdnet.com/article/the-do-not-track-standard-has-crossed-into-crazy-territory/
[74] http://arstechnica.com/business/2015/11/fcc-wont-force-websites-to-honor-do-not-track-requests/
[75] http://www.zdnet.com/article/twitter-abandons-do-not-track-privacy-protection/

advertising and more personalised services, their surveillance doesn't always benefit us, the watched.

Big Bad Data

In late 2016, the British car insurance company Admiral announced a new policy called "firstcarquote" which would, in the wording of Admiral's press release, let "first-time drivers share their social data to produce a personality-based risk assessment to secure a steep discount on their car insurance". Admiral said it would start with people's Facebook page likes and their posts on the social network – all they needed to do was give the insurance company access to their account, in order to start claiming those discounts. "It's scientifically proven that some personalities are more likely to have an accident than others. But standard insurance questions don't tend to measure personality," the company said. "At firstcarquote, we look at a driver's personality by analysing some of their Facebook data and if we see indicators that you will be a careful driver, we will give you a discount of between 5 and 15 percent off the price you would get off admiral.com."

Privacy advocates such as Jim Killock, director of the UK's Open Rights Group, warned that this could set a dangerous precedent. "Such intrusive practices could see decisions being made against certain groups based on biases about race, gender, religion or sexuality – or because their posts in some way mark them as unconventional," he said. "Ultimately, this could change how people use social media, encouraging self-censorship in anticipation of future decisions."[76] Within a day, Facebook scuppered the scheme, saying it broke the social network's terms and conditions and threatened people's privacy.[77] Specifically, Admiral was breaking a rule that bans using Facebook data "to make decisions about eligibility, including whether to approve or reject an application or how much interest to charge on a loan".

---

[76] http://www.wired.co.uk/article/admiral-facebook-policy
[77] https://www.theguardian.com/money/2016/nov/02/facebook-admiral-car-insurance-privacy-data

But programmes like this are really just continuations of an ongoing trend that's particularly prevalent in the insurance industry. Insurers such as Progressive in the US and Discovery in South Africa ask their customers to agree to being tracked as they drive, using a little device that plugs into the car, so that the company can constantly assess their behaviour. In exchange, drivers get discounts on their premiums – as long as the insurer likes what it sees. What the insurer classifies as bad behaviour isn't just limited to driving above the speed limit and regularly braking too quickly; it can also include things like driving at night. Bad luck if you happen to be someone who works far from home and has to commute in the dark. Bad luck if your insurance company decides that your car spends too much time in an undesirable neighbourhood where the perceived risk of damage or theft is higher.

This car data can reveal very valuable things. It can tell you how to drive more safely and reduce emissions, and it can help businesses keep a closer eye on their fleets. However, the data can also entrench people's situations by punishing them for their misfortune. If your neighbourhood is seen by the insurance company as risky because it's poor, then chances are you don't have a lot of money either, and are more likely to be hurt by higher premiums.

The insurance business is intrinsically about discrimination – looking at people's circumstances and trying to classify them into different categories so that they pay what the insurer thinks is an appropriate amount for their insurance. Many places have laws that try to limit the kinds of discrimination that insurers can use, for example by banning them from discriminating on the basis of ethnicity or religion.[78] However, these protections are not universal. Without meaningful protection against unfair or unethical discrimination, "big data" becomes many people's enemy, intruding into their lives without giving them the benefits. Previously, insurers would not have known when and where their customers drive or park their cars, so those poor

---

78

http://repository.law.umich.edu/cgi/viewcontent.cgi?article=1163&context=law_econ_current

neighbourhoods and night-time driving didn't affect their premiums. Sure, the same intrusion may benefit people in more fortunate circumstances, but a societal shift like this should not be regressive in nature.

This isn't just a problem in the realm of insurance – and, perhaps counterintuitively, the problem isn't just about getting too much accurate information about people. In early 2016, the US Federal Trade Commission issued a warning about how the data broker and credit reporting industries are using big data. One particular risk, it said, lies in making predictions about a person's creditworthiness by using data from many sources – sources that may have nothing to do with the person in question. "Some credit card companies have lowered a customer's credit limit, not based on the customer's payment history, but rather based on analysis of other customers with a poor repayment history that had shopped at the same establishments where the customer had shopped," the report noted.[79] That could mean getting punished for living in a certain area and, if that area happens to be most populated by a minority, the net effect may be racial discrimination.

"Big data offers companies the opportunity to facilitate inclusion or exclusion," the FTC report said. "Companies can use big data to advance education, credit, and employment opportunities for low-income communities or to exclude them from these opportunities. They can use big data to target products to those who are most interested or to target products in ways that could exclude certain populations."

To that extent, the issue is not so much the fact that the data is being collected, but the ways in which the data is cross-referenced and ultimately used. These algorithms can have deeply unfair outcomes if they are not carefully and ethically formulated. Where anti-discrimination laws exist, those outcomes may even be illegal. The problem, though, is figuring out how these algorithms come to their conclusions. Algorithms can be deeply complex and, if they are

---

[79] https://www.ftc.gov/system/files/documents/reports/big-data-tool-inclusion-or-exclusion-understanding-issues/160106big-data-rpt.pdf

proprietary to the company rather than being open to inspection, they're hard to analyse in the first place. Their biases may even be accidental.

For example, researchers from Carnegie Mellon University developed a tool called AdFisher, which they used in 2015 to study how Google shows ads to different people. AdFisher created 1,000 simulated people, half of them male and half female, who then "visited" various top employment sites in order to get Google to start showing them ads relating to new jobs. The researchers found that Google's ads seem to show better-paying positions to men than to women. "The male users were shown the high-paying job ads about 1,800 times, compared to female users who saw those ads about 300 times," said researcher Amit Datta.[80] Why did this discrepancy exist? The researchers had no idea, because they couldn't look at Google's algorithms.

The same big data principles are being taken to extremes in a new social control system being devised in China, with an intended roll-out date of around 2020. Under state-approved pilot projects, companies such as Alibaba's Sesame Credit are building databases that combine each person's civic information, such as traffic violations, with their financial information in order to come up with an algorithmically-derived "social credit" score.[81] Also included in this data stew is information about the items and services that people buy and consume. Incessant video-game playing, for example, might negatively affect the score by suggesting idleness. The credit-scoring systems that most people already take for granted can be bad enough, sometimes punishing people for having lived in the same house as strangers who didn't pay their bills. But the penalties proposed by the Chinese government are something else. Poor scores, denoting low trustworthiness, could result in restrictions on holding a company directorship, becoming a senior executive in a state-owned enterprise, becoming a civil servant, joining the military, working with food or being able to use natural resources such as grasslands or rivers. People

---

[80] https://www.cmu.edu/news/stories/archives/2015/july/online-ads-research.html

[81] http://www.bbc.com/news/world-asia-china-34592186

may also be banned from riding first class on trains or planes, visiting restaurants, staying in good hotels, sending their children to private schools, or building houses.[82]

China's social credit scheme is a continuation of the country's longstanding system of maintaining a *dang'an*, or secret file, on each citizen. The state's massive collection and collation of citizen data is not just aimed at deciding who is worthy of reward or punishment; the government also wants to use this information to try predicting who might commit a terrorist act in the future.[83] Ultimately, China's profiling mania is about securing the future of its ruling elite and entrenching control over Chinese citizens. If that were not the case, the transparency would go both ways. It doesn't; the Chinese government is used to operating in secrecy. If you can't look back at those who are looking at you, the surrender of your privacy probably isn't in your best interest.

Out Of Your Hands

When it comes to big data, the disempowerment doesn't stop with being only semi-aware of all the tracking and remaining unable to stop it. Too often, we have no way to find out what happens to the data once it's been collected and shared, or even to find out what the data actually entails.

The data broker Acxiom has a website called AboutTheData.com that lets you check out your record in order to correct it – a good thing for you, obviously, but also for Acxiom, which after all wants to sell accurate profiling information. It also lets you opt out of being included in Acxiom's databases. However, the site only works if you're in the US and willing to give up your social security number for identification. As

---

[82] https://chinacopyrightandmedia.wordpress.com/2016/09/25/opinions-concerning-accelerating-the-construction-of-credit-supervision-warning-and-punishment-mechanisms-for-persons-subject-to-enforcement-for-trust-breaking/

[83] https://www.bloomberg.com/news/articles/2016-03-03/china-tries-its-hand-at-pre-crime

Acxiom holds data on hundreds of millions of people outside the US, that's less than useful.

Facebook's terms explain that it shares its users' data with "third-party companies who help us provide and improve our services or who use advertising or related products, which makes it possible to operate our companies and provide free services to people around the world," which is nice, but the terms leave users none the wiser as to who those third-party companies are. It is, however, possible to find out the information Facebook holds on you. And that's largely thanks to an Austrian law student named Max Schrems, who has waged a long-running campaign against the social network's privacy abuses – with far-ranging consequences.

Schrems studied for a semester at the Santa Clara University School of Law in California, where he witnessed lawyers from Silicon Valley tech firms boast about ignoring European privacy laws. The penalties for breaking them were so low that they didn't have to take notice, they said. So in 2011 Schrems asked Facebook to give him all the data it held on him – a right he held under EU data protection law – in order to see how well the company would comply.[84] After repeatedly emailing the company, he finally received a CD containing 1,222 pages of data encompassing his Facebook history, including all his actions on the platform and even stuff he thought he had deleted.

Shocked to see that this information included a supposedly-deleted private chat with a sick friend, and concerned about how hard it had been to get his data, Schrems and his "Europe v Facebook" activist group decided to take action. They complained to the data protection authority in Ireland, where Facebook has its European headquarters, and the regulator eventually asked Facebook to become more transparent about the data it holds, and to let people access their data more easily. As a result, in 2012 Facebook offered its users the ability to easily download an "expanded archive" of their information. Schrems and his group were not impressed, though, noting that

---

[84] https://www.nytimes.com/2015/10/11/business/international/behind-the-european-privacy-ruling-thats-confounding-silicon-valley.html

Facebook was still holding back a lot of data. For example, Facebook has a record of the webpages each user has browsed that have "like" buttons embedded in them, but it didn't give Schrems this information. As Schrems noted, even some porn pages have "like" buttons on them, so this record is sensitive to say the least.[85]

This was far from Schrems's crowning achievement, though. A few years later, the privacy crusader would become better known for sinking a major transatlantic agreement – the "Safe Harbour" scheme, which was supposed to give US companies an easy way to import Europeans' personal data. The scheme's destruction caused transatlantic panic. And the spark that lit that particular fuse was a man called Edward Snowden.

**

Our reality has both online and offline layers, which is why it can be so frustrating to see people treating "cyberspace" as some separate place. The online layer is spreading across the offline at a great pace, as more elements of our world and our existence get connected to the internet. And as we inhabit this online layer – as we live, work and play in it – we develop our online selves. The problem is, we're not the only ones involved in that development. Our online selves are partly our own construction, via social media, blogs and other platforms, but they are also built by giant corporations, many of whom remain obscure to the general public.

As the profiles compiled by these data merchants can have real consequences for us, it's important that we have control over them. But that's not happening yet. The profilers hold most of the power. Yes, we get to flip a privacy switch here and block a tracking cookie there, but there's really no escape from being profiled online – if one cookie doesn't toss you into the big data stew, others will. For most of us, there's limited scope for shaping what our profiles looks like, or being

---

[85] https://gigaom.com/2012/04/12/students-force-facebook-to-cough-up-more-user-data/

able to see what they look like at all. It's a heavy toll to pay for being part of online society, and one that people shouldn't really have to pay.

There are several ways in which we can deal with this situation. The first is obvious, if unfortunate: limit your online activities, as well as the things you reveal online. Ideally, this wouldn't be necessary, though it may seem like the simplest solution to many people. At the other extreme, you could just surrender to what the tech journalist Jack Clark called "data feudalism". Back in 2009, he wrote: "… People yoke themselves to the providers by handing over their data in exchange for use of the services. It's like a feudal system: the social-networking companies are sustained by the data flooding into them, and gain in power from the exchange. People upload their photos, their messages and other data from their personal life, but the service providers control how that information is presented to the world."[86]

There's an argument for saying that the trend is irreversible, and that more data is the solution, in order to at least ensure that the great, shadowy profiling systems paint accurate images of us. That argument may work for some, but for those who fear that big data will extend and intensify the discrimination they already experience in the offline world, it's cold comfort. For a fairer solution, we can try to ensure that people get increased agency over their digital selves through real controls and real lines in the sand. That means enforceable regulations.

In 2016, the European Union passed the world's most comprehensive privacy law, the General Data Protection Regulation (GDPR), which will come into effect in May 2018.[87] Unlike the bloc's existing Data Protection Directive, the GDPR doesn't give EU countries leeway to bend the rules, and those rules include giving people the right to tell companies to stop profiling them and to delete the information they already hold. What happens to personal data is supposed to

---

[86] http://www.zdnet.com/article/facebook-google-welcome-to-the-new-feudalism/

[87] http://eur-lex.europa.eu/legal-content/EN/TXT/?uri=uriserv:OJ.L_.2016.119.01.0001.01.ENG&toc=OJ:L:2016:119:TOC

become clearer, and our data is supposed to become better-protected under this law. EU privacy law has already proven influential around the world, and the GDPR will hopefully follow suit. But for now, these principles remain far from universal.

With accountability and restrictions, of course the big internet beasts will do what they like with our digital representations. So, just as human rights are supposed to protect us from physical harm, they need to protect us in the online layer. This equivalence isn't just about freedom from exploitation by commercial concerns; it's about freedom in the civic, political sense. After all, it's not just corporations that are interested in knowing more about us.

CHAPTER 3: HIJACKING THE MACHINE

Edward Snowden was a contractor for the National Security Agency (NSA), the American signals intelligence agency. Like Government Communications Headquarters (GCHQ) in the UK, and the *Bundesnachrichtendienst* (BND) in Germany, the NSA's primary mission is to spy on the communications of foreign adversaries such as terrorists or government officials in rival countries. However, Snowden was uncomfortable with what he saw in reality: mass surveillance operations in which the NSA and partners such as GCHQ were scooping up the communications of billions of ordinary people. And so, in mid-2013, Snowden downloaded scores of NSA documents onto a memory stick and fled to Hong Kong, where he met with journalists from the *Guardian* and revealed operations that would shock the world.

The first story was published on 5 June 2013, before Snowden identified himself as the whistleblower. It involved the telecoms operator Verizon, which had been secretly passing on Americans' call records – in bulk – to the country's intelligence services.[88] The next day, the *Guardian* revealed the existence of a programme called PRISM, through which the spy agencies got information on their surveillance targets from some of the biggest web firms.[89] An NSA PowerPoint presentation, dated April 2013, described PRISM as "collection directly from the servers of these US Service Providers: Microsoft, Yahoo, Google, Facebook, PalTalk, AOL, Skype, YouTube, Apple."

The agencies' co-opting of corporate systems didn't always necessarily happen with the companies' knowledge. As shown in a *Washington Post* story based on the Snowden leaks, the NSA and GCHQ found a way to use Google's profiling cookies to follow suspects around the web. They were also intercepting mobile apps'

---

[88] https://www.theguardian.com/world/2013/jun/06/nsa-phone-records-verizon-court-order
[89] https://www.theguardian.com/world/2013/jun/06/us-tech-giants-nsa-data

location data, in order to figure out where mobile devices were physically located.[90] This is more like hijacking a system than winning over its operator.

If you're keen on maintaining your privacy, commercial surveillance is problematic enough. However, one thing that makes such systems outright dangerous is their vulnerability to being commandeered by others with a different agenda. The fact that these services are so centralised does not help matters – everything you do on Facebook or Google is funnelled through those companies' servers, making such corporate systems an obvious target for anyone who wants to know what you've been doing. Whatever your stance on privacy, you probably don't set up a Google or Facebook account in order to share your personal information with intelligence services. And you're particularly unlikely to want foreign spies nosing through your communications.

Just because they can, doesn't mean they should. And, as Snowden's further revelations went on to show, there are disturbingly few limits to what intelligence services are capable of doing as they exploit the opportunities presented to them by the internet.

Google For Spies

The PRISM revelation sparked a storm in Silicon Valley and around the world, with the named companies scrambling to assure their users that the NSA did not actually have a direct connection to everything going on in their systems. The exact truth remains murky, but what the NSA definitely did have was the ability to demand, via the Federal Bureau of Investigation (FBI), the data that those companies hold on their users – while banning the web firms from telling people they were handing over this data. The whole process was supposedly kept in check by the secretive Foreign Intelligence Surveillance Act (FISA) Court, whose hearings were closed to the public.

---

[90] https://www.washingtonpost.com/news/the-switch/wp/2013/12/10/nsa-uses-google-cookies-to-pinpoint-targets-for-hacking/

The Snowden revelations horrified many people around the world because, for those who were not American, the NSA faced no restrictions in demanding and searching through their data. Combined with the fact that the web services they use are frequently American, this left billions of people in a vulnerable position. For European users of those services, it also meant that the web firms and US agencies were potentially stomping all over their fundamental privacy rights – human rights that were supposed to be guaranteed by European law.

That said, many European countries were themselves partnering with the US agency. PRISM was only part of an arsenal of surveillance tactics that also included tapping into core communications infrastructure with international cooperation. In its now-famous PowerPoint presentations, the NSA recommended that agents use PRISM in conjunction with Upstream, the umbrella name for a series of direct taps on the arteries of the internet. By accessing these core networks, it's possible to scoop up vast quantities of the data that flows around the world. The UK's GCHQ is a particularly useful partner when it comes to collecting such information, thanks to a top-secret programme that was subtly named "Mastering the Internet".[91] Partly because of its location on Europe's periphery, dozens of undersea internet cables come ashore in the UK, making it an ideal place to monitor the data that's passing through. In exchange for information gleaned from this deep-level monitoring, the US tells its partners when it has detected terrorist threats that may affect them. It also lets them use its custom-built software for sifting through intercepted data – a kind of Google Search for spies, called XKeyscore.[92]

The American and European legal systems approach privacy and surveillance in significantly different ways. In the US, agencies can relatively freely collect people's data, with the law only seriously restricting what they can do with the data afterwards. In other words,

---

[91] https://www.theguardian.com/uk/2013/jun/21/gchq-mastering-the-internet

[92] https://www.theguardian.com/world/2013/jul/31/nsa-top-secret-program-online-data

the US sees "surveillance" as something that only happens when someone decides to look at what's been collected – at least, that's what the intelligence agencies argued after Snowden blew his whistle. In the EU, merely collecting the data can qualify as surveillance. In the US, data belongs to whoever collects it, such as an online profiling operation. In Europe, personal data belongs to the person and, outside of certain exceptions, they are supposed to be able to control what happens to it, including its collection. And in Europe, unlike in the US, privacy and data protection are classed as fundamental rights, which means they are legally enforceable human rights.[93]

Following the Snowden revelations, Max Schrems, the Austrian law student who made it his mission to fight Facebook's privacy practices, sprang into action. He complained to the Irish data protection commissioner that his Facebook data was not properly protected when transferred to the US, because of the NSA's surveillance programmes. As Schrems had complained to the Irish watchdog several times before, the regulator decided he was a "frivolous and vexatious" complainant and refused to investigate, pointing to a deal between the US and the EU called Safe Harbour.[94]

The Safe Harbour programme began in 2000, giving US firms an easy way to legally import Europeans' personal data – a pretty big deal, seeing how important US online services are. Under EU data protection law, companies in foreign countries can only import the personal data of Europeans without restrictions if the European Commission has decided that those countries' data protection laws are "adequate", meaning they protect Europeans' privacy rights as effectively as EU law protects them. Because the US did not have "adequate" data protection laws and because so many US firms import European people's data, the Commission came up with Safe Harbour as a way of working around the issue, to keep data flowing across the Atlantic. By signing up to the Safe Harbour register, US companies could promise that *they* abided by

---

[93] http://eur-lex.europa.eu/legal-content/EN/TXT/?uri=CELEX:12012P/TXT
[94] http://uk.reuters.com/article/us-eu-ireland-privacy-schrems-idUKKCN0S02NY20151006

EU-strength data protection standards, even if their own country did not force them to do so.

The Irish privacy regulator told Schrems it could not investigate his complaints because Facebook had signed up to the Safe Harbour register; the regulator said it had no authority to question the system that the Commission had set up. Schrems disagreed and took his case all the way up to the Court of Justice of the European Union, the EU's highest court. In 2015, he won. The court ruled not only that EU countries' privacy regulators had the power to investigate all potential abuses of fundamental privacy rights, but that Safe Harbour was itself invalid. The Commission should not have decided 15 years before that the system would provide enough protection for Europeans' rights, because Safe Harbour in no way stopped the US authorities from poking their noses around Europeans' data at will.

The ruling was a bombshell, because it suddenly left thousands of US companies without a legal basis for importing and processing the personal data of European customers and employees. There were other legal mechanisms they could use, but those took a lot of time and effort to set up – Safe Harbour had been the easy route, and it was gone. The Commission and the US government had to quickly come up with a new scheme. This arrived in mid-2016 in the form of a system called "Privacy Shield" that was similar to Safe Harbour, but that was supposed to come with additional safeguards. Companies on the Privacy Shield register had to agree to more monitoring of their data-handling practices by US regulators, more restrictions on passing on data to third parties, and a new complaint mechanism for Europeans who want to challenge the treatment of their data by US authorities. However, within months Privacy Shield was already subject to a legal challenge by privacy activists. [95] Although the Commission said in its first annual review of Privacy Shield that the new system was working well enough to provide adequate protection for Europeans – a statement

95

https://www.theregister.co.uk/2016/10/28/irish_advocates_fight_euus_priva cy_pact_as_tech_giants_flock_to_sign_up/

that was to be expected, seeing as the Commission didn't want Safe Harbour scrapped in the first place – it said some of the new safeguards were yet to be fully implemented.[96] Privacy Shield's long-term outlook seems shaky, to say the least.

The fundamental problem is one of targeting – the US agencies still claim the right to collect people's data in bulk, for broad reasons such as investigating cybersecurity issues and terrorism. There will always be cybersecurity and terrorist threats out there, so there will always be an excuse to collect everyone's data. EU law only allows surveillance when it's properly targeted, otherwise it's just mass surveillance, and therefore disproportionate and illegal.

There is, theoretically at least, broad consensus around the world that privacy is a human right. When international human rights law emerged after the Second World War, in the form of the Universal Declaration of Human Rights, many countries agreed: "No one shall be subjected to arbitrary interference with his privacy, family, home or correspondence, nor to attacks upon his honour and reputation. Everyone has the right to the protection of the law against such interference or attacks." Almost identical language made it into the International Covenant on Civil and Political Rights, which was adopted by the United Nations General Assembly in 1966. To date, 169 countries have signed and ratified the later treaty – 19 countries have neither signed nor ratified it, including Malaysia and Saudi Arabia, and seven countries have signed but not ratified the treaty, including China and Cuba.

However, although it is a well-defined human right, privacy is not generally seen as an absolute right, like the rights to life and freedom of thought and freedom from torture. In the international treaties, it's "arbitrary" interference with privacy that's banned. Someone's right to privacy can still be overridden, but only when there's a good reason for doing so. For example, if the authorities suspect someone is a criminal and they're trying to catch them out, it may be acceptable to monitor their communications with others, even if doing so infringes on their

---

[96] http://ec.europa.eu/newsroom/just/item-detail.cfm?item_id=605619

privacy and the privacy of the people with whom they're communicating. Depending on the circumstances, this may be seen as proportionate. But it would never be proportionate to monitor the communications of everyone in the city where the target lives, or the whole country.

Most people accept the idea of law enforcement and the need for intelligence services, because some people do pose threats to the rest of us. We need to have spies and investigators who can fight threats in a targeted way. However, mass surveillance is an entirely different matter, constantly infringing the privacy rights of the majority of people who have done nothing to warrant such treatment. Might there be a situation in which mass surveillance *was* proportionate? Perhaps, but it would have to be literally extraordinary – a genuine state of emergency, not a way of life.

Targeted surveillance can involve hacking into someone's phone, to make it possible to listen to calls and see what's on their screen. It can involve going through their Gmail emails, which the spies can get using the PRISM scheme. However, mass surveillance programmes generally involve monitoring what's known as metadata – data about data, such as the information about where and when an email is sent or a call is made, or which website somebody is visiting, rather than the contents of that email or call or website. After Snowden, the agencies were very keen to point out that metadata is not the same as the actual substance of people's conversations and the details of what they do online. They claimed they do not poke around in that amount of detail until they've launched a targeted investigation. However, there's an enormous amount you can tell about a person from their metadata. You can map their networks, figure out their movements, get a good idea of their leanings and even make predictions about what they might do. By looking at someone's communications metadata, you may be able to figure out if they're a terrorism risk, but you'll also know if they called a suicide prevention hotline or accessed a drug counselling website. You'll know if they visited specialist pornographic websites, or regularly called the same number when their partner was out of town.

Sometimes the metadata tells you as much as the contents of communications.

In late 2016, the UK passed a very invasive law called the Investigatory Powers Act. This was what's known as a "data retention" law, as (among other things) it forced internet service providers to keep records of their customers' communications and web-browsing histories. The act gave all sorts of agencies – even the Food Standards Agency – the ability to see what citizens were doing online. The government stressed that the records would only include the main domains of the websites people visit, rather than the contents of specific pages. So, for example, the records would show that a person visited "bbc.com", as opposed to a specific news article on the BBC's website. But that metadata can be highly revealing on its own. As tech law lecturer Paul Bernal wrote after the bill went through: "The data that will be gathered – known as 'internet connection records' — was characterised as the equivalent of an itemised phone bill for the internet. In reality, it's a record of our movements, interests, friends, health, sexual preferences and even our tastes in music. And even more information about us could be derived from that data."[97]

Shortly after the Investigatory Powers Act came into force, the Court of Justice of the European Union ruled that it was illegal for EU countries to introduce blanket data retention programmes of this sort, unless they were limited to fighting serious crime and subject to independent oversight.[98] In the light of that ruling, the UK's Investigatory Powers Tribunal asked the Court of Justice to assess whether the British snooping law was itself illegal under EU law.[99] It may take a while to arrive, but the ruling is predictable. The EU court has been hammering home the same point about targeting for some time now. In 2014, it struck down a 2006 directive that forced EU

---

[97] https://theconversation.com/how-the-uk-passed-the-most-invasive-surveillance-law-in-democratic-history-69247
[98] http://www.dw.com/en/european-court-of-justice-rules-against-mass-data-retention-in-eu/a-36859714
[99] https://techcrunch.com/2017/09/09/europes-top-court-must-rule-on-uk-spies-bulk-powers-says-tribunal/

governments to have data retention laws.[100] The next year, it struck down Safe Harbour over mass surveillance concerns. Meanwhile, later in the same year, the European Court of Human Rights censured Russia for allowing its spies to monitor people's mobile communications with no real safeguards.[101]

European law seems fairly clear on the issue of mass surveillance's lack of proportionality and safeguards, but that doesn't stop governments and agencies from repeatedly trying their luck. They insist it's the best way to figure out who really deserves a closer look – though plenty of experts insist otherwise.

Chilling the Web

Even if everyone with access to mass surveillance systems was an angel, it would be rather important to know whether the system did what was intended. There are wildly differing opinions about how well mass surveillance functions as a gateway to targeted surveillance. The computer security guru Bruce Schneier has long argued that indiscriminate data collection actually makes it harder to identify genuine threats, because it increases the number of false positives. "Finding terrorism plots is not a problem that lends itself to data mining. It's a needle-in-a-haystack problem, and throwing more hay on the pile doesn't make that problem any easier," he wrote back in 2005, discussing the counter-terrorism authorities' post-9/11 "Total Information Awareness" drive.[102] The programme was de-funded after a public outcry, but was a forerunner to the programmes Snowden revealed.

100

http://curia.europa.eu/juris/document/document.jsf?docid=162437&mode=req&pageIndex=1&dir=&occ=first&part=1&text=&doclang=EN&cid=30671
[101] http://hudoc.echr.coe.int/eng#{"itemid":["001-159324"]}
102

https://www.schneier.com/essays/archives/2005/03/why_data_mining_wont.html

Others have echoed Schneier's point. Computer scientist Ray Corrigan, for example, wrote in 2015: "It is statistically impossible for total population surveillance to be an effective tool for catching terrorists. Even if your magic terrorist-catching machine has a false positive rate of 1 in 1,000 – and no security technology comes anywhere near this – every time you asked it for suspects in the UK it would flag 60,000 innocent people."[103]

On the other side of the argument, former GCHQ intelligence officer David Wells wrote the following that, if agents were overwhelmed by data, it wasn't because there was too much data. Instead, he said, there were "too many intelligence targets" – too many people that the government needed to spy on.[104] "Bulk collection has allowed intelligence analysts to ask smarter questions. And to do so with greater confidence, knowing they are querying a broader and more comprehensive dataset," he wrote. Wells also pointed to a review of the British intelligence agencies' mass surveillance powers by the country's independent reviewer of terrorism legislation, David Anderson.[105] After going through multiple case studies, Anderson concluded that there was a "proven operational case" for the agencies' mass spying. It's worth noting that Anderson did not go into whether these powers were desirable or whether they should have more safeguards, but he did say that without them investigations "would often be less effective, more dangerous, more resource-intensive, more intrusive or slower".

It's not hard to believe that mass surveillance makes the jobs of intelligence and law enforcement agencies easier. However, that doesn't justify what the spies and cops are doing. After all, police states make life easier for investigators, because they don't have to worry about

---

103

http://www.slate.com/articles/health_and_science/new_scientist/2015/01/mass_surveillance_against_terrorism_gathering_intelligence_on_all_is_statistically.html

[104] http://www.computerweekly.com/opinion/Investigatory-Powers-Bill-the-case-for-mass-surveillance

[105] https://terrorismlegislationreviewer.independent.gov.uk/bulk-powers-review-report/

human rights slowing them down, but that's not a desirable way of running things. This cannot be said enough: mass surveillance is a massive infringement on human rights. At the very least, it creates a tool of great power that could become incredibly dangerous in the wrong hands. The systems for mass surveillance might sometimes be set up by governments that have good intentions, but their successors may be authoritarians who want to stamp out opposition, whether by blackmail or by simply making it impossible for the opposition to organise its next moves in secret.

Even in the "right" hands, surveillance powers are often abused. For example, a number of NSA officers have been caught using their resources to spy on their love interests. The agency admitted in 2013 that one employee had listened in on the calls of the woman with whom he was sleeping. Meanwhile, a female employee found a foreign phone number on her husband's phone and, suspecting infidelity, used her privileges to collect his calls.[106] Snowden also claimed that NSA employees collecting people's data would sometimes find sexually compromising pictures that they'd pass around their colleagues.[107]

Journalists and their sources are popular targets for surveillance. The UK's Investigatory Powers Act of 2016 made sure that investigators had to get a proper warrant if they wanted to spy on journalists, to try to uncover who it was that gave them confidential information. But that was only because of the degree to which the British police abused earlier surveillance laws. Indeed, the National Union of Journalists complained that authorities used the earlier legislation to spy on journalists in a "systemic and institutionalised" way.[108] For example, in 2012, reporters in Cleveland, in the north-east of England, were following up on a racial discrimination case involving the local police force. Cleveland Police prosecuted an officer from a minority

[106] http://edition.cnn.com/2013/09/27/politics/nsa-snooping/

[107] http://www.forbes.com/sites/kashmirhill/2014/07/17/nsa-responds-to-snowden-claim-that-intercepted-nude-pics-routinely-passed-around-by-employees/#67948a7cbf96

[108] https://www.theguardian.com/media/2014/nov/04/police-ripa-powers-spy-journalists-sources

background, who had complained about discrimination, for theft. The officer, who said he had been stitched up, won more than £800,000 in compensation for the malicious prosecution. Cleveland Police still claimed the force was not institutionally racist, but an anonymous tipster told reporters from *The Northern Echo*, a local newspaper, that an internal police report had found institutional racism. Furious at the leak, the police force put the reporters under surveillance, seizing records of a million minutes of the journalists' phone calls.[109]

This isn't just a British problem, of course. In 2013, US investigators seized the phone records of Associated Press reporters without explaining why. "There can be no possible justification for such an overbroad collection of the telephone communications of The Associated Press and its reporters," thundered AP president Gary Pruitt.[110] And in 2017, *Der Spiegel* revealed that Germany's BND spy agency had systematically spied on foreign journalists for years, trying to identify their sources.[111] The BBC, whose employees were among those targeted, complained they "should be able to operate freely and safely, with full protection for their sources."[112] Journalists have an ethical responsibility to protect their sources' identities. If they're being monitored in this way, they can't keep their promises, with the result that people are less likely to contact them with valuable tips about corruption and wrongdoing. If they're being watched, we're kept in the dark.

Mass surveillance also undermines the confidentiality that other professionals need to be able to offer their clients, such as doctors and lawyers. Following the Snowden leaks, the British government admitted that it spies on lawyer-client communications, including in

---

109

http://bigstory.ap.org/article/791aa30b21c5467499babf130754c593/reporters-spy-saga-gives-glimpse-uk-surveillance-culture

[110] http://www.nytimes.com/2013/05/14/us/phone-records-of-journalists-of-the-associated-press-seized-by-us.html

[111] http://www.spiegel.de/international/germany/german-intelligence-spied-on-foreign-journalists-for-years-a-1136188.html

[112] http://www.bbc.com/news/world-europe-39080256

cases where the client is trying to sue the government. This admission came following a lawsuit against the government by members of two families who had been kidnapped and tortured by US and UK intelligence – those taken included children and a pregnant woman. In the course of that lawsuit, the lawyers representing the al Saadi and Belhaj families said they were worried that the intelligence services were spying on their communications with their clients.[113] The government was forced to release internal guidelines that said it was fine to "target the communications of lawyers" and use the results "just like any other item of intelligence".

Surveillance also has what's sometimes called a "chilling" effect on regular people and their inquisitiveness. Mass surveillance works by monitoring internet traffic for suspicious keywords and other things that might be of interest, such as visits to certain websites. Snowden may have done a great service to the world by exposing the existence and reach of these programmes, but the flipside is that we're now more likely to be cautious in our intellectual exploration, because we're more likely to suspect that we're being watched. A 2016 study found that, following the Snowden revelations a few years earlier, people were at least 10 percent less likely than before to visit Wikipedia pages that discussed terrorism.[114] This didn't just apply in the immediate aftermath of the Snowden news; it appeared to be a long-term effect. A separate study in 2015 suggested the revelations were followed by a 5 percent drop-off in web searches for privacy-sensitive terms.[115] A survey of American writers in late 2013 found around one in six were avoiding researching certain topics, in order to avoid coming to the attention of the authorities.[116]

113

http://www.reprieve.org.uk/press/2014_11_06_uk_govt_force_release_spying_lawyers/

[114] https://papers.ssrn.com/sol3/papers.cfm?abstract_id=2769645

[115] https://papers.ssrn.com/sol3/papers.cfm?abstract_id=2412564

[116] https://pen.org/press-release/2013/11/13/pen-american-center-report-shows-impact-nsa-surveillance-american-writers

Ironically, this again highlights a key difference between modern mass surveillance and the kind practiced in the pre-internet age, for example in the Soviet Union and East Germany. Along with the monitoring of phone calls and letters, the intelligence services of both countries relied heavily on informants. At the time of the Berlin Wall's fall in 1989, the East German Ministry for State Security (commonly known as the Stasi) had more than 90,000 full-time employees and around 180,000 full-time, unofficial collaborators from the local populace.[117] The entire population of East Germany numbered 17 million, so more than 1 percent of East Germans were informants. These were sprawling operations that could not be kept secret from their populations. Indeed, one of the aims of the KGB and Stasi was to chill dissent by making people too scared to oppose the government line. By contrast, today's liberal, capitalist democracies have tried to build their surveillance states in secret, a task made easier by the fact that everyone's social and commercial activities are going online. These activities are conducted on platforms owned by companies that have to submit to a court order when they receive one. There's no need to recruit hundreds of thousands of informants, when the providers of the commercial services that underpin modern life will do the job more discreetly and reliably.

At least the modern alternatives to the Stasi don't turn citizens into conscious traitors to their friends and families. But personal treachery aside, mass surveillance clearly threatens not just privacy, but also free expression, freedom of information and even fair trials. It threatens democracy itself, because it places too much power in the hands of those who control the surveillance systems or have access to them, and makes it more difficult to challenge that power. It's a system of control, wielded by individuals who, at least in democracies, are supposed to be servants of the people. And we can't escape it. Faced with the monitoring of both private corporations and the intelligence services that piggyback on their systems, it is currently near-impossible to evade

---

[117] http://www.spiegel.de/international/germany/east-german-domestic-surveillance-went-far-beyond-the-stasi-a-1042883.html

the vast dragnets of mass surveillance unless one simply doesn't use the internet. In the words of programmer and entrepreneur Maciej Cegłowski, "opting out of surveillance capitalism is like opting out of electricity, or cooked foods – you are free to do it in theory. In practice, it... means opting out of much of modern life."[118]

Given the risks and demonstrably negative effects of mass surveillance, you might think that Snowden's revelations would have prompted reforms to better protect citizens and make the internet more trustworthy. But you'd be wrong.

Entrenching Control

Politicians and officials in Europe may be largely keen to protect citizens from corporate surveillance, but the story has been quite different when it comes to state surveillance. The most depressing outcome of Edward Snowden's revelations is that, certainly in Europe, they have merely resulted in the legitimisation of the illegal activities he revealed.

After Snowden told the world what the UK intelligence services were up to, human rights groups complained about GCHQ to the Investigatory Powers Tribunal. The partially-secret tribunal found that British agencies had been illegally receiving data from the US intelligence services' mass surveillance programs. However, it said the illegality came from the programme's extreme secrecy – now that Snowden had revealed what was going on, the sharing was now magically legal.[119] The UK's Investigatory Powers Act of 2016 also explicitly legalised many of the mass surveillance and mass hacking activities that had previously remained in the shadows (although it may yet be deemed illegal by the EU courts).

In Germany, chancellor Angela Merkel expressed great outrage at the news that the NSA was spying on her communications. However, when the German Bundestag subsequently held an enquiry into

---

[118] http://idlewords.com/talks/sase_panel.htm
[119] https://www.privacyinternational.org/node/482

Snowden's revelations and the German intelligence services' own activities, it turned out that the country's signals intelligence service was itself monitoring huge amounts of data. The BND was taking advantage of the fact that the world's largest internet exchange point – where data flows between different parts of the internet's infrastructure – is situated in Frankfurt.[120] The law allowed the agency to scoop up a maximum 20 percent of the traffic flowing through the hub, which is called De-Cix, but the BND was monitoring far more than that. In 2016 De-Cix's operators sued the government over BND surveillance. The solution? In October 2016, the German government voted through a new law allowing the BND to monitor *all* the internet traffic flowing through the country.[121]

The problem is that politicians at the European Commission and Parliament can make new EU privacy laws, but they can't tell national governments what to do when it comes to national security issues. That's crucial, because few national politicians stand up for people's privacy when national security is the issue. Security is seen as a far more emotive factor for voters, and any politician who promotes privacy above security is opening themselves up to future criticism by their opponents when there is a terrorist attack in the country.

There's an argument for saying it's a good thing that governments are now explicitly legalising their spies' murky activities. The logic goes like this: now that these activities exist within a framework that is written down in statute, the framework can be improved over time, through the democratic process. But this is a naïve hope, for two reasons. Firstly, in an environment governed by the politics of fear – of terrorism, immigration, international insecurity and serious crime – there's no political will to roll back the intelligence agencies' powers. The only thing likely to change this reality would be a strong backlash against a highly authoritarian regime that has demonstrated the dangers of mass surveillance. Given that such a regime would likely be using its

---

[120] https://netzpolitik.org/2015/how-the-german-foreign-intelligence-agency-bnd-tapped-the-internet-exchange-point-de-cix-in-frankfurt-since-2009/
[121] http://www.reuters.com/article/us-germany-spying-idUSKCN12L1ER

surveillance powers to entrench its power, the backlash might have trouble getting traction. What's more, the types of personal data that spies can spy on are proliferating at speed, as we connect more and more things around us to the internet. Legislative improvements take place over many years, if they take place at all, and these laws are new. They're not going to improve anytime soon, and in the meantime they will be exploited in increasingly invasive ways.

Many of the new data sources will be sensors that measure things and use the internet to report back to the companies that run them. Smart meters already report energy-use measurements to utility companies; smart cars send driving and location data to insurers. Our phones are packed with sensors for measuring movement and light, or photographing stuff – a camera is a sensor too. All this is what's known in the tech industry as the "internet of things". It's a spy's dream. Smart electricity meters can reveal when someone is at home. Home surveillance cameras send data back to providers that would, if legally compelled, have to give law enforcement access to their systems. Our phones don't just track us all the time (even if they're turned off), but the sensors embedded in them can be used to identify us, too.

Here's what CIA chief technology officer Gus Hunt said at a pre-Snowden conference in 2013, regarding fitness trackers that are packed with sensors: [122]

"You guys know the Fitbit, right? It's just a simple three-axis accelerometer. We like these things because they don't have any – well, I won't go into that. What happens is, they discovered that just simply by looking at the data what they can find out is with pretty good accuracy what your gender is, whether you're tall or you're short, whether you're heavy or light, but what's really most intriguing is that you can be 100 percent guaranteed to be identified by simply your gait – how you walk.

"Now this could be a really good thing. Think about this as a security app. If you're walking along and you want to access your bank

---

[122] https://gigaom.com/2013/03/20/even-the-cia-is-struggling-to-deal-with-the-volume-of-real-time-social-data/2/

code, maybe it could become simplified because they can with absolute assurance know it's you by your gait trying to do something with your bank. On the other hand, if you don't want to be found or you want to protect yourself, maybe you don't want to have somebody know what your gait looks like so they can figure out where you are at all times."

When Hunt referred to the intelligence services appreciating the lack of something in the internet of things, it's not hard to figure out what he meant: decent security. The agencies don't just passively intercept communications. When they want to set up mass surveillance, or when they want to conduct targeted investigations, spies find it very useful to break into things. And unfortunately they're not the only ones.

***

For all its benefits and potential, the internet is a surveillance machine. Where data retention laws exist, your internet service providers are essentially drafted as spies by the authorities, and they have to follow you around the online layer even if they don't want to. We wouldn't accept this in the physical realm, certainly in democratic societies. There is certainly a very strong case for using tools such as virtual private networks (VPNs) to hide your activities from your broadband company. If you've done nothing wrong, you have no reason to reveal yourself.

It's disturbing that so many politicians seem happy to introduce draconian surveillance mechanisms in their countries, but many of those supporting such measures probably don't see them that way. Whether it's down to a general lack of technical knowledge or the pleadings of the intelligence agencies, it's easy to rationalise data retention and taps on internet infrastructure as mere mechanisms for identifying targets and carrying out investigations on them. The problem is that they go further than that – to get to the desired result, mass surveillance is taking place. It happens as soon as the authorities' and internet service providers' systems record all that data about what people are doing. At that point, people's fundamental rights are infringed, even if no-one looks at the data afterwards. The spies have done their job.

These are tools for tyrants – the kind of social control structures that denoted authoritarian regimes in the past, and that still do so today. They're dangerous. If they're not abused today, they will be abused tomorrow. While we have the democratic capacity to do so, we must push back. We need to make it clear to our elected representatives that our societies don't flourish by being tightly controlled, but by enjoying the freedoms that previous generations won at great personal cost.

To be clear, spies have to spy and investigators have to investigate. But the principles of human rights dictate that interference with people's privacy must remain proportionate to the threat that's being investigated. We need to maintain boundaries on investigators' activities that ensure regular people maintain control over the privacy of their digital selves – something that's impossible under systems of mass surveillance. And while we're at it, we need to make sure that our spies and investigators going about their work don't end up leaving us less, rather than more, secure.

On 29 November 2012, as Syria's civil war intensified, the internet suddenly went down across the country. The Syrian government denied responsibility, blaming rebels for cutting internet cables. CloudFlare, a prominent American provider of content delivery and website protection services, pointed out that this explanation appeared "unlikely" as the internet had gone down everywhere in Syria.[123] The rebels would have had to have simultaneously cut all four of the telecommunications cables carrying data in and out of the country. CloudFlare pointed out that the state-run Syrian Telecommunications Establishment was the country's sole internet access provider, and its gateways to the Syrian internet had shut down within the space of a couple minutes, in a "systematic way". It looked like the government was responsible. Internet access in Syria only returned a few days later.

Almost two years after the incident, Edward Snowden offered another explanation. In an interview with *Wired*, he said that, when he was a contractor at the US National Security Agency, an officer there told him the NSA had been responsible for the big Syrian outage.[124] According to that officer, the incident was an accident. Tailored Access Operations (TAO), the NSA's elite hacking unit, had broken into one of the core Syrian internet routers in order to install a wiretap, but had accidentally knocked out the router. The TAO staff tried to fix it but, since it was out of action and they were not physically in front of it, they failed. Oops.

Snowden also revealed that, between 2010 and 2011, the UK's GCHQ spy agency had hacked into the systems of Belgacom, the largest telecommunications company in Belgium.[125] Belgacom served high-profile customers such as the European Commission, European Parliament and European Council. However, it was also possible that

---

[123] https://blog.cloudflare.com/how-syria-turned-off-the-internet/
[124] https://www.wired.com/2014/08/edward-snowden/
[125] https://theintercept.com/2014/12/13/belgacom-hack-gchq-inside-story/

the British were trying to track the phones of suspects travelling within Europe, or gain access to the internet infrastructure that Belgacom operates in regions like North Africa and the Middle East. GCHQ had plentiful access to core internet infrastructure, partly because of geography but also thanks to secret deals with telecoms companies like BT, Vodafone and Verizon Business. As Snowden's documents revealed, the agency got these operators to let it tap their undersea cables, which carry data between countries and between continents. GCHQ was able to copy and store enormous amounts of information. According to the *Guardian*, the tapped cables could have carried as much as 21 petabytes a day. It kept the data for up to 30 days, giving it time to search for particular people's activities if it wanted to.[126]

The British spy agency was able to look through its troves of collected data to find the information it needed about Belgacom's engineers. The spies found traces of cookies from Google, Yahoo and LinkedIn that they were able to correlate with the engineers' suspected IP addresses – the numbers identifying their internet connections – in order to confirm their identities. GCHQ's hackers picked three engineers as targets and tracked which websites they visited. Then, in early 2011, the spies played a trick on their targets. When the engineers thought they were visiting LinkedIn, they were in fact redirected to a dummy LinkedIn page that contained malware. The malware infected their computers, giving the spies access to Belgacom's systems. Thanks to that access, GCHQ was able to tap into the traffic passing over Belgacom's networks. Game over – at least, until 2013, when Belgacom finally cottoned onto the fact that it had been hacked, and embarked on an expensive clean-up operation.

Of course, most of us are unlikely to be targeted by national intelligence agencies – we're just not that useful or interesting to them. But other people may take an interest in us. Maybe we hold corporate secrets. Maybe we have money. And maybe our computers would just make useful weapons.

---

[126] https://www.theguardian.com/business/2013/aug/02/telecoms-bt-vodafone-cables-gchq

The principles of good and bad security remain constant, whether we're talking about intelligence agencies or garden-variety criminals. In the Belgacom case, the spies' trick could only have worked with very speedy access to their targets' traffic. This may have been the result of having access to the engineers' own internet service providers, or perhaps they already had access to part of Belgacom's systems – either way, this was an expert cyberattack and a lesson in what well-resourced agencies can do.[127] But the principle was quite simple: identify targets and dupe them into clicking on something they shouldn't, in order to infect their computer.

This is often called "social engineering" these days, though it's really just an evolution of the good old-fashioned confidence trick. Perhaps you've had a pop-up window appear from nowhere on your screen, telling you that your computer is infected with malware and you need to download a program to clean it up. Of course, that program itself contains the malware. You will surely have received "phishing" emails that claim to come from a popular web service or bank, asking you to log into your account to verify your details. The link they provided would take you to a dummy page, and, if you entered your credentials, they're now in the hands of criminals. And maybe your bank account has less money in it. Sometime spies and criminals even work together. In 2017, the US indicted a Russian hacker named Evgeniy Bogachev for allegedly hacking into thousands of computers and stealing millions of dollars from people's bank accounts. Officials told *The New York Times* that Russian spies had piggybacked on Bogachev's activities – as his victims probably included government officials and contractors, the hacking provided a great opportunity for conducting espionage.[128]

---

[127] http://www.csoonline.com/article/2914236/cyber-attacks-espionage/fox-it-releases-answer-to-nsas-quantum-insert-attack.html

[128] https://www.nytimes.com/2017/03/12/world/europe/russia-hacker-evgeniy-bogachev.html

Whatever the hackers' motives might be, they mostly rely on exploiting bad security. Sometimes their path is opened up by our very human gullibility, but the biggest technical problem is insecure software. Modern computer programs contain a vast amount of code and, partly due to the complexity of that code, it's common for them to contain flaws. These "bugs" can, under certain circumstances, cause the program to operate in unintended ways. If someone can figure out what those circumstances are, and if they have the capacity to prompt a predictable malfunction by, say, feeding the program a carefully crafted string of malicious code, then they can exploit that flaw. The result might be that the program crashes, or that it lets someone do something with it that they shouldn't be able to do.

Fixing these bugs means finding them first. If the code is proprietary to the company providing the software, no-one but that company (or whoever it pays to audit the code) will be able to find the bugs. If the code is "open-source" – available to the public for inspection, use and modification – then anyone with sufficient skill could theoretically spot the flaws. However, they can only find the bugs if they're looking. Defence requires resources, the will to deploy those resources, and the time to find and patch up all the vulnerabilities. Sometimes the attacker is better-resourced and more motivated than the defender, and all they have to do is find one flaw that will let them in.

These flaws, when discovered but not yet patched, are known as zero-day vulnerabilities – as in, the software provider has had zero days in which to patch them with an update. There's a whole industry of hackers who make a living by finding zero-days and figuring out how to exploit them. The question is, once they have this knowledge, what do they do with it? In the best-case scenario, the hackers will take the zero-days back to the companies or organisations behind the software, so that they can patch them up before anyone else finds and exploits them. Companies and organisations that make popular software, and the devices and online services that run it, will often have "bug bounty" schemes to encourage people to test the security of the software, and discreetly tell them about the results. Some individuals have earned more than $100,000 through the bug bounty programs of companies like Facebook[129] and Microsoft.[130] Banks and even the Pentagon have also run such schemes.[131]

In the industry, researchers who use their bug-finding skills for good, and who first ask for permission to test a system's defences, are known as "white hat" hackers. The whole point of bug bounty schemes is to encourage hackers to take this path. However, the same skillset could also let them be "black hat" hackers who supply their findings to criminal syndicates and hostile states, or who exploit the flaws for their own illegal purposes. There are also "grey hat" hackers who may not be out to help criminals and spies target others, but who don't stick to the ethical guidelines of the white hats – they might, for example, expose flaws to the world before the company behind the software has a chance to fix them.

Intelligence agencies sometimes buy zero-day exploits from hackers, but they also try to find their own ways to break through security protections. Some of Snowden's most explosive revelations regarded efforts by the NSA and GCHQ to break the encryption that everyone uses to keep data secure as it flows through the internet. Leaked slideshows showed GCHQ marvelling that the NSA's $250-million-a-year decryption program meant "vast amounts of encrypted internet data which have up till now been discarded are now exploitable".[132]

Unfortunately, the agencies don't just try to find examples of broken security; they encourage it, too. Snowden showed that the NSA took a major role in drafting flawed security standards, thanks to its influence at the US National Institute of Standards of Technology (NIST). In

---

[129] https://www.facebook.com/notes/facebook-security/an-update-on-our-bug-bounty-program/10151508163265766/
[130] https://blogs.technet.microsoft.com/bluehat/2013/10/08/congratulations-to-james-forshaw-recipient-of-our-first-100000-bounty-for-new-mitigation-bypass-techniques/
[131] https://hackerone.com/resources/hack-the-pentagon
[132] https://www.theguardian.com/world/2013/sep/05/nsa-gchq-encryption-codes-security

particular, the agency enthusiastically pushed the adoption of a weakened cryptographic algorithm. The tool was a random number generator called "Dual_EC_DRBG" – random numbers are a core part of encryption, but Dual_EC_DRBG's output was easy to guess if you knew certain constants that the NSA had inserted into the algorithm. NIST accepted the NSA's submission, but few adopted it because it was slow in practice. However, according to a Reuters report from the end of 2013, the NSA paid an influential security firm called RSA $10 million to make Dual_EC_DRBG the default random number generator in its security software.[133] RSA denied the allegations that it had knowingly accepted money to put out a weakened product, but the revelation severely tarnished the company's name in the industry, leading many experts to boycott its previously-popular security conference.[134]

When you deliberately weaken a widely-used security tool in order to make it easier for you to hack stuff, the ploy will only work if you can be certain that no-one else also finds the flaw. If you're going to make sure everyone's locks are broken rather than simply making better lockpicks, then you'd better keep that information to yourself.

That idea seemed hopeful enough after Edward Snowden walked out the door with reams of NSA secrets, but it seemed downright insane after further leaks in 2016 and 2017. The first set of leaks didn't come from some conscience-plagued NSA worker trying to warn the world of major power imbalances and the vulnerability of billions of people. It was a bunch of hackers calling themselves the "Shadow Brokers" and making a very public appeal for someone to buy what they had to sell: an NSA trove of zero-day exploits, which seemed to have been hacked back in 2013, probably after Snowden fled to Hong Kong. To prove they had the real goods, the Shadow Brokers – who wrote in enthusiastically mangled English – released exploits that anyone could

---

[133] http://www.reuters.com/article/us-usa-security-rsa-idUSBRE9BJ1C220131220
[134] https://gigaom.com/2014/01/08/if-rsa-was-hoping-nsa-furor-would-fade-away-it-was-mistaken/

use to break into software from companies such as Microsoft and Cisco.[135] They didn't just release proof that they had these exploits; they gave the tools to anyone who fancied downloading them.[136]

Snowden hypothesised that a foreign intelligence agency had broken into a server used by the NSA to launch attacks, and was demonstrating to the world that it had done so.[137] US investigators later also said they were focusing on the possibility that an NSA operator accidentally left software on an open server that then fell victim to Russian hackers.[138] Scores of NSA hacking tools were also among files that were allegedly taken from the agency by contractor (again!) Harold Martin, who was arrested in August 2016 for theft of government property and the mishandling of classified information.[139] Martin had worked in the elite Tailored Access Operations team, and US officials claimed he made off with three-quarters of TAO's arsenal.[140] Another TAO employee was also arrested in 2015 for taking secret files home (Russian hackers stole them from his home computer), but, fifteen months after the Shadow Brokers leak, investigators still weren't really sure whether that trove was stolen by an NSA insider or via an outside hack.[141]

Then, in early 2017, WikiLeaks published more than 8,000 pages of CIA documents, including the code for many of the intelligence agency's hacking tools, and details of the zero-day vulnerabilities that allow these tools to work. Some of these vulnerabilities lay in iPhones and Android devices, routers, antivirus programs and even Samsung's

---

[135] https://www.us-cert.gov/ncas/current-activity/2017/04/15/Microsoft-Addresses-Shadow-Brokers-Exploits-0

[136] https://blogs.cisco.com/security/shadow-brokers

[137] https://twitter.com/Snowden/status/765513662597623808

[138] http://www.reuters.com/article/us-cyber-nsa-tools-idUSKCN11S2MF

[139] http://www.nytimes.com/2016/10/20/us/harold-martin-nsa.html

[140] https://www.washingtonpost.com/world/national-security/prosecutors-to-seek-indictment-against-former-nsa-contractor-as-early-as-this-week/2017/02/06/362a22ca-ec83-11e6-9662-6eedf1627882_story.html?utm_term=.3841b6f103f4

[141] https://www.nytimes.com/2017/11/12/us/nsa-shadow-brokers.html

microphone-equipped smart TVs.[142] It's not clear that the CIA managed to develop successful exploits for all those flaws, such as the vulnerabilities in the smart TVs, but there were successful hacking tools in the stash. And, as with the Shadow Brokers trove before it, anyone could now use them.

This isn't some theoretical worry. In May 2017, organisations and individuals across the world were hit by a massive "ransomware" attack known as WannaCry or WannaCrypt. Ransomware is a nasty phenomenon where malware infects people's computers and networks and encrypts their files, or even entire drives. The victim is then shown a message urging them to send money – usually in the form of a cryptocurrency such as bitcoin – to the attackers as ransom for their files. If they pay up, victims then have to hope that the attackers will indeed decrypt their files as promised. WannaCry was a particularly bad strain that managed to infect hundreds of thousands of computers in one day. It spread via emails, using the phishing tactic of getting people to click on things they shouldn't, but it was able to subsequently infect computers thanks to one of the NSA exploits that the Shadow Brokers had given to the world. This tool, dubbed EternalBlue, exploited a flaw in a component of Windows, particularly older variants such as Windows XP that were no longer officially maintained by Microsoft.[143] The UK's National Health Service was badly hit, with hospitals having to shut down their systems and turn away patients.[144] Other victims included Deutsche Bahn, the telecoms giant Telefónica and the logistics multinational FedEx.[145] The attack was only stopped from infecting more computers because a security researcher studied its

---

[142] http://www.rollingstone.com/culture/wikileaks-cia-document-dump-what-you-need-to-know-w471532

[143] https://www.fireeye.com/blog/threat-research/2017/05/smb-exploited-wannacry-use-of-eternalblue.html

[144] http://www.telegraph.co.uk/news/2017/05/13/nhs-cyber-attack-everything-need-know-biggest-ransomware-offensive/

[145] http://www.businessinsider.de/telefonica-and-other-firms-have-been-infected-by-wannacry-malware-2017-5

code and found a reference to a long web domain that didn't exist – he registered the domain and WannaCry stopped spreading.

WannaCry's success was partly down to people running outdated operating systems that are riddled with security vulnerabilities, but there's no getting round the fact that the NSA was largely to blame. The agency knew about these vulnerabilities and, instead of telling the software companies about them to make sure everyone was protected, it developed tools to exploit them for its own purposes. This hidden knowledge got out into the wild, and in just this one incident it caused billions of dollars' worth of damage.[146] A month later, EternalBlue popped up again as part of another piece of malware called NotPetya, which had the appearance of ransomware but was seemingly designed to destroy data, not hold it for ransom.[147] This is, in many ways, even more worrying than a digitised shakedown.

According to a 2017 Rand Corporation study, zero-day exploits have an expected lifespan of almost seven years. An exploit is good as long as the underlying vulnerability hasn't been patched, and Rand found three quarters of the tools remained viable a year and a half after being created.[148] With the tools lasting so long, these stockpiles are pretty toxic. And, as the world found out in 2017, the consequences of their exposure can be dire.

So if insecurity is rife and secrets don't remain secret, why is there still an ongoing debate about putting secret holes into regular people's everyday security mechanisms, in the hope of keeping everyone safe?

The Encryption Debate

We all need encryption to do what it promises – stopping outsiders from reading electronic communications – otherwise modern life gets

---

[146] http://www.cbsnews.com/news/wannacry-ransomware-attacks-wannacry-virus-losses/
[147] https://www.theregister.co.uk/2017/06/28/petya_notpetya_ransomware/
[148] http://www.rand.org/pubs/research_reports/RR1751.html

scarily dangerous. Why is online banking safe? Encryption. Cloud storage for your photos? Encryption. Filing your tax returns online? Keeping your online dating habits private? Remotely viewing the feed from the camera watching your sleeping baby? You get the idea. However, all encryption is not created equal.

It's important to remember that for every lock there is a key, and whoever holds the key to an encrypted piece or stream of data is able to unscramble it. Some companies that deploy encryption will use it to protect transmissions of their users' data, but will hang onto the cryptographic keys to that data themselves. For example, Google encrypts Gmail emails as they flow through the internet and the company's internal systems. This means that anyone collecting the data while it's in transit will only see gobbledegook, so it does provide a lot of protection. However, if a court or intelligence agency comes knocking, Google has to turn over the data in decrypted form.

This cannot happen with what's known as "end-to-end" encryption. Here, the key stays with the user, and even the provider cannot decode their communications. For communications, end-to-end encryption is the only genuinely strong and trustworthy kind.

Before Snowden, end-to-end encryption was rare and cumbersome. There is, for example, a venerable method of encrypting and decrypting emails called Pretty Good Privacy (PGP) – it's not incredibly difficult to use, but it's not straightforward either, and it represents too much hassle for most people. However, after Snowden, many new communications providers such as Signal, Telegram and Wire started popping up to offer people "secure" tools that were simpler to use. Some big communications providers, such as WhatsApp, responded by introducing end-to-end encryption in their own services (indeed, WhatsApp now uses the same underlying technology as Signal's to encrypt its messages). Unlike with PGP, users of these services don't need to go through the tricky process of storing, managing and using their cryptographic keys. The keys are just stored in the app on their phone, but they still make it so that no-one can read those messages unless they have direct access to the phone or computer. Probably thanks to Snowden, end-to-end encryption is now so easy to use that people don't even realise they're using it.

Apple and Google, the producers of the most widely used mobile operating systems, also reacted to the post-Snowden paranoia by letting people encrypt their iOS and Android devices. The promise was that, even if someone had the device in their hands, they would not be able to read what was on it unless they could unlock it. The code for unlocking that phone or tablet was in the head of the user. Yes, that might just mean a four-digit series of numbers, and computerised code-crackers can easily run through all the possible permutations of those numbers within seconds, but extra security measures can stymie these automated systems. For example, Apple lets its customers set their iPhones and iPads so that their data will be permanently scrambled if someone enters a certain number of incorrect passcodes.

Strong encryption is not just valuable to people trying to stop the authorities from reading their communications. Phone encryption combats theft on the street, by making it harder to sell a stolen handset. Encrypted messaging can help an executive protect their communications from corporate rivals who are willing to play dirty and hire a hacker. These are the realities of modern life. However, governments and their agencies often have very ambivalent feelings on the subject of encryption.

Spy agencies and quite a few politicians have a dream: encryption that only keeps out bad people, but lets the authorities through the gates. Various methods for achieving this have been proposed and even attempted. During the Clinton administration in the 1990s, the NSA developed a tiny encryption chip that phone companies were supposed to install in their products, at the government's urging, to make it harder for outsiders to intercept the conversations of phone users. Each "Clipper chip" came with its own cryptographic key that the government would hold onto – a concept known as "key escrow". If investigators wanted to decrypt someone's communications, then they and (in theory) no-one else would have the key to let them do so. Officials said this would strike a balance between individual privacy and safety from crime, but security experts warned that no-one would trust devices with Clipper chips in them, because the government would be able to spy on them.[149] In the event, there were myriad problems with the scheme. Security researchers found serious flaws in the device's encryption algorithms that could allow people to listen in on communications, even if they weren't officials.[150] Anyone who really wanted to communicate in secret had freely-available alternatives, like PGP email, that they could use instead. And even if all US phone manufacturers had agreed to use the Clipper chip – which they didn't – there was the slight issue of all the other manufacturers in the world that export their phones to the US. No-one was going to force *them* to put Clipper chips into their products. The scheme was dead three years after its announcement.

The Clipper chip debacle provided lessons that have informed the encryption debate ever since – and it's a debate that apparently refuses to die. In 2014, when Apple responded to Snowden by encrypting iPhones, *The Washington Post* reached for its smelling salts. "With all their wizardry, perhaps Apple and Google could invent a kind of secure golden key they would retain and use only when a court has approved a search warrant," the paper suggested.[151] Again, the idea of a golden key is a lovely one, but the reality is that such a key, if it was leaked, would wreak havoc. And again, Apple and Google's overseas rivals would have a golden opportunity to create alternative operating systems that weren't fitted with backdoors for the benefit of the US intelligence services.

The debate flared up again a couple years later, this time with a different twist. In December 2015, an apparently radicalised Muslim couple massacred 14 people in San Bernardino, California. The killers, Syed Rizwan Farook and Tashfeen Malik, were themselves killed in a shootout with police. In February 2016, the FBI said it had Farook's

---

[149] http://www.nytimes.com/1993/04/16/us/electronics-plan-aims-to-balance-government-access-with-privacy.html
[150] http://www.crypto.com/papers/eesproto.pdf
[151] https://www.washingtonpost.com/opinions/compromise-needed-on-smartphone-encryption/2014/10/03/96680bf8-4a77-11e4-891d-713f052086a0_story.html

iPhone but couldn't access it to see what evidence might lie inside, because the phone was encrypted. So the agency tried to force Apple to create a special version of its iOS operating system that would bypass the iPhone's security mechanisms, in particular the one that permanently scrambles the phone after multiple incorrect passcode guesses. The idea was that this special iOS could then be installed on Farook's phone, and only that device.

However, Apple's lawyers told a federal judge that the FBI actually wanted the company to install the software on phones from a dozen other cases, too.[152] Apple pushed back with the support of most of the tech industry and even former law enforcement officials. Former homeland security chief Michael Chertoff said making a specially weakened version of iOS would be like "creating a bacterial biological weapon".[153] In the end, the FBI dropped its attempts to use the terrorist attack as an emotive catalyst for its long-held encryption-busting hopes, and instead bought software from hackers to unlock Farook's phone, at a reported cost to the US taxpayer of around $900,000.[154] They did not find any evidence of Farook making contact with other plotters.[155]

One of the main problems with getting the big tech companies to create backdoors, or golden keys, or special cracked versions of their software, is that these companies do not purely serve their domestic market and those of western allies. Android, iOS, Windows and WhatsApp are used across the world, and if you build a special way into them for one set of authorities, the authorities in many other countries will also want in. Some of those countries have governments that have little respect for human rights, and some are hostile to the west. If they cannot legally compel the western companies to give them

[152] https://www.theatlantic.com/technology/archive/2016/02/apple-is-right-the-fbi-wants-to-break-into-lots-of-phones/470607/

[153] http://fortune.com/2016/03/03/apple-support-former-government-officials/

[154] https://www.macrumors.com/2017/05/08/fbi-paid-900k-hacking-tool-iphone/

[155] http://edition.cnn.com/2016/04/19/politics/san-bernadino-iphone-data/index.html

such access, they may fine them or forbid them to operate in their countries. Or, they might just seek help from hackers – after all, if there's a way through or past these devices' encryption, a lot of deep-pocketed organisations will be offering big bucks to anyone who can find and exploit it.

The encryption debate may be repetitive, but the basic facts don't change: there's no way to make a system insecure only for certain people, while keeping it secure against all the bad guys. And in any case, encryption often won't stop truly determined investigators from doing their job.

Legalised Hacking

If investigators tapping the internet do encounter encrypted data and they can't crack it or get the key, then there is sometimes a way around the problem, as long as the target is still using their device. If it's possible to hack into that phone or tablet or computer, then encryption doesn't matter – investigators can secretly install surveillance software that tells them what's on that person's screen, or what they're typing. After all, people don't type in encrypted text and they need to decrypt it before they can read it. The keyboard and screen give everything away.

There's understandably an ongoing debate over whether it's such a great idea for agencies to stockpile the zero-day exploits that aid their hacking activities, due to the risk of others finding out about those techniques. However, aside from this issue – and it's a big issue for sure – hacking into people's computers is not necessarily objectionable from a human rights perspective. If the hacking targets specific individuals, and if the threat being investigated is serious enough, then it may be proportionate. After all, nobody really objects to the cops being able to pick someone's front door lock and bug their apartment when they really have to, so long as they've got a proper warrant. Investigators are supposed to investigate.

But what if the cops were to send robots to break into lots of people's apartments at once? That would cause a great deal of outrage, but it's essentially what spies and law enforcement are doing in the virtual realm these days. The UK government only admitted for the first time in 2015 that its agents engaged in hacking at all. But British warrants for "targeted" hacking can be broad, covering an entire place, or computers anywhere that are being used for a particular activity.

Why hack computers and phones *en masse*? To look for patterns that might single out individuals for closer examination. For example, the spies might want to find out who's been both using a particular piece of communications software that terrorists are known to use, and accessing a certain extremist website.[156] By hacking lots of devices, investigators can identify those that have been doing both these things. They then have their lead and can look in depth at particular computers' contents. However, getting to that point means breaking into and spying on a number of computers that may have nothing to do with terrorists. This mass hacking technique, a form of fishing expedition, was first made explicitly legal in the Investigatory Powers Act passed by the British parliament in late 2016.[157]

Mass hacking is almost always disproportionate because of the number of innocent people that get caught up. However, sometimes the target group really is large and distributed. In late 2016, Motherboard reported that the FBI had hacked into the computers of 8,000 people in 120 countries, all under a single warrant.[158] The agency was investigating a child sexual abuse site called Playpen that operated on the "dark web", a term referring to parts of the web that require special software to access, and that aren't indexed by the likes of Google. The site's users connected to it using a service called Tor, which encrypts and repeatedly reroutes a user's traffic. The beauty of Tor is that it makes it almost impossible for anyone spying on the network to figure out where or who the user really is – it's used by dissidents in

---

156

https://www.gov.uk/government/uploads/system/uploads/attachment_data/file/504187/Operational_Case_for_Bulk_Powers.pdf

[157] http://www.theverge.com/2016/11/23/13718768/uk-surveillance-laws-explained-investigatory-powers-bill

[158] https://motherboard.vice.com/read/fbi-hacked-over-8000-computers-in-120-countries-based-on-one-warrant

oppressive countries, spies and just regular people trying to stay private. In this case, though, it was being used by paedophiles, and investigators needed to identify them. So the FBI quietly seized Playpen's servers. When people visited the site, the agency dumped malware onto their computers – around 1,000 of them in total. The malware then copied data from the computers and sent it back to the FBI, essentially letting the investigators search through the malware-infested computers from afar. Hundreds of Playpen users were identified and arrested.

Few people will shed a tear at the takedown of a child abuse website, and the arrest of people who used it. However, having seized Playpen in order to set a trap for its users, the FBI kept the site up and running for a couple weeks, in order to let people fall into that trap. That meant the agency was itself distributing child sexual abuse pictures. What really upset digital rights activists, however, was the mass hacking precedent. "These cases are laying the foundation for the future expansion of law enforcement hacking in domestic criminal investigations, and the precedent these cases create is likely to impact the digital privacy rights of internet users for years to come," warned the Electronic Frontier Foundation (EFF).[159]

Mass hacking is sometimes a matter of targeting everyone who's at a certain location. For years, many law enforcement agencies around the world have been using devices called IMSI catchers (also known as "stingrays" or "cell site simulators") to conduct surveillance, notably at protests. When connecting to mobile networks, phones look for the cell towers that offer the strongest signals, typically those that are closest. An IMSI catcher impersonates a network's cell tower, so that nearby phones connect to it rather than a genuine cell tower. The owner of the phone can't tell the difference. Once the phone is hooked up to the IMSI catcher, the device can record its unique international mobile subscriber identity (IMSI). These codes identify individual devices, effectively revealing who's at the protest. By moving around the IMSI catcher and

[159] https://www.eff.org/deeplinks/2016/09/playpen-story-fbis-unprecedented-and-illegal-hacking-operation

recording the strength of its connection to each phone, investigators can track people's movements more accurately than they could by reading the connection data from real, stationary cell towers.[160]

What's more, these devices can be used to help tap into phones' microphones. As the American Civil Liberties Union (ACLU) of Northern California discovered following a legal battle, US Justice Department guidelines said IMSI catchers may be used to update the firmware of a handset "so that you can intercept conversations using a suspect's cell phone as the bug".[161] Some IMSI catchers can jam phones or make them turn off. A British company called Datong sold such a system to the London Metropolitan police in the late 2000s. According to reports, the system's ability to cut off phones' communications was intended for use in demonstrations, riots and war zones.[162]

There's a great deal of secrecy around these devices, but reporters and activists have established that they've been used by agencies and police forces in the UK,[163] the US[164] and elsewhere. In Germany, agencies have to tell a parliamentary committee when they use IMSI catchers.[165] In the US, federal guidelines[166] and those of several states demand a warrant for the use of an IMSI catcher, and in some cases block investigators from using them to bug people's phones.[167] It's worth noting that criminals use similar fake base stations too. In 2014, Chinese authorities arrested over 1,500 people who were using them for spamming – once they'd fooled people's phones into connecting to the

---

[160] https://www.wired.com/2016/05/hacker-lexicon-stingrays-spy-tool-government-tried-failed-hide/
[161] https://www.aclunc.org/docs/20151027-crm_lye.pdf
[162] https://www.wired.com/2011/10/datong-surveillance/
[163] https://www.theguardian.com/world/2016/oct/10/controversial-phone-snooping-technology-imsi-catcher-seven-police-forces
[164] https://news.vice.com/article/vice-news-investigation-finds-signs-of-secret-phone-surveillance-across-london
[165] https://www.privacyinternational.org/node/454
[166] https://www.wired.com/2015/09/feds-need-warrant-spy-stingrays-now/
[167] https://www.eff.org/deeplinks/2016/08/illinois-sets-new-limits-cell-site-simulators

devices, they'd pump out messages containing dodgy links, or even just advertising local businesses' wares.[168]

According to the UK anti-terror watchdog, mass hacking may become necessary as "the spread of encryption" successfully stops spies from snooping on the traffic flowing through the internet.[169] However, Privacy International has argued that broad warrants are disproportionate. "They lack any element of individualised suspicion, preventing effective judicial authorisation and increasing the risk of arbitrary action," the activist group warned.[170]

When it comes down to it, mass hacking is generally a form of mass surveillance. Its purpose is to get around the encryption that proliferated as a result of people finding out about other mass surveillance programmes. And, certainly in Europe, mass hacking may have the same legal weakness that sunk other mass surveillance techniques: a lack of proportionality and proper safeguards.

Worst-Case Scenarios

It's essential that we have safeguards on both bulk and targeted surveillance. There are plenty of examples from around the world that show us what happens without human rights protections, when torture-happy regimes get their hands on these tools.

Bahrain was one of the countries where protestors took to the streets in the so-called Arab Spring of 2011. Its repressive monarchy successfully crushed the protests, with authorities using devious tactics to unmask those behind anonymous dissident social media accounts. Bahraini activists were sent emails that appeared to come from an Al Jazeera journalist, with an attachment that was supposedly a picture of a human rights report. The attachment was actually an executable file

---

168

https://www.theregister.co.uk/2014/03/26/spam_text_china_clampdown_police/

[169] https://terrorismlegislationreviewer.independent.gov.uk/wp-content/uploads/2016/08/Bulk-Powers-Review-final-report.pdf

[170] https://www.politico.eu/wp-content/uploads/2016/09/PI_Lords.pdf

that infected the targets' computers with malware, which in turn let the authorities steal their information. According to Reporters Without Borders, the authorities also created fake email, Twitter and Facebook accounts that impersonated known dissidents. If people clicked on the links in those accounts' tweets, posts and emails, their phones got infected with malware.[171] This malware recorded device information that could then be cross-referenced against mobile phone operators' records, to identify the subscriber.

According to the pro-democracy group Bahrain Watch, the authorities in the country have also used software called FinFisher to spy on lawyers, human rights activists and politicians, some of whom were subsequently tortured.[172] The spyware allows the user to see everything their target is doing on their computer, and tap into their webcam and microphone. For example, in 2011 the Bahraini activist Moosa Abd-Ali Ali – who lived in the United Kingdom – discovered someone had hijacked his Facebook account. That someone was talking to a friend of his in Bahrain, under his identity. According to a report in *The Verge*, someone posing as him also "solicited his female Facebook friends for sex", possibly in order to gather blackmail material. It turned out his phone and computer had been infected with FinFisher.[173]

FinFisher is the product of an Anglo-German company called Gamma International. Accused of violating the UK's laws on surveillance equipment exports, Gamma claimed the Bahrainis had stolen and modified a demo version of the software. However, Bahrain Watch and Citizen Lab, a team of security experts at the University of Toronto, found evidence to the contrary: the Bahraini's FinFisher installation was still getting security updates from Gamma's systems.[174]

---

[171] https://surveillance.rsf.org/en/bahrain/

[172] https://bahrainwatch.org/blog/2014/08/07/uk-spyware-used-to-hack-bahrain-lawyers-activists/

[173] http://www.theverge.com/2015/1/21/7861645/finfisher-spyware-let-bahrain-government-hack-political-activist

[174] https://bahrainwatch.org/blog/2013/02/06/uk-spyware-in-bahrain-companys-denials-called-into-question/

An Italian spyware company called HackingTeam – a key rival to Gamma – was greatly embarrassed in 2015 when it was itself hacked. The hackers leaked 400 gigabytes of the firm's emails, invoices and espionage tools, showing that HackingTeam's clients included Bahrain, Kazakhstan, Sudan, Ethiopia, Azerbaijan, Egypt, Russia and Saudi Arabia. Citizen Lab found that the Ethiopian authorities had probably used HackingTeam's spyware to monitor the activities of diaspora journalists in the US.[175] Ethiopia is a prolific jailer and torturer of journalists. The Egyptian government also has a dreadful human rights record. After the HackingTeam leak, and perhaps in connection with the Egyptian authorities' killing of Italian student Giulio Regeni, the Italian authorities cancelled the company's export license.[176]

South Africa's VASTech, France's Amesys and China's ZTE sold surveillance systems to the regime of Libyan dictator Muammar Gaddafi, helping it to spy on the country's populace.[177] Amesys's EAGLE software was used by the Libyan secret police to monitor the online activities of journalist Khaled Mehiri, who ended up having to go into hiding. It was likely used to identify other dissidents who were subsequently tortured. Human rights activists filed a complaint against Amesys in 2011, but are still waiting for a resolution from the French courts.[178]

It's certainly true that repressive regimes spied on people before the advent of personal computing and the internet – surveillance has a long and inglorious history. However, because so much of our personal activities and communications now take place through our smartphones and PCs, secret police can now invade our lives so much more easily

---

[175] https://citizenlab.org/2014/02/hacking-team-targeting-ethiopian-journalists/
[176] https://www.privacyinternational.org/node/826
[177]

http://www.wsj.com/articles/SB10001424053111904199404576538721260166388
[178] https://www.fidh.org/en/region/north-africa-middle-east/libya/16959-the-amesys-case-the-victims-anxious-to-see-tangible-progress

and comprehensively than before. But on we go, connecting ever more things to the internet without making sure they can't be used against us.

Proliferation and Confusion

The more we live our lives online, and the more devices we connect to the internet that measure and track us, the more we're opening ourselves up to being monitored or attacked. This applies not only to the surveillance machines we carry around in our pockets, but also to the "internet of things" sensor systems that are being installed in our houses and cities to measure everything from environmental conditions to traffic flow. "In the future, intelligence services might use the [internet of things] for identification, surveillance, monitoring, location tracking, and targeting for recruitment, or to gain access to networks or user credentials," US director of national intelligence James Clapper testified in early 2016.[179] Even if you don't find anything wrong with that, consider this: the same vulnerabilities that make mass surveillance possible are also attack points for criminals and other people who might want to spy on us or coerce us. We really, really need security to work, to a degree that no-one – not even the "good guys" – gets to circumvent it.

Sadly, the security of the "internet of things" is generally dismal. Just a few months before Clapper's testimony, the FBI was warning US citizens that their new fitness devices, smart lighting systems and home security cameras create "opportunities for cybercrime", making consumers vulnerable to spying or even home break-ins.[180] As the agency noted, the companies that produce these products often don't patch them regularly or effectively enough, leaving them with open security holes. Sometimes, the manufacturers do very silly things like shipping products that all have the same, hard-wired security password

---

[179] https://www.theguardian.com/technology/2016/feb/09/internet-of-things-smart-home-devices-government-surveillance-james-clapper
[180] https://www.ic3.gov/media/2015/150910.aspx

– effectively like selling mass-produced locks that can all be opened by the same key.

The internet of things includes many kinds of devices, but connected toys and baby products have repeatedly provided emotive examples of what can go wrong. In 2015, US media reported that a couple had found a strange man talking through their infant son's baby monitor. "Wake up little boy, daddy's looking for you," he said. The baby monitor was designed to send video and audio to a smartphone app. It had been hacked, and someone was remotely controlling it.[181] A company called CloudPets makes cuddly toys that can read out messages to kids through a speaker, and also record their replies through a microphone. These messages are, of course, passed over the internet, and stored on CloudPets' servers along the way. In early 2017, people discovered that the company's database had no protection. Unsecured online databases are easy to find with commonly available tools. The information in the database made it easy to hack into the accounts of hundreds of thousands of users. Millions of recordings were there for the taking, and criminals repeatedly held the data to ransom, demanding that CloudPets pay them to return it. Despite this, and the fact that multiple people found and tried to warn CloudPets about the vulnerability, the company didn't tell its customers about the mess-up.[182]

Also in early 2017, Germany's federal cybersecurity agency banned a kids' doll called My Friend Cayla, which again comes with a microphone. Cayla records voice commands and sends them off to a speech recognition service in the cloud, so that it can understand what was said. "Items that conceal cameras or microphones and that are capable of transmitting a signal, and therefore can transmit data without detection, compromise people's privacy," said agency chief Jochen Homann. The agency also warned of toys that don't have good security

---

[181] http://newyork.cbslocal.com/2015/04/21/seen-at-11-cyber-spies-could-target-your-child-through-a-baby-monitor/
[182] https://www.troyhunt.com/data-from-connected-cloudpets-teddy-bears-leaked-and-ransomed-exposing-kids-voice-messages/

on their network connections, allowing "anyone in the vicinity to listen in on conversations undetected.[183] Some people thought the privacy-obsessed Germans were going overboard – they told parents to literally destroy the dolls – but the scale of the problem suggests they weren't.

This isn't just about the vulnerability of the people buying these products. Poorly-secured internet-of-things devices can also be quietly exploited by criminals who are building so-called botnets. These are swarms of hijacked computers, routers and other devices that are used to pump out spam or quietly launch massive attacks on online targets. There's a growing phenomenon of what's known as distributed denial of service (DDoS) attacks, where lots of computers band together to flood a target's systems with data until the target overloads and shuts down. These attacks are getting more powerful every year. In October 2016, a major US internet infrastructure company called Dyn was hit by a doozy of a DDoS. Popular websites such as Twitter, Amazon and Spotify went down for hours.[184] It turned out that the Dyn attack was largely the work of a botnet known as Mirai, and most of Mirai's power was based on terrible internet-of-things security.[185] The botnet had commandeered thousands of security cameras that used vulnerable components from a Chinese supplier called XiongMai, which subsequently had to issue a major recall in the US. Weeks later, a Mirai botnet was found launching major attacks on internet infrastructure in Liberia.[186] The attacks lasted two weeks and crippled the network of a

---

183

https://www.bundesnetzagentur.de/SharedDocs/Pressemitteilungen/EN/201 7/17022017_cayla.html?nn=404422

[184] http://searchsecurity.techtarget.com/news/450401962/Details-emerging-on-Dyn-DNS-DDoS-attack-Mirai-IoT-botnet

[185] http://arstechnica.com/information-technology/2016/10/inside-the-machine-uprising-how-cameras-dvrs-took-down-parts-of-the-internet/

[186] https://medium.com/@networksecurity/shadows-kill-mirai-ddos-botnet-testing-large-scale-attacks-sending-threatening-messages-about-6a61553d1c7#.2sf25v378

major internet service provider, Lonestar MTN, affecting 60 percent of the country.[187]

As security expert Bruce Schneier has suggested, nation states may be testing their capabilities for taking down target countries' internet on a wide scale.[188] The scary thing about DDoS attacks, though, is how easy it is to launch them. For years, people have been hiring out their botnets to people who are willing to spend quite a modest amount – even just $2 an hour – to make life very difficult for the target of their choice.[189] We can see the risks in the example of an attack that took place in the eastern Finnish city of Lappeenranta in late 2016. Someone launched a long-running DDoS attack against the internet-connected heating systems used in a couple of residential buildings, forcing them to constantly reboot. With sub-zero temperatures outside, the systems were out of order for around a week. According to local reports, the buildings' maintenance staff didn't know what to do, as they were understandably not trained in the intricacies of network security.[190]

Hackers can cause costly physical damage. In late 2014, Germany's federal information security agency reported that hackers managed to access the systems of a steel plant somewhere in the country. They caused outages that made it impossible for the plant's operators to properly shut down a blast furnace, damaging it in the process. Details of the attack were scarce, although we do know that the hackers used good old social engineering to con their way into the plant's systems.[191] People often provide the most exploitable flaws in any defensive structure.

---

[187] http://allafrica.com/stories/201611080863.html

[188] https://www.schneier.com/blog/archives/2016/09/someone_is_lear.html

[189] http://blogs.wsj.com/tech-europe/2012/11/05/where-to-rent-a-botnet-for-2-an-hour-or-buy-one-for-700/

[190] http://metropolitan.fi/entry/ddos-attack-halts-heating-in-finland-amidst-winter

[191] http://www.securityweek.com/cyberattack-german-steel-plant-causes-significant-damage-report

Many in the security industry worry about the implications of electronic voting. [192] This is partly because, if you're voting over the internet, it's near-impossible to cast a vote that's not linked to your identity – votes in a democracy are supposed to be cast in secret, to ensure the legitimacy of the election. [193] However, experts are also worried about the poor security of the technology that's involved. Electronic voting machines at physical polling stations can be bad enough. Virginia officials decertified a machine in 2015 because it could be hacked and manipulated by a nearby smartphone, or by someone inserting a malicious USB stick into it.[194] Online voting systems seem especially risky. When the Australian state of New South Wales carried out a 2015 election using an online voting system called iVote, security researchers said they found vulnerabilities that meant "vote verification... was itself susceptible to manipulation".[195] Estonia has been a trailblazer in allowing online voting, but security experts examining the country's systems found "staggering gaps in procedural and operational security". They also warned that "the architecture of the system leaves it open to cyberattacks from foreign powers, such as Russia". [196] These attacks, the experts said, could alter votes.

After the Ukrainian revolution in 2014, the country held a presidential election. Shortly before the country went to the polls, officials discovered that CyberBerkut, a pro-Russian "hacktivist" group, had hacked into the central election computers and made them inoperable. CyberBerkut then published documents to prove that it had "destroyed" the electoral network infrastructure. Officials restored the systems from backups but then, just minutes before the announcement of the election results, they found and removed a virus that would have

[192] https://www.engadget.com/2016/09/02/should-we-be-worried-about-election-hacking/

[193] http://www.secretballotatrisk.org/Secret-Ballot-At-Risk.pdf

[194] https://freedom-to-tinker.com/2015/04/15/decertifying-the-worst-voting-machine-in-the-us/

[195] http://people.eng.unimelb.edu.au/vjteague/iVoteSecurityAnalysis.pdf

[196] https://estoniaevoting.org/

declared the far-right Dmytro Yarosh as the winner.[197] Yarosh actually got less than 1 percent of the votes. The Ukrainian officials concluded that this had been a failed attempt to discredit the elections. It would have backed up Russian propaganda claiming neo-Nazis were behind the Ukrainian revolution that deposed pro-Russian president Viktor Yanukovych.

According to US intelligence assessments, Russian hackers also played a significant role in the 2016 presidential election, in a variety of ways. First, the Department of Homeland Security said Russian hackers had tried to access the voter database systems in several states, downloading information on 200,000 people in Illinois.[198] But in terms of impact, that was nothing compared to the hacking of the Democratic National Committee (DNC) and Hillary Clinton's campaign manager, John Podesta. These intrusions used unremarkable social engineering tactics, such as sending a fake "account reset" link to Podesta, but they may have helped tip the election to Donald Trump.[199] The hacks yielded emails and voicemails that were then publicised through WikiLeaks and other conduits in an apparent attempt to discredit Clinton and her team. WikiLeaks chief Julian Assange had a great deal of animosity for Clinton ever since, as secretary of state under Barack Obama, she criticised WikiLeaks for publishing classified US military cables.[200] Although Assange denied receiving the DNC documents from the Russian government,[201] the Central Intelligence Agency (CIA)

---

[197] http://www.csmonitor.com/World/Passcode/2014/0617/Ukraine-election-narrowly-avoided-wanton-destruction-from-hackers-video
[198] http://fortune.com/2016/10/01/hackers-targeted-election-systems/
[199] http://www.theverge.com/2016/12/13/13940514/dnc-email-hack-typo-john-podesta-clinton-russia
[200] https://www.buzzfeed.com/jamesball/heres-what-i-learned-about-julian-assange
[201] https://www.rt.com/news/365164-assange-interview-wikileaks-russia/

reportedly established that they at least came from hackers working for Russian intelligence.[202]

The hacked documents made Clinton and her team look bad, for example by showing how concerned they were about presentation. More damningly, they suggested the DNC had favoured Clinton over rival Bernie Sanders in the primaries – one official suggested encouraging the media to write that Sanders' campaign was "a mess". DNC chair Debbie Wasserman Schultz subsequently had to step down just as the party was crowning Clinton at its conference.[203] The documents did not show anything illegal, but they did provide fuel for the right-wing media's constant attacks on Clinton. These emails and voicemails were not encrypted. If they had been less vulnerable, the 2016 US election might have turned out a different way. Anyhow, the DNC and the House Democrats now use encrypted messaging for their communications.[204]

Candidates and parties, individuals, institutions and the internet's infrastructure all need defences against criminals and hostile states. But the same protections would also make life harder for spies and law enforcement officials who want a broader, deeper view of what their own citizens are up to. Hackers are powerful because they have the skill to exploit flaws that lie everywhere, just waiting to be found, but also because it's so difficult to identify who was responsible for an attack.[205] Clever hackers can leave false trails that implicate someone else. The answer is to stop them getting in in the first place.

In short, we will always need more security, not less. It's unlikely that we'll ever be able to build totally impregnable defences, so even widespread "strong" security is unlikely to stop law enforcement and

---

[202] https://www.washingtonpost.com/world/national-security/obama-orders-review-of-russian-hacking-during-presidential-campaign/2016/12/09/31d6b300-be2a-11e6-94ac-3d324840106c_story.html

[203] https://www.theatlantic.com/politics/archive/2016/07/the-fall-of-debbie-wasserman-schultz/493019/

[204] https://www.engadget.com/2017/07/18/house-democrats-encrypted-messaging-hack/

[205] http://www.tandfonline.com/doi/full/10.1080/01402390.2014.977382

intelligence services from doing their jobs. Somehow, they and their criminal counterparts will probably find cracks in the armour. However, intelligence and law-enforcement agencies should certainly not be allowed to actively undermine the building of the best security mechanisms that can be offered.

***

When it comes to issues around hacking, encryption and surveillance, we need to keep asking two questions: what's generally desirable, and what's practically feasible? It's feasible to hack into lots of computers and phones at once, but doing so will in most cases be undesirable from a human rights perspective. For an example of desirable but unfeasible, look to the magic key that would allow authorities, but not criminals, access to citizens' encrypted communications. (As if eager to demonstrate this unfeasibility in the most ironic way possible, Australian prime minister Malcolm Turnbull insisted in 2017 that it must be possible to let the good guys in while keeping the bad guys out, because "the laws of mathematics are very commendable, but the only law that applies in Australia is the law of Australia".[206])

And what of the agencies' stockpiles of toxic hacking tools? When they discover that a certain piece of software has a gap in its armour, what should they do: tell the company that makes it, or hoard the knowledge for exclusive exploitation? The first result would help protect people, particularly as less benevolent organisations might know of the same flaw. The second would bring power. In countries such as the UK and US, the same agencies are tasked with both improving security to protect people, and breaking security to spy on people. That's a clear conflict of interest, and these functions of GCHQ and the NSA should be separated into different agencies, as the security

---

[206] http://www.zdnet.com/article/the-laws-of-australia-will-trump-the-laws-of-mathematics-turnbull/

expert Bruce Schneier has recommended.[207] But even then, we know that it's dangerous to hoard vulnerabilities. We've seen them get out into the wild, giving criminals the tools to try holding the world to ransom. We've also seen whistleblowers reveal the secrets of supremely secretive agencies. As soon as you introduce conscience or greed or other human motivations into the equation, all bets are off. And when the agencies' hacking tools themselves break free, there are far too many losers.

As the author Cory Doctorow has argued, we should treat security like public health: "If you discovered that your government was hoarding information about water-borne parasites instead of trying to eradicate them; if you discovered that they were more interested in weaponising typhus than they were in curing it, you would demand that your government treat your water-supply with the gravitas and seriousness that it is due."[208] Vulnerabilities do help spies spy, and there will be times where it's appropriate to use them. But given the vulnerability of vulnerabilities, hoarding should be avoided. The emphasis should be on patching them, in order to protect all of us who use the software or rely on a service that uses it.

Meanwhile, the whole tech industry needs to accept the responsibilities that come with connecting absolutely everything to the internet. Security is always going to be an ongoing struggle. Unless everyone is willing to keep fighting to maintain the security of that connected home surveillance camera, or car, or voting system, keeping it offline is by far the smarter option. And people buying tech products also have a responsibility, to themselves and those around them, to check that the internet-connected products they're buying have decent security. If tech companies find people are seriously complaining about their slack practices, maybe they'll start taking the security of their customers more seriously.

---

[207] http://edition.cnn.com/2014/02/20/opinion/schneier-nsa-too-big/index.html
[208] https://www.theguardian.com/technology/2014/mar/11/gchq-national-security-technology

If we all try hard enough, perhaps we can make ourselves safer from criminals and spies. But that's not all we need to keep ourselves safe online. These days we must keep our eyes open for new threats that warp and commandeer our notions of society itself.

After the ousted Ukrainian president Viktor Yanukovych fled to Russia in 2014, Russia's hacking efforts extended further than the attacks on revolutionary Ukraine's election systems. While Russia annexed Crimea and backed an uprising in the Ukrainian east, organisations operating from within Russia, such as the St Petersburg-based Internet Research Agency, unleashed thousands of fake social media accounts to flood conversations around the world. This was an information war, too.

As Buzzfeed described it, each staffer at the Internet Research Agency had to post 50 comments a day, maintaining six active Facebook accounts that each pumped out posts and comments. On Twitter, they had to tweet 50 times a day from 10 accounts.[209] They insulted Western journalists and anyone taking an anti-Russian stance. They sang the praises of Vladimir Putin and his strength. When a Russian-made missile downed a commercial airliner in Ukraine, these accounts moved to muddy the waters about who was responsible for the incident – when they spotted people discussing the tragedy on Twitter, they would start pushing out theories about who else might have brought down the plane.[210] Just as denial-of-service attacks overload servers with excessive data, armies of trolls aim to swamp and derail online conversations, and to change some people's minds if they can. Even if the Russian trolls failed to convince many Western people's minds about Russian claims to Crimea in 2014, they would certainly make their presence felt a couple years later, during the US presidential election.

When people hijack social media to disrupt and divide people, they are exploiting its core traits of interactivity and a low-to-non-existent

---

[209] https://www.buzzfeed.com/maxseddon/documents-show-how-russias-troll-army-hit-america

[210] http://www.politico.com/story/2016/09/donald-trump-twitter-army-228923

bar to entry, but they are also subverting the business models of the social media companies – business models that are themselves exploitative, and that encourage corner-cutting wherever possible. Another vulnerability lies in our persistent uncertainty about how the online layer of our lives maps to the offline; the technology is new and we are in a state of flux, so only experience can make us wise to the dangers we face. And then there's basic human nature, which at times doesn't need much encouragement to create strife.

The internet's control shifts don't just relate to the power exerted over us from above. The medium also gives us power that we can wield over one another. The internet is a battleground for competing ideas and, as on any battleground, people get hurt. Dealing with this problem means balancing the right to free expression with the right to freedom from abuse and harassment. It's a societal task that will involve facing up to the realities of our online "public" spaces, and getting the operators of those spaces to accept the responsibilities that come with their riches. It will not be easy.

Open To Abuse

Almost anyone's voice can carry far and wide on a service like YouTube or Twitter. All you need is a cheap smartphone, the ability to string words together in a compelling way, and the social intelligence to promote your voice through the right channels.

This is particularly useful for minorities and activists whose voices have been underrepresented in traditional media. Consider the Black Lives Matter movement, which began with a Twitter hashtag and, through a combination of online activism and on-the-street protests, pushed its message into the international conversation. The movement originated after the 2012 killing of 17-year-old Trayvon Martin by a Florida neighbourhood watch volunteer named George Zimmerman. Zimmerman thought Martin, an African-American, looked suspicious. After calling the police to tell them about him, he confronted and shot the boy in the street. The police initially didn't even arrest Zimmerman, but the outcry forced them to charge him. He was ultimately acquitted of second-degree murder and manslaughter. "Stop saying we are not surprised. That's a damn shame in itself. I continue to be surprised at how little Black lives matter. And I will continue that," wrote activist Alicia Garza in a Facebook post, coining the phrase that would name the movement. The attorneys for both Zimmerman and Martin's family agreed that social media was key to the case reaching the court in the first place. "We didn't engage social media. It's almost as if social media engaged us," said Martin attorney Benjamin Crump. "All the world is watching because they want to see if everybody gets equal justice in America."[211]

The #BlackLivesMatter hashtag became even better known after the 2014 killings of two black men, Michael Brown and Eric Garner. Both men were killed by police; in both cases, juries decided not to indict the officers responsible. More cases followed, and social media served not just to highlight the trend, but to allow people from around the world to join the conversation. "The thing about [Martin Luther] King or Ella Baker is that they could not just wake up and sit at the breakfast table and talk to a million people," said Black Lives Matter activist DeRay Mckesson in an interview with *Wired*. "The tools that we have to organise and to resist are fundamentally different than anything that's existed before in black struggle."[212]

The internet has also had much to offer those promoting a non-mainstream, feminist critique of modern culture. In 2014, through the works of cultural critic Anita Sarkeesian and game creators such as Brianna Wu and Zoë Quinn, a new wave of feminist gamer culture began to push back against games' stereotyped depiction of women as busty victims. Using online platforms, these people were able to spread their ideas far beyond what would have been possible in the realms of academia, where such discussions have traditionally been concentrated.

---

[211] http://articles.orlandosentinel.com/2013-04-27/news/os-benjamin-crump-mark-omara-20130427_1_benjamin-crump-trayvon-martin-george-zimmerman

[212] https://www.wired.com/2015/10/how-black-lives-matter-uses-social-media-to-fight-the-power/

However, the same openness of these platforms allowed a clash with a group of mainly male gamers and "men's rights" activists who adopted the "Gamergate" tag for their counter-movement, opposing what they claimed was excessive political correctness. The confrontation turned very ugly indeed, becoming emblematic of social media's abuse problem.

Gamergate began when Eron Gjoni, Quinn's former boyfriend, wrote on his blog that she had repeatedly cheated on him with other men including Nathan Grayson, a reviewer for the game blog Kotaku. The denizens of 4chan, an image-sharing forum whose users have a reputation for trolling people, discussed Gjoni's post and decided Quinn had slept with Grayson in exchange for a positive review of her indie game, *Depression Quest*. Despite the fact that Grayson never even reviewed her game, the trolls went wild. Here was the spark for a rage-fuelled backlash against so-called "social justice warriors" – a term intended as an insult – who wanted to fight misogyny.[213]

Both sides of an emerging culture war were finding their voices through online platforms, exerting power on a new kind of intellectual battleground that allows for direct conflict between people who would probably have never crossed paths before. However, one side abused its power appallingly. As Quinn wrote shortly after the attacks began: "Long story short, the Internet spent the last month spreading my personal information around, sending me threats, hacking anyone suspected of being friends with me, calling my dad and telling him I'm a whore, sending nude photos of me to colleagues, and basically giving me the 'burn the witch' treatment."[214]

Quinn was not the only target. Sarkeesian, a keen gamer who had been publishing video critiques of misogyny in games for a couple of years, was subjected to horrific abuse. One man tweeted her home

---

[213] https://www.bostonglobe.com/arts/2014/09/20/gaming-summer-rage/VNMeHYTc5ZKoBixYHzi1JL/story.html
[214] http://www.cracked.com/blog/5-things-i-learned-as-internets-most-hated-person/

address and threatened to "rape [her] to death".[215] She had to cancel a speech at Utah State University after the administrators refused to allow people attending her lecture to be screened for guns. Someone claiming to be a student had previously emailed university staff, warning of "the deadliest school shooting in American history" if they did not stop Sarkeesian from speaking. "Feminists have ruined my life and I will have my revenge, for my sake and the sake of all the others they've wronged," the author claimed.[216]

Although the Gamergate movement later fused with underground neo-Nazi groups to create the Trump-backing "alt right" scene, it is still relatively rare for such abuse to spill out from online forums into the real world to this degree.[217] However, abuse on platforms such as Twitter is anything but unusual, particularly for women and people of colour. A study carried out for the anti-racism-in-football organisation Kick It Out looked at abusive social media posts between August 2014 and March 2015. It found 134,400 instances of abusive posts, almost a third of which were directed at players themselves rather than their teams. More than a quarter of the posts were racist. Interestingly, 88 percent of the discriminatory posts were made on Twitter, and only 8 percent on Facebook.[218] This last statistic was particularly telling because Twitter, unlike Facebook, allows its users to use pseudonyms rather than insisting they use their real names.

This is an extraordinarily complex and nuanced issue. Firstly, it's important to note that the use of aliases is not always a successful shield against identification. British trolls John Nimmo and Isabella Sorley found that out in 2013 when they were caught sending threatening tweets to the feminist campaigner Caroline Criado-Perez. Nimmo was identified by journalists who linked his Twitter handle to a

---

[215] https://twitter.com/femfreq/status/504718160902492160/photo/1
[216] http://www.standard.net/Police/2014/10/14/Utah-State-University-student-threatens-act-of-terror-if-feminist.html
[217] https://medium.com/@DaleBeran/4chan-the-skeleton-key-to-the-rise-of-trump-624e7cb798cb
[218] http://www.kickitout.org/news/kick-it-out-unveils-findings-of-research-into-football-related-hate-crime-on-social-media/#.VTEHvRPF8bM

gaming profile, and Sorley did not hide her IP address (which identified her internet connection) when she sent the abuse.[219] Both were jailed.[220] But in most cases, people can get away with abusing someone while hiding behind a pseudonym.

There's something about using an assumed name that allows many people to feel freer about what they say online. As the classic 1993 *New Yorker* cartoon caption noted, "on the internet, nobody knows you're a dog", and this freedom is liberating and empowering.[221] While too many people abuse that power, others do use it for good. For one thing, anonymity or pseudonymity is essential if you live under an oppressive regime and want to use the internet to organise with other dissenters or leak information that is embarrassing to the government. It's also extremely useful for, say, women trying to lead an online existence while avoiding an abusive ex-partner, or people who simply feel more comfortable under an identity that is not their legal name, such as gay people who might want to express themselves in online communities without disclosing their sexuality to family members or employers. You can't force trolls to identify themselves without forcing innocent people to remove protections they might need to lead a happy online existence.

Facebook's real-name policy, which is largely aimed at discouraging abuse, has even proved to be a tool for abuse in itself. In 2014, the company apologised to many of its transgender and drag-queen users, who were using adopted or stage names and whose accounts had been reported as fake.[222] It turned out that one person had reported "several hundred" such accounts, probably as a homophobic action. The social network then demanded birth certificates or drivers' licenses from the affected users and told them to either set up "fan pages" under their

---

[219] http://www.newstatesman.com/media/2014/01/john-nimmo-and-isabella-sorley-tale-two-trolls

[220] https://www.theguardian.com/uk-news/2014/jan/24/two-jailed-twitter-abuse-feminist-campaigner

[221] https://en.wikipedia.org/wiki/On_the_Internet,_nobody_knows_you're_a_dog

[222] https://www.facebook.com/chris.cox/posts/10101301777354543

assumed names or switch back to their legal names.[223] Once it figured out what was really going on, Facebook promised to improve its reporting mechanisms.

It's also not entirely clear that the use of real names dissuades abusive online behaviour. A 2016 German study of online "firestorms" suggested that, when abusive people see themselves as enforcing a moral point, many are fine with using with real names. If you're on a mission to convince people of something, then pseudonyms can decrease the impact of what you're trying to achieve.[224] And it's worth noting that Facebook does still play host to a lot of hate speech, even with its real-name policy. From individuals saying ignorant and offensive things, to organised hate groups such as the Islamophobic Britain First, there is plenty on Facebook that incites hatred and, in some countries, breaks the law by doing so.

However, Twitter's abuse problem is in another league, and this is largely down to the fact that it's full of people – and automated accounts, known as "bots" – with an agenda to push and little accountability for their actions. "We suck at dealing with abuse and trolls on the platform and we've sucked at it for years," admitted then-CEO Dick Costolo in a leaked internal memo, back in 2015.[225] The next year, Twitter belatedly made it easier for people to fight abuse by expanding its "mute" feature so that users no longer had to see the nasty messages that were being hurled at them.[226] A few months later, Twitter also stepped up its automated detection of abusive accounts, and it let people avoid seeing messages from accounts with no profile picture.[227] But the possibility for pseudonymity on Twitter remains.

---

[223] https://gigaom.com/2014/09/12/facebook-is-under-fire-from-gay-and-transgender-users-who-are-being-forced-to-use-real-names/

[224] http://journals.plos.org/plosone/article?id=10.1371/journal.pone.0155923#sec018

[225] https://www.wired.com/2015/02/dick-costolo-trolls/

[226] https://blog.twitter.com/2016/progress-on-addressing-online-abuse

[227] https://blog.twitter.com/2017/our-latest-update-on-safety

Facebook and Twitter offer very different environments, in a way that's best explained using an offline analogy. Twitter is like a giant field, where you may surround yourself with people of your choice, but where anyone can walk over and start talking to (or at) you. Because of the retweet function, which usually re-broadcasts messages without restrictions, Twitter users are constantly experiencing the outpourings of people they've never encountered before, and who may not be what they seem. Facebook, on the other hand, is like being in a house with people you already know. You'd hope those people have broad enough interests to occasionally surprise you with the information they share, but overall it's a much more predictable experience.

Both platforms can prove highly divisive in their own ways. In Twitter's case, the discord comes from mixing people who might never meet offline, while allowing people to obscure their identities as they push out their messages. But in Facebook's case, the danger lies not in encouraging clashes but in exacerbating division through the reinforcement of people's existing beliefs, thanks to a phenomenon known as the "filter bubble".

The Things You Know

The filter bubble was conceptualised by Eli Pariser, the CEO of an influential media company called Upworthy that focuses on stories that go "viral" – as indeed do most media outlets these days. If you're sick of headlines that end on a click-me-now formulation such as "You won't believe what happens next", you have Upworthy to thank for that.

Pariser's "filter bubble" refers to the excess of personalisation that takes place on Facebook and services like it. Just as Google's algorithms carefully track what you're searching for over time, in order to present ever-more-relevant results to your queries, Facebook monitors your use of its service in order to figure out what you like and show you more of it. This can be handy – after all, if you have hundreds of friends who post things regularly, that's a lot of information to take in. Algorithmic prioritisation pushes things and people to the top of your newsfeed, based on the likelihood that you'll find those things and people interesting. That's why you see certain people feature more than others in your feed. For Facebook, the benefits relate to advertising. The more relevant you find its service, the more you will use it and the more ads you will see. The more Facebook understands about you, the better it can tailor those ads to you, and the more it can prove to advertisers that they're getting their products and services in front of the right eyeballs.

However, this approach has a major social impact. As Pariser noted in his book, *The Filter Bubble*: "Democracy requires citizens to see things from one another's point of view, but instead we're more and more enclosed in our own bubbles. Democracy requires a reliance on shared facts; instead we're being offered parallel but separate universes... Politically, I lean to the left, but I like to hear what conservatives are thinking, and I've gone out of my way to befriend a few and add them as Facebook connections. I wanted to see what links they'd post, read their comments, and learn a bit from them. But their links never turned up in my Top News feed."[228]

If you're liberal or progressive, Facebook will deduce that fact from your likes and associations and use it to select the stories it pushes to the top of your feed. If you're conservative, it will encase you ever more in the conservative worldview; if you're liberal, your ideas will be correspondingly reinforced. Many people spend a significant amount of time each day using Facebook's services – nearly an hour on average.[229] This one company is so powerful that it can shape your experience of the world. And you won't believe what happens next.

During the 2016 US election, *The Wall Street Journal* ran a fascinating test called "Blue Feed, Red Feed", in an attempt to show people how different the left and right experiences of Facebook are.[230] The test allowed people to click on a subject, then see what kinds of stories on that subject were being posted to Facebook by popular liberal

---

[228] Eli Pariser – The Filter Bubble: What The Internet Is Hiding From You
[229] http://www.nytimes.com/2016/05/06/business/facebook-bends-the-rules-of-audience-engagement-to-its-advantage.html?_r=0
[230] http://graphics.wsj.com/blue-feed-red-feed/

and conservative news sources. For example, in December, immediately after the election of Donald Trump, a click on the subject of Trump showed the "blue feed" carrying an "RIP America" post from the Daily Kos, while the "red feed" had Fox News's Sean Hannity crowing about Donald Trump still being on top after the Wisconsin recount. If you clicked on the subject of abortion, on the left a Mic story complained about restrictive Texan abortion laws, and on the right LifeNews.com decried the "hypocrisy" of being pro-choice but against the death penalty.

Once it was the news media itself that prioritised certain stories over others, creating a set of stories that might lean one political way or another, but that did so under the banner of the publisher or broadcaster. When wielded by the media, we call this editorial power.[231] But now everything, no matter the source, is being shoved through the same funnel, with the prioritisation performed by algorithms that have been wholly designed to pander to people and to help them show off to their peers, all so that the system can better profile them for advertising purposes. As Sean Parker, Facebook's founding president, said in late 2017, the whole point of Facebook was always to consume as much of people's time and attention as possible.[232] "That means that we need to sort of give you a little dopamine hit every once in a while, because someone liked or commented on a photo or a post or whatever. And that's going to get you to contribute more content, and that's going to get you... more likes and comments," he said. "It's a social-validation feedback loop... exactly the kind of thing that a hacker like myself would come up with, because you're exploiting a vulnerability in human psychology."

This is still editorial power, but – perhaps through wilful ignorance – misused in a way that manages to be both sociopathic and extremely blinkered. Because the system can be gamed, and it can be gamed hard.

---

[231] http://fortune.com/2016/05/09/facebook-media-principles/
[232] https://www.axios.com/axios-am-2508003126.html

It's one thing to reap the ad revenue that comes from being people's primary portal to the online world. It's quite another to accept responsibility for how that portal presents the world.

"We are a tech company, not a media company," Facebook CEO Mark Zuckerberg said in 2016, responding to a question about whether Facebook sees itself as having an editorial role.[233] However, that's just not true. Facebook's system chooses which stories get put in front of its users' eyeballs. When people share articles and videos, the platform suggests related articles and videos that people might also want to read or view. The service also shows people "trending" articles, providing amplification for pieces that have already started to take off.

Crucially, this has not been a purely automated system. Facebook caught a lot of flak in early 2016 after the tech news site Gizmodo published an investigation into Facebook's "news curators", the contract staff that the company used to help determine what showed up as trending.[234] Former curators told Gizmodo that they had routinely suppressed stories of a conservative bent. Facebook denied this, but a few months later it got rid of its human curators, leaving its algorithms in charge of deciding what should be pushed into prominence. The results were immediate and humiliating: within days, the algorithm started serving up a false story about Fox News host Megyn Kelly being fired for supporting Democratic presidential candidate Hillary Clinton (she didn't, and wasn't), and a piece about someone masturbating into a chicken sandwich.[235]

In the words of media commentator Mathew Ingram: "We've grown accustomed to the idea that media outlets such as *The New York Times* and *Washington Post* and CNN have at least some sort of

---

[233] http://www.reuters.com/article/us-facebook-zuckerberg-idUSKCN1141WN
[234] https://gizmodo.com/former-facebook-workers-we-routinely-suppressed-conser-1775461006
[235] https://www.theguardian.com/technology/2016/aug/29/facebook-fires-trending-topics-team-algorithm

notional commitment to journalistic principles, including fairness, balance, accuracy, and the greater good of society. What commitment does the Facebook algorithm have to any of these principles?"[236]

In September of that year, Facebook drew heavy criticism for censoring *The Terror of War*, Nick Ut's iconic photograph of a naked young girl running in terror from a napalm attack in the Vietnam War. Facebook deleted a post by Norwegian writer Tom Egeland that included the photo, because of the subject's nudity. Norwegian newspaper *Aftenposten* reported on this censorship incident, and posted its article to Facebook, including the contentious photo. Again, Facebook removed the post. "First you create rules that don't distinguish between child pornography and famous war photographs," *Aftenposten* editor Espen Egil Hansen wrote in an open letter to Zuckerberg. "Then you practice these rules without allowing space for good judgement. Finally you even censor criticism against and a discussion about the decision – and you punish the person who dares to voice criticism... You are the world's most powerful editor. Even for a major player like *Aftenposten*, Facebook is hard to avoid. In fact we don't really wish to avoid you, because you are offering us a great channel for distributing our content... I think you are abusing your power, and I find it hard to believe that you have thought it through thoroughly."

Norwegian prime minister Erna Solberg also wrote a post to support the newspaper, and Facebook deleted it. Eventually, the company backed down. In October Facebook changed its policy to "begin allowing more items that people find newsworthy, significant, or important to the public interest — even if they might otherwise violate our standard."[237] In other words, Facebook started to acknowledge that it was not just running a community; it was also the editor of a major news service.

---

[236] http://fortune.com/2016/05/09/facebook-media-principles/
[237] http://petapixel.com/2016/09/14/facebook-coo-apologizes-norway-prime-minister-photo-censorship/

Then the 2016 US election happened, and social media's dangerous influence slowly became clearer. As people tried to understand how Donald Trump won the presidency, they started to point fingers at the "fake news" stories that had recently been circulating on social media platforms. There's a whole ecosystem of sites that run hoax stories, such as the one about Megyn Kelly backing Clinton, or the one about the Amish backing Trump,[238] or the one about an FBI agent involved in Clinton's email leaks being "found dead in [an] apparent murder-suicide",[239] or the one about Clinton's campaign paying people $3,500 each to protest at Trump's rallies.[240] As a Buzzfeed investigation showed, such hoaxes are often the products of operations in unlikely places like Macedonia. People set up websites filled with attractive nonsense, put ads next to the nonsense, watch their stories go viral on Facebook and then rake in thousands of advertising dollars when gullible people click through.[241] As pro-Republican accounts shared these false stories more often than pro-Democrats accounts did, some drew a connection with Trump's surprising victory, which defied most pre-election polls.[242]

"Personally I think the idea that fake news on Facebook, of which it's a very small amount of the content, influenced the election in any way is a pretty crazy idea," Zuckerberg argued, leaving many wondering how that could be the case when Facebook's pitch to

---

[238] https://www.buzzfeed.com/ishmaeldaro/paul-horner-amish-trump-vote-hoax

[239] http://www.denverpost.com/2016/11/05/there-is-no-such-thing-as-the-denver-guardian/

[240] http://www.politifact.com/truth-o-meter/statements/2016/nov/17/blog-posting/no-someone-wasnt-paid-3500-protest-donald-trump-it/
https://www.washingtonpost.com/news/the-intersect/wp/2016/11/17/facebook-fake-news-writer-i-think-donald-trump-is-in-the-white-house-because-of-me/

[241] https://www.buzzfeed.com/craigsilverman/how-macedonia-became-a-global-hub-for-pro-trump-misinfo

[242] https://www.buzzfeed.com/craigsilverman/partisan-fb-pages-analysis

advertisers is based on their ability to influence its users.[243] A week later, outgoing president Barack Obama weighed into the debate, fretting that the jumble of real and fake news on social media meant "everything is true and nothing is true".[244]

"An explanation of climate change from a Nobel Prize-winning physicist looks exactly the same on your Facebook page as the denial of climate change by somebody on the Koch brothers' payroll," Obama said in a *New Yorker* interview. "And the capacity to disseminate misinformation, wild conspiracy theories, to paint the opposition in wildly negative light without any rebuttal – that has accelerated in ways that much more sharply polarise the electorate and make it very difficult to have a common conversation."

A couple days later, Zuckerberg said Facebook was working on various ways to combat the "misinformation" problem but wanted these techniques to centre on users reporting stories they think are hoaxes.[245] "We do not want to be arbiters of truth ourselves, but instead rely on our community and trusted third parties," he wrote. Indeed, since 2015 the company has offered people the ability to report articles that they think are hoaxes, but it's not clear how many do so, and whether they abuse the mechanism to target information with which they disagree.[246] In December 2016, Facebook finally took a further step to deal with the problem, teaming up with professional fact-checkers – in other words, journalists – to evaluate reports of fake news on the platform.[247]

The fact is that traditional media involves editors and other expensive humans who try to make sure that they tell their readers the truth. An enormous, highly automated service like Facebook, which is

[243] https://variety.com/2016/digital/news/mark-zuckerberg-facebook-donald-trump-win-1201915811/

[244] http://www.newyorker.com/magazine/2016/11/28/obama-reckons-with-a-trump-presidency

[245] https://www.facebook.com/zuck/posts/10103269806149061

[246] https://newsroom.fb.com/news/2015/01/news-feed-fyi-showing-fewer-hoaxes/

[247] https://newsroom.fb.com/news/2016/12/news-feed-fyi-addressing-hoaxes-and-fake-news/

aggregating the output of these relatively small-scale operations, does not want to pay the many, many humans who would be needed to make sure the end-result is a fair representation of reality. Instead, it would rather use algorithms to do the same job – to prioritise worthwhile articles over nonsense. With two billion users, there is probably no other way for Facebook to live up to its responsibilities in a cost-effective way, in the long term. But its technology cannot yet determine truth, so it must use humans for now, where it's forced to do so. And even then, it's not clear that it takes the issue seriously enough for the humans to help as much as they'd like. "I don't feel like it's working at all. The fake information is still going viral and spreading rapidly," one fact-checker told the *Guardian*. "It's really hard to hold [Facebook] accountable. They think of us as doing their work for them. They have a big problem, and they are leaning on other organisations to clean up after them."[248]

As was established in 2017, the Russians tried to influence the previous year's election in a variety of ways, one of which involved the use of Facebook ads – that is, paid-for posts, targeting people based on what the social network knows about them. So, some people were shown an "LGBT United" ad for a colouring book that depicted Clinton running mate Bernie Sanders "in muscle poses". Others saw an "Army of Jesus" ad showing Jesus arm-wrestling Satan. Its text: "Satan: If I win Clinton wins! Jesus: Not if I can help it! Press 'Like' to help Jesus Win!"[249] Another group was called "Blacktivist" – a fake black activism group that tried to organise actual rallies through Facebook. According to CNN, the Blacktivist Facebook group had more likes than the verified Black Lives Matter account.[250] Facebook's system was doing what it was supposed to: allow a broad base of advertisers to find their marks and target them with carefully tailored information. When your

---

[248] https://www.theguardian.com/technology/2017/nov/13/way-too-little-way-too-late-facebooks-fact-checkers-say-effort-is-failing

[249] https://www.nytimes.com/2017/11/01/us/politics/russia-2016-election-facebook.html

[250] http://money.cnn.com/2017/09/28/media/blacktivist-russia-facebook-twitter/index.html

only missions are to grow and to profile everyone, you will design your algorithms to achieve these things, not to protect people from disinformation and division.

It wouldn't be fair to single out Facebook on the issue of misinformation. Many of these fake groups and personas had Twitter accounts, too. Twitter, with its lax policies on real identities, is full of automated accounts – according to a 2017 study by US academics, as many as 15 percent of Twitter accounts are bots.[251] Sometimes, organisations set up these bots simply in order to follow other accounts. Some people will pay good money to boost their follower count, because they think it gives them more credibility. If people follow the bots back, they might also click on the spam links in their tweets. But bots are also useful for pumping out hoaxes and attacking people. All they need is a keyword or phrase to trigger them. Russian hackers deployed them during the Crimea crisis, and they did it again in the US election of 2016. And in the Brexit vote earlier the same year – according to *The Times*, more than 150,000 Russian Twitter accounts talked about the UK's proposed withdrawal from the EU, and they pumped out almost 45,000 messages about it in the two days around the vote.[252]

At the time of writing, the extent of Russia's social media hijacking is starting to be determined through congressional hearings and federal investigations. However, although we don't yet know how much was done or how effective it was, the kind of manipulation that we are seeing should be instructive in itself. And already, Facebook and Twitter have said they will work with news organisations to accredit their real news. Facebook said its adoption of the new "Trust Indicators" content-badge system was part of its "ongoing efforts to

---

[251] https://arxiv.org/pdf/1703.03107.pdf
[252] https://www.thetimes.co.uk/edition/news/russia-used-web-posts-to-disrupt-brexit-vote-h9nv5zg6c

enhance people's understanding of the sources and trustworthiness of news on our platform".[253]

When any profile can position itself as a genuine teller of truth, and when the platform can't or won't catch it out, people will abuse the obvious potential for spreading lies. Some countries are starting to take this threat seriously. For example, the German government passed a law in mid-2017 that forces social networks to take down posts containing hate speech or fake news within a day, or within a week in particularly complex cases. If the tech firms don't comply, they face fines of up to €50 million. Civil rights activists don't like the fact that this just creates an incentive for companies like Facebook to take down anything that they think might be hate speech, without taking time to properly evaluate the post in its context, to figure out if it's maybe a joke or just fair comment.[254] A lot of people make comments, and using humans to read them is expensive. Inevitably, automated systems will police the social networks – our privately-held, modern-day version of the town square.

Will those algorithms prioritise people's free expression, or their proprietors' avoidance of fines? Will they help to make truth great again? Time will tell, but there are stark implications to getting it wrong. And this is not just a problem for social media platforms.

The Worst Lessons

Google also signed up to support the online media industry's Trust Indicators standard, which is good, because Google also has a truth problem. As the *Guardian* reported in December 2016, a search for "Did the Holocaust happen?" generated results topped by an article from the neo-Nazi Stormfront website, denying that the Holocaust took place. And just to compound matters, Google's autocomplete function

---

[253] https://media.fb.com/2017/11/16/launching-new-trust-indicators-from-the-trust-project-for-news-on-facebook/
[254] http://www.zdnet.com/article/social-media-giants-face-50m-fines-under-new-german-law/

suggested the "Did the Holocaust happen?" question whenever anyone typed into their search bar: "Did the ho..."[255] The paper previously noted that, if people typed in "Are Jews...", Google would suggest that the phrase they might be looking for was "Are Jews evil?" Similarly, the search engine suggested to people that they might want to know whether women are evil, or whether Muslims are bad.[256] Four months after this coverage, Google started allowing its users to report offensive autocomplete suggestions and misinformation-spreading articles that come up in search results.[257]

These results and suggestions weren't deliberate in the sense that Google would like people to consider anti-Semitism, Islamophobia and misogyny as lifestyle choices. But Google's system, which tries to reflect the most popular search terms and content, can be manipulated. Want to push a hate-speech website to the top of the list? Create lots of webpages that link out to that site, in order to tell Google that it's popular. Have lots of people search for it. The algorithms controlling the search results are smart, but they can be outsmarted.

A similar syndrome was on display when Microsoft created an automated Twitter account called Tay. An experiment in a research field known as machine learning, Tay was a bot that Microsoft wanted to train in "conversational understanding", by having it interact with humans. The bot would "talk" to people over Twitter and use the experience to constantly become more human-like. Tay's socialisation did not go as planned. Many people decided it would be funny to teach Tay how to act like a terrible person by conversing with "her" in terrible terms. Microsoft's pet project responded accordingly. After Tay

[255] https://www.theguardian.com/commentisfree/2016/dec/11/google-frames-shapes-and-distorts-how-we-see-world
[256] https://www.theguardian.com/technology/2016/dec/04/google-democracy-truth-internet-search-facebook
[257] https://www.recode.net/2017/4/25/15415428/google-updating-search-flagging-fake-news

began tweeting out praise for Hitler and comparing feminism with cancer, Microsoft halted the experiment.[258]

Tay was embarrassing for its creator, but it hardly had a great impact on the world. Google and Facebook's services do have a great impact, though, and not merely because they are widely used. Remember that Google and Facebook are primarily advertising companies, and as such they have designed their core services to be able to influence their users. If they could not achieve this influence, through their fine-grained analysis of what people want to see, why would advertisers place ads on their platforms?

In their native US, which has strong protections for freedom of speech, the big social media platforms mostly get to do what they like with their algorithmic ranks and recommendations. For example, in 2014, a San Francisco court dismissed a lawsuit against Google by a man who was angry that the search engine shoved his website down the list in its results, even though rival search engines such as Bing and Yahoo gave it more prominence. The judge sided with Google's lawyers, who argued that the firm's "search results express Google's opinion on which websites are most likely to be helpful to the user in response to a query and are thus fully protected by the First Amendment".[259]

However, Google does have to abide by more restrictive expression laws in other countries. There's Germany and its strict approach to policing hate speech, but also countries that censor the internet based on moral concerns or to stamp out political discussions, such as China and Saudi Arabia.[260] Even in the US, Google adjusts its results and suggestions when the searched-for terms may relate to copyright

---

[258] https://techcrunch.com/2016/03/24/microsoft-silences-its-new-a-i-bot-tay-after-twitter-users-teach-it-racism/

[259] https://www.theguardian.com/technology/2014/nov/18/google-search-judge-free-speech

[260] https://www.theguardian.com/world/2017/mar/04/chinese-official-slams-internet-censorship

infringement.[261] In 2011, it stopped suggesting file-sharing tools and services like "BitTorrent" and "Rapidshare" to autocomplete users.[262] The next year, Google told its users: "Starting next week, we will begin taking into account a new signal in our rankings: the number of valid copyright removal notices we receive for any given site. Sites with high numbers of removal notices may appear lower in our results."[263] When it really has to, Google will censor or edit what it tells people.

Search results and autocomplete suggestions are already very powerful ways of telling people that something is important and true, but this power is only likely to increase as algorithms assume a more influential role in our lives. Today, when we enter queries into Google Search, we usually get a list of results. However, the tech industry is veering towards a very different way of presenting information. When you ask a question of a virtual assistant such as Apple's Siri, Google's Assistant or Microsoft's Cortana, the aim of these programs is to give you one answer, not many. Ultimately, these new assistant services are trying to simulate very well-informed people, and if you ask a smart person something, you expect them to tell you the truth. If these assistants tell a lie, that's a problem – what they say can't even be checked against results further down the list, because there's no list.

For example, Google these days puts a snippet from a popular article at the top of its results for certain search terms. It also uses the same snippets to provide answers read out by its Home device, a device that contains a microphone and speaker so people can interact with Google Assistant. In early 2017, after Donald Trump assumed the presidency, if you asked Google Home the question "Is Obama planning a coup?", you got this response: "According to Secrets of the Fed, According to details exposed in Western Center for Journalism's exclusive video, not

---

[261] https://torrentfreak.com/google-adds-pirate-bay-domains-to-censorship-list-120910/

[262] https://www.theregister.co.uk/2011/01/27/google_bittorrent_terms_killed_on_autocomplete/

[263] https://search.googleblog.com/2012/08/an-update-to-our-search-algorithms.html

only could Obama be in bed with the communist Chinese, but Obama may be in fact be planning a communist coup d'état at the end of his term in 2016."[264] Needless to say, Secrets of the Fed is a conspiracy website, and the newly vacation-happy Obama was far more interested in waterskiing than overthrowing his successor. But if you took your virtual assistant at its word, you might have thought otherwise.

The question of what constitutes "artificial intelligence" (AI) is as open as that of what constitutes intelligence itself. Some argue that true AI will only exist when machines become sentient. However, although they are far from being autonomous beings, it's useful to classify tools such as Siri, Assistant, Cortana, and perhaps IBM's Watson, as proto-AIs. They're increasingly advanced question-and-answer machines that try to provide a human-like interface, to make life easier for us. Once they become really good at this, it won't really matter if they're sentient or not – from the human perspective, they'll be close enough. These systems are getting better and better at interpreting meaning in what we say, so that they can respond in an appropriate and useful manner.

For these proto-AIs, interpreting meaning in words and nuggets of information is not simply a matter of methodically teaching the system more words and factoids. Rather, the key is to teach the system how to "learn" – essentially, how to find patterns in a large amount of data that help it identify certain things and act accordingly. It's not about instruction, so much as using applied statistics to make decisions.[265] This is machine learning, the field in which Microsoft's Tay was abortively playing.

Machine learning has a huge range of uses. Gmail, for example, uses machine learning techniques to figure out which emails are spam, so it can route those emails to the spam folder. Facebook uses comparable techniques to analyse all the photos that its users upload, so it can

---

[264] https://www.independent.co.uk/life-style/gadgets-and-tech/news/donald-trump-barack-obama-coup-google-home-assistant-question-fake-news-a7614421.html

[265] http://www.fudzilla.com/news/41763-google-assistant-uses-ai-machine-learning-to-become-people-friendly

recognise people its systems have seen before, and offer up their identities as tag suggestions. The development of self-driving cars is largely about teaching the software how to recognise road markings, other vehicles, people crossing the road, and things by the roadside such as kerbs and trees, then optimising the car's decision-making process so that it reacts to those things as a good driver would.

The fuel for this auto-education is the data that you feed into the machine: the more you put in, the more it can learn from. That's why Google and Facebook are among the companies making the biggest strides in this field: their millions of users upload so much information and create so much data through their activities – all those searches; all those likes – that the companies behind the platforms have the richest resources with which to feed their proto-AIs.

However, there's a major issue with machine learning that is both part of its magic and a serious potential problem: it means letting the system develop its own methods of doing what it does, and the people who build the system do not necessarily understand those methods. It's not simply a matter of, say, telling the system how to be a good driver – indeed, we're hoping that automated cars will be better drivers than we are. What we're interested in is the results, and if our "AIs" come up with ways of getting there that are alien to the human thought process but more efficient, then all the better. However, it's risky to train a system without being exactly sure what it sees as worth learning from.[266]

One of the biggest dangers here is that, because the machine-learning system constantly takes in new data and readjusts its pattern-seeking methods accordingly, it's extremely difficult to track how biases in the data are affecting those methods. Because these systems are opaque in their workings, we ought to be very, very careful about the data on which we train them. What we don't want to do is create racist, misogynistic artificial intelligences. As the Tay experiment demonstrated, this is not a fanciful threat. Microsoft Research chief

---

[266] http://spectrum.ieee.org/cars-that-think/transportation/self-driving/why-ai-makes-selfdriving-cars-hard-to-prove-safe

Peter Lee wrote after that debacle: "Looking ahead, we face some difficult – and yet exciting – research challenges in AI design. AI systems feed off of both positive and negative interactions with people. In that sense, the challenges are just as much social as they are technical. We will do everything possible to limit technical exploits but also know we cannot fully predict all possible human interactive misuses without learning from mistakes."[267]

Google takes the problem of opacity and control seriously. As Gary Illyes of the company's search team explained in a 2016 interview with Search Engine Land, Google is experimenting with machine learning as a way of looking for new kinds of "signals" – the factors that it uses to rank its results. However, it's unlikely to employ the technique more deeply "any time soon or in the foreseeable future".[268] The problem, Illyes noted, is that it's "close to impossible" to figure out why a machine learning system makes the decisions it makes, and "that would limit our with our ability to improve search in general".

This caution is eminently sensible, but let's see whether it holds. Perhaps machine learning will end up producing smarter results than Google's human-made core algorithm can produce. Perhaps another company using these techniques will displace Google. These are distinct possibilities. And if we end up with an AI making decisions that are based on the information we have to offer – and acting as our mediator to the world around us – we had better make sure that this information is as factual and fair-minded as possible. There are too many clashing viewpoints out there for us to treat the internet's output in a casual way.

***

---

[267] https://blogs.microsoft.com/blog/2016/03/25/learning-tays-introduction/#sm.00001557aaxn9mf0gpwmelm41bmsx
[268] http://searchengineland.com/google-uses-machine-learning-search-algorithms-261158

One solution to the problem of misinformation is better media literacy. People – and not just kids – need to be educated about the dangers of online lies and shown how to spot them. Essentially, people should become better fact-checkers, employing timeless techniques like always looking for the original source of a claim, and being extra-skeptical when a claim seems to reinforce their own prejudices. The power to misinform people on social media is insidious, but it is possible to push back. The principles of critical thinking need to be burned into our collective consciousness, but doing so will take time and effort. Not all countries will be keen on teaching citizens these principles, either. A credulous populace is more likely to grant great power to its leaders.

Looking to the future, we're going to need to find ways to keep our virtual assistants honest. Right now they're still a novelty, helping us with basic tasks while amusing us with their failure to appear truly human-like. But the more we use them, the more they will evolve. Eventually, they will become truly useful, bundling up the search capabilities of Google with the networking nous of Facebook, and in the process learning about us in minute detail. But if we're going to let them into our lives as confidantes, companions, advisors and agents, we'll need to trust them. As these proto-AIs become more sophisticated and influential, we'll need to know and understand their motives. Are they there to serve our own agendas, or those of someone else? If we ask them to tell us about some event that's just happened, which version of events will they relate?

There will come a time when authorities demand to see the inner workings of these algorithms, to check they're complying with the law, to force changes in how they operate, and potentially to influence what they tell us. Although they may sometimes have very good reasons for doing so, it's really not clear whether this will be possible, because those training the algorithms are themselves frequently ignorant of their inner workings. But let's assume there is a way for the authorities to meaningfully poke around inside the box. If so, regular people should ideally have a similar view.

Our assistants are today entirely proprietary and shut off from inspection. If they were open-source – if the code were open to public auditing and improvement – we would be closer to figuring out if they're trustworthy. This is the approach the security community takes with encryption algorithms: if they're not open to scrutiny, the experts shy away because they worry about hidden components that betray the user. Perhaps there will be a gap in the market for open-source virtual assistants that don't feed data back to some corporate mothership, but that genuinely act as our agents, always with our interests in mind, and always trying to figure out the unvarnished truth.

We'll need to fight for the truth as these technologies evolve. But the fight for free expression may prove even more difficult. When the German government cracked down on online hate speech and disinformation in 2017, it almost forced the social networks to install mechanisms that would have proactively filtered out law-breaking posts. Again, technology cannot yet determine the truth, and in any case EU law forbids forcing online platforms to monitor all their users' activities, so the clause was removed before the "Enforcement on Social Networks" bill was passed. But over time, other governments will be tempted to mandate these mechanisms.

After all, offline laws must apply online too. Particularly where those rules restrict what people can and cannot say, it stands to reason that enforcement must take place on platforms such as Facebook and Twitter. The question is, whose rules? These are global services. Who gets to decide what's true and fair, what information should be suppressed and how insulting people are allowed to be? Countries around the world have wildly differing opinions on issues such as free speech. How, in the context of the global internet, can they lay down the law?

CHAPTER 6: WHOSE RULES?

In 2012, the Iranian government announced it was building high-speed broadband infrastructure to get more people using the internet.[269] However, this project was not about making it easier for Iranians to access the likes of Google and Facebook. Quite the opposite.

The government was creating what it called *Internet-e Paak*, a "pure internet" that would be "compatible with religious and revolutionary values". In other words, it was an alternative to the global internet and all its terrible, non-halal influences. According to the government, it would be "free from immoral, corrupt and violent content", carrying only services and content that's hosted on Iranian servers. Of course, with everything on the *Internet-e Paak* being local, it would also be firmly under the theocratic regime's control. That meant the government wouldn't need to filter anything out to enforce its strict religious laws, as it does with the regular internet.

Iran launched its halal internet in 2016, promising that citizens would only have to pay half as much to access it as they do with the international internet.[270] The government also said the *Internet-e Paak* would be faster and more reliable than its global counterpart. Iranian authorities have repeatedly insisted that the development of this local internet will not lead to a cut-off of the full-fat internet. But why else would the government have developed it? It's expensive and almost impossibly difficult to stop the internet from ushering unwanted foreign influences through the door. Closing the door is far easier.

The internet is a system that does not inherently respect borders – if something is available online, it is by default available to everyone with internet access, regardless of where they are. At the same time, countries do not have one set of laws for what happens online and a separate set for the equivalent offline actions. Nor should they, as

---

[269] https://citizenlab.org/2012/11/irans-national-information-network/
[270] http://en.mehrnews.com/news/119304/Iran-launches-National-Information-Network

"online" and "offline" are just two layers of the same reality. This presents governments and regulators with a massive dilemma. They need to be able to enforce their domestic laws – a basic principle of the centuries-old Westphalian concept of the sovereign state. But they are, under the norms of international law, only supposed to do so within their domestic borders.[271] So how can they maintain national sovereignty when faced with the technical realities of the borderless internet? Is it possible to maintain a balance between the rule of law and the global nature of this platform of platforms? And where systems clash, who chooses the winner?

The answers to these questions are starting to emerge, but so far they're looking deeply unattractive – a mix between the ineffective, the confused and the downright dangerous. This is a classic clash between what's desirable and what's technically feasible. And if the battle between the internet and the nation state is going to leave both sides intact, we're going to need to start paying a lot more attention to this quandary.

Building Walls

When Edward Snowden revealed the existence of the PRISM program, through which US authorities can secretly get access to information stored in the big tech companies' systems, countries around the world scrambled to figure out how to protect their citizens. In several cases, their first major reaction was to call for what's known as "data localisation" or "data sovereignty" – essentially the idea of keeping citizens' personal data stored in their own country, rather than letting it cross over into foreign jurisdictions. Brazil considered introducing a requirement for data localisation in its 2014 Civil Rights Framework for the Internet (the "Marco Civil da Internet"), but the government dropped the idea after a major outcry from the internet sector. Companies such as Google said the move would have increased

---

[271] http://internationalrelations.org/peace-of-westphaliatreaty-of-westphalia/

132

their costs.[272] Russia did introduce a data localisation law in 2014 that came into effect two years later. Companies such as LinkedIn, which refused to set up Russian datacentres for storing Russian users' personal information, found themselves blocked in the country.[273]

The idea of building data walls also proved briefly attractive in Europe. After Snowden revealed in 2014 that the US had tapped Angela Merkel's phone, the German chancellor proposed enhancing the EU's internet infrastructure, as Europeans "shouldn't have to send emails and other information across the Atlantic".[274] The big German email providers – T-Mobile, GMX and web.de – had by that point already responded to the NSA scandal by launching a service called "Email Made in Germany", that made sure emails sent between their services never left the country.[275]

This is not how the internet is supposed to work, technically speaking. The internet is a network of networks connected by routers that, as their name suggests, always try to steer data down the most efficient route to its destination. Perhaps counterintuitively, the most efficient route may not be the shortest one, as networks vary in quality and congestion. As data passes through the internet, it might also be used and altered by a variety of outsourced services. For example, a website might use one service to translate its users' information into different languages, another service to profile its users, another to let them share things they found on the site, and so on. These different services may be run from locations around the world, even if it seems to the user like they're only using the service provided by one website. So, geographically speaking, data typically goes all over the place, even though it's trying to get where it's going as quickly as possible. Of course, many of the services people use – and many of the companies

---

[272] http://www.law360.com/articles/520198/brazil-nixes-data-localization-mandate-from-internet-bill

[273] https://techcrunch.com/2016/11/17/linkedin-is-now-officially-blocked-in-russia/

[274] https://www.ft.com/content/dbf0081e-9704-11e3-809f-00144feab7de

[275] http://www.spiegel.de/international/germany/growing-demand-for-german-email-providers-after-nsa-scandal-a-918651.html

providing core infrastructural services that internet users never even know about – are based in the US. In short, it's very, very difficult to stop the average internet user's data from passing through the US at some point.

There's another, rather ironic problem with the idea of keeping non-US data safe from the American intelligence agencies. While those agencies can force US-based online service providers to give them access to their users' data, there are certain safeguards in place for doing so.[276] These safeguards may not be sufficient – the court that deals with surveillance requests hardly ever turns them down – but they're there.[277] When people's data is stored or travelling outside US borders, American agencies face comparatively weak restrictions if they want to spy on it. The strongest protections lie inside the country. Most countries have a similar legal split between what their spies can do inside and outside their domestic territory, in order to stop governments from spying on their own citizens. However, there are ways around such restrictions. When Snowden sent testimony to the European Parliament in 2014, describing what he knew about the surveillance of EU citizens, he painted a picture where countries effectively pool their spying efforts in order to help the NSA, which then shares data with them in return:

"The result is a European bazaar, where an EU member state like Denmark may give the NSA access to a tapping centre on the (unenforceable) condition that NSA doesn't search it for Danes, and Germany may give the NSA access to another on the condition that it doesn't search for Germans. Yet the two tapping sites may be two points on the same cable, so the NSA simply captures the communications of the German citizens as they transit Denmark, and the Danish citizens as they transit Germany, all the while considering it entirely in accordance with their agreements," Snowden testified.

---

[276] https://www.whitehouse.gov/the-press-office/2014/01/17/presidential-policy-directive-signals-intelligence-activities
[277] http://www.zdnet.com/article/us-spy-court-didnt-reject-a-single-secret-government-demand-for-data/

"Ultimately, each EU national government's spy services are independently hawking domestic accesses to the NSA, GCHQ, [Sweden's] FRA, and the like without having any awareness of how their individual contribution is enabling the greater patchwork of mass surveillance against ordinary citizens as a whole."[278]

In other words, keeping data within a non-US region is far from a guarantee that the data will be safe from the US intelligence services. And what's more, the nature of the internet means anyone can hack into data from anywhere in the world, making the physical location of data even less relevant.

So why, then, are some governments so keen on data localisation? In certain cases, the aim really does seem to be the protection of citizens' data. For example, Australia has a law that bans anyone from storing or sending Australians' electronic health records outside the country, with a few exceptions. This approach could make it easier for Australian health services to keep an eye on where those records are going.[279] However, some countries clearly just want to be able to get at their own citizens' data without having to go through the tedious process of formally requesting it from the US authorities – something they can already do through a "mutual legal assistance treaty" (MLAT), if indeed they have such an agreement with the US. Russia's data localisation law makes it easy for the Russian intelligence services to quickly access their citizens' data. Vietnam has a similar law, demanding for example that social network operators have "at least [one] server system in Vietnam serving the inspection, storage, and provision of information at the request of competent authorities".[280]

278

http://www.europarl.europa.eu/document/activities/cont/201403/20140307
ATT80674/20140307ATT80674EN.pdf

[279] http://www.globaltradealert.org/measure/australia-data-localisation-requirement-electronic-health-records

280

http://www.itpc.gov.vn/investors/how_to_invest/law/Decree_No.72_2013/
mldocument_view/?set_language=en

In countries with strong censorship, data localisation also makes it easier to force social networks, blogging platforms and web hosts to comply with national laws on what can and cannot be said. Russia has long had restrictions on what newspapers and broadcasters can say. At the same time as it brought in its data localisation law, it also extended these traditional media laws to apply to bloggers with 3,000 or more readers each day. This meant bloggers were no longer allowed to write anonymously, they had to avoid hate speech and "extremist calls", they could not swear and they could not slander anyone.[281] Importantly, they could also no longer publish any information without first verifying it. It would certainly be nice, in an ideal world, if all online reporting was fully verified. However, a restriction like this makes it extremely difficult to publish leaked information that's in the public interest, but impossible to verify without placing yourself in great danger.

In 2016, China also announced that foreign media would only be able to publish online in China if they hosted all their content on servers within the country.[282] It had already told foreign tech firms to store Chinese people's personal data on Chinese servers the year before. Apple is one company that was forced to comply. It had to do so if it was to continue its lucrative expansion into the Chinese market, although the company insisted that China Telecom – the state-owned telecommunications firm whose servers Apple is using – would have no access to the contents of users' accounts.[283]

Of course, if a foreign web service provider won't submit to your laws, you can simply order your country's internet service providers to block access to it. In 2011, the UK started doing this to services that break copyright laws, but that aren't physically located within the UK's jurisdiction. The previous year, the film studio Twentieth Century Fox had won an injunction forcing a file-sharing site called Newzbin to stop

---

[281] https://gigaom.com/2014/08/01/the-registration-of-russian-bloggers-has-begun/

[282] http://fortune.com/2016/02/20/china-foreign-media-rules/

[283] http://www.reuters.com/article/us-apple-data-china-idUSKBN0GF0N720140815

infringing on its copyrights. Newzbin shut down but swiftly re-emerged in the form of the near-identical Newzbin2, which was run from outside the country. So the High Court told BT to block Newzbin2.[284] The same tactic is spreading beyond the realms of copyright. In 2017, the British government passed legislation forcing internet service providers to block access to pornographic websites that don't verify users' identities in order to check their age, or that show sexual acts that would lead to a DVD being banned from sale under the country's film classification laws.[285]

China famously blocks access to many outside web services with what's known as the "Great Firewall" – a filter that forms part of a wider censorship and surveillance project called "Golden Shield". In probably the world's most prominent demonstration of internet sovereignty, China blocks access not only to media such as *The New York Times* and *Bloomberg*, but also to services such as Google and Dropbox. China has also moved to stop its citizens using tools such as proxies and virtual private networks (VPNs) to try to circumvent the Great Firewall. The authorities often block access to VPNs as soon as they identify them, making circumvention a dangerous cat-and-mouse game.[286] They've also forced app store providers such as Apple to remove VPN apps from their catalogues.[287]

China's model is starting to prove attractive to other repressive countries, such as Iran.[288] But in China, the Great Firewall has more benefits than merely controlling information. It's also been great for

---

[284] http://www.zdnet.com/article/film-studios-win-newzbin2-blocking-case-against-bt/
[285] https://www.theregister.co.uk/2017/04/28/digital_economy_bill_royal_assent/
[286] http://www.scmp.com/news/china/policies-politics/article/1922677/china-blocks-vpn-services-let-users-get-round-its-great
[287] https://www.cnbc.com/2017/07/31/apple-removes-vpn-apps-in-china-app-store.html
[288] http://www.themedialine.org/news/iran-introduces-halal-internet/

Chinese ecommerce and web communications giants such as Baidu, Alibaba and Tencent, because they're effectively shielded from big US rivals like Google.[289] In a country with such a large domestic market and a serious tech industry to serve it, data sovereignty is a splendid mechanism for protectionism. If we are entering a new era of post-globalisation, as the rise of nationalist forces in countries such as the US suggests, then we can perhaps expect to see more of this sort of thing.[290]

Although protectionism may not be a purely bad thing, seeking as it does to stimulate local economies, it's a risky business when it comes to the internet. Not only is data localisation often motivated by a desire to control and censor, but it could damage the internet's potential as the framework for a sort of global, collective intelligence. The internet provides the mechanisms for unprecedented collaboration across borders that can benefit humanity as a whole. Services such as ResearchGate, for example, allow researchers in a variety of fields and countries to peer-review one another's work and come up with cross-disciplinary solutions to the problems they face. The globalised internet could also make easier to track the spread of diseases by gathering together social media data from different countries, so researchers can look for patterns in the places where people are mentioning that they've fallen ill.[291] A system that links humanity together is something to be protected and nurtured.

People sometimes refer to the internet as a "commons" – a shared resource like the oceans and the air.[292] This is a somewhat utopian way of looking at things; after all, the internet is a network of commercially-run systems that are physically situated within national jurisdictions. However, aspects of the characterisation ring true. The fact of the

[289] http://blogs.wsj.com/chinarealtime/2015/01/28/china-owns-great-firewall-credits-censorship-with-tech-success/

[290] https://www.theguardian.com/business/2016/nov/09/globalisation-backlash-us-economy

[291] https://www.ncbi.nlm.nih.gov/pmc/articles/PMC3261963/

[292] https://www.theguardian.com/commentisfree/2014/mar/31/capitalism-age-of-free-internet-of-things-economic-shift

matter is that the internet may sometimes operate like a commons, and this may indeed be the most natural way for the internet to exist, but countries do have the power and the right to assert their jurisdictions if they think things are getting out of hand.

But where do those jurisdictions begin and end? The answer to that question is starting to look scarily complicated.

The Right to be Forgotten

Since 1995, people in the European Union have had the right to demand certain things from the people and organisations that hold or control their personal data, which includes things like names, phone numbers, financial information, photos and documents. Specifically, they can tell these people and organisations to make sure that the data is "adequate, relevant and not excessive in relation to the purposes for which they are collected and/or further processed". If the data doesn't meet these terms, then the data subject – the person who the data is about – can demand its deletion.

In 2009, a Spanish man named Mario Costeja González was annoyed about the fact that, when people searched the web for his name, they easily discovered that he had debt problems a decade before. Back then, on the order of the Spanish labour ministry, the newspaper *La Vanguardia* had published announcements about the forced sales of repossessed houses. Costeja's name was listed in one of those announcements, and he was tired of people finding it online. The newspaper refused to take down the announcements, so Costeja complained to the Spanish data protection authority, which also refused to make *La Vanguardia* unpublish what it had, after all, been officially ordered to publish in the first place. However, the regulator agreed with Costeja that Google should remove the links from its results. Google appealed and the case ended up going to the EU's highest court, the Court of Justice of the European Union. The CJEU ruled in 2014 – against the advice of its advocate-general – that Google had to respect Costeja's wish to have the story delisted.

The ruling was significant in two particular ways.[293] Firstly, it made it clear that Google's core search business fell under Spanish jurisdiction, even though the company maintained that it processed the data elsewhere. Google tried to argue that its only activities in the country were those carried out by Google Spain, a small subsidiary that deals with local advertising clients. The CJEU didn't play along. Instead, the court said that Google Inc, the US-based parent company, was operating on Spanish soil by offering its search service there, and that this was "inextricably linked" with Google's ad business. In other words, if Google wants to let Spanish people use its search engine, it has to play by Spanish rules.

Secondly, the ruling established that people across the EU could tell search engines to remove links about them if they don't want them up anymore. However, the court stressed that the search engine could refuse takedown requests if there was an overriding public interest in helping people find the information in question. The ruling was a bombshell, not least because it left the EU's data protection authorities scrambling for a way to handle hundreds of thousands of de-linking requests. In what's becoming a theme in the relationship between online platforms and law enforcement, the regulators decided that the search engines themselves should handle the requests. As Google has over 90 percent market share in the EU, that decision effectively made Google the judge of what constitutes the public interest in Europe.

The media was livid, and stories abounded of Google accepting de-linking requests from a disgraced referee,[294] a former Merrill Lynch chairman and other subjects of legitimate public interest.[295] These links may have gone down, but that meant Google was making bad decisions

---

293

http://curia.europa.eu/juris/document/document_print.jsf?doclang=EN&text=&pageIndex=0&part=1&mode=DOC&docid=152065&occ=first&dir=&cid=667631

[294] https://www.theguardian.com/commentisfree/2014/jul/02/eu-right-to-be-forgotten-guardian-google

[295] http://www.bbc.com/news/business-28130581

that weren't in line with the ruling. After all, the public interest should have led the company to reject those requests.

The ruling itself had a positive impact for many people, as Google itself made clear in a later transparency report.[296] The report noted that, for example, a rape victim had been able to use the mechanism to remove a link to an article about the crime that named her. A woman whose husband had been murdered decades before was able to stop that fact coming up in Google's results when people searched for her name. If it weren't for the everlasting index of facts that is Google, these people would have found it easier to move on with their lives and make new acquaintances that don't view them through the prism of long-past bad experiences that weren't their fault. Why shouldn't they have that right in the online age?[297] Why shouldn't Señor Costeja be able to move on from being known for his past debts? After all, it's what the EU's privacy law is supposed to ensure. It's worth noting that the ruling inspired a similar new law in Russia, only without the public interest defence. That's a recipe for abuse, as bad people could use the law to cover up pasts that people should know about. But that doesn't mean the CJEU's ruling, which was designed to protect the public interest, wasn't fair or an accurate reading of EU law.

It's also fair that the bloc's laws should apply to companies serving EU citizens, even if the companies aren't based in Europe – a point made even more explicit in the EU's new General Data Protection Regulation, which will replace the rules in the 1995 privacy directive in 2018. If we draw an analogy to the offline layer, a service provided online is like the service you might get if you go to a physical store or a social meeting place. Just because the service is now virtual, and can therefore be provided from anywhere in the world, that doesn't mean that you, sitting in your country, should suddenly give up your local rights.

---

[296] https://www.google.com/transparencyreport/removals/europeprivacy/
[297] http://press.princeton.edu/titles/9436.html

However, European privacy regulators took things a step further by deciding that Google should remove links around the world, not just in the EU.[298] The French data protection authority, CNIL, told Google in 2015 that it had to remove links from "google.com" and all its various national versions, not just the European sites like "google.es" and "google.fr".[299] Although the EU court's ruling didn't specifically say this was necessary, CNIL said this was the only way to meaningfully enforce the law, because anyone in France could still access the unwanted links by using a foreign version of Google. On the other side, Google argued that the regulator had no right to affect what people outside European jurisdiction could or could not see. In July 2017, the disagreement was finally referred up to the CJEU, which will need to determine where the line should be drawn.[300]

This disagreement perfectly demonstrates the clash between local laws and the internet's borderless nature – the struggle to strike a new balance where the old relationship between national authorities and industry has been rendered obsolete. The French regulator is trying to enforce French law on French soil, which is a fair aim, but the only way to make this enforcement truly effective is to apply it across the world. This means stomping all over the rights of people in countries with different laws on such things, and therefore interfering with those countries' own sovereignty.

The US and the EU both recognise the right to privacy and the right to free expression, but they prioritise different rights. In the EU, the right to privacy generally overrules the right to free expression, and in the US, free speech usually wins out. These are two conflicting legal systems, so if one tries to enforce its laws in the other's turf, that's a problem. What if you're an American who finds links disappearing from your search results because of a complaint somebody made in

---

[298] https://gigaom.com/2014/11/26/why-the-eus-right-to-be-de-linked-should-not-go-global/
[299] http://fortune.com/2016/03/24/france-google-right-to-be-forgotten/
[300] http://www.conseil-etat.fr/Actualites/Communiques/Portee-territoriale-du-droit-au-dereferencement

Bulgaria? The Bulgarian might be happy, but your own country's laws are supposed to stop that sort of censorship from affecting you.

The real danger here is that we all end up buried under overlapping laws from around the world, from democratic countries with good public-interest safeguards to oppressive regimes that want to make valuable information hard for anyone, anywhere, to find. That would trample over a lot of people's right to free information, but Google, which has to obey the laws of each country where its search service runs, would have no way to push back. Legislators and regulators around the world are going to have to think long and hard about proportionality in the online context. The obvious temptation is to opt for very strict enforcement in order to achieve effectiveness and assert sovereignty, but what's effective might also be unjust and undesirable.

Is there an international solution to this problem? Some, such as the Internet & Jurisdiction Project, argue that we should come up with international agreements that set the rules for these clashes of legal systems – not just over issues like de-linking and takedown requests, but also over the activities of various intelligence and law enforcement agencies.[301] Ultimately, the organisation has suggested, there should be treaties covering these issues.

However, there's a problem with getting more international cooperation on internet matters: the countries that currently have an outsized influence over the internet are very wary about giving more influence to their rivals.

The Battle Over Internet Regulation

To understand why there's so little international agreement about the future of the internet, it's important to look at the history of the network. This explains why western countries currently have such a disproportionate influence over what policy wonks call "internet governance".

---

[301] http://fortune.com/2016/04/08/internet-jurisdiction-trade/

The internet evolved from ARPANET, a network born in the US defence department at the end of the 1960s as a way of linking research teams and making it easier to quickly communicate nuclear threats between military installations. The public only started using the internet in significant numbers decades later, after Tim Berners-Lee's invention of the web browser in 1989. Berners-Lee was a Briton working at the CERN nuclear research facility in Switzerland, but the industry he spawned initially grew most vigorously in the US. Crucially, the US is also the home of the domain name system, or DNS. This is the system that translates human-recognisable website names (word-based domain names, like "facebook.com") into the mostly number-based IP addresses that computers use to talk to one another. It's a bit like a phone book, linking names to numbers, except it's constantly updated rather than being static. After all, websites' IP addresses often change, but you want a domain name such as "google.com" to always bring up the same service.

The DNS was a hugely important function in the earlier days of the web, though its importance is diminishing as people access websites via search and apps rather than by typing in addresses. Those running the directory get to do things like assign IP addresses to users and manage the creation of new top level domains – web address extensions such as ".com" and ".xxx". From 1998, the Internet Corporation for Assigned Names and Numbers (ICANN) managed the DNS under a contract with the government's commerce department. ICANN, a US-based non-profit organisation, is a "multi-stakeholder" group that includes all sorts of players: governments, businesses, technical experts, human rights groups and academics. The arrangement gave the government oversight over ICANN's operations, and it was only in 2016 that the government let the contract expire, finally giving up control over the internet's core routing system. ICANN was now officially in charge of DNS management – mostly a symbolic move, as nothing really changed on the technical level.

However, a lot of people in the US were not happy with the Obama administration's decision to officially pass control to this multi-stakeholder group.[302] Senator Ted Cruz tried to block the transfer because it would give countries like Russia, China and Iran more influence over how the internet is managed. He warned of "significant, irreparable damage... not only on our nation, but on free speech across the world". Donald Trump also opposed the deal while campaigning for the presidency.[303] Now, it's true that ICANN did have problems with transparency and accountability – for example, the internet community had a lot of trouble getting a clear answer about how the organisation spends money on lobbying.[304] But the transition was going to have to happen at some point. The internet came from the US but is now critical infrastructure for the world. Some argued for delaying the handover of power so that ICANN could first be improved, but the US – particularly in the wake of Edward Snowden's revelations – desperately wanted to demonstrate the internet's neutrality to the world.

This whole affair may seem dramatic, and US politicians and media certainly portrayed it as such. But the handover was arguably designed to effect as little change as possible, ensuring that anti-free-speech countries don't really get much more influence over the internet. The US has mostly had a very *laissez-faire* attitude towards internet regulation, particularly when it comes to free expression. In 1996, the Clinton administration passed the Communications Decency Act, in response to a moral panic over online pornography – the act made it illegal to show "obscene or indecent" material to people under the age of 18. However, it only took a year for the Supreme Court to strike it down as an unconstitutional affront to free speech.[305] From that point on, internet regulation in the US largely became a matter of soft power – a model subsequently adopted by many countries in Europe and

---

[302] https://www.icann.org/news/announcement-2016-10-01-en

[303] https://www.donaldjtrump.com/press-releases/donald-j.-trump-opposes-president-obama-plan-to-surrender-american-internet
[304]

http://www.theregister.co.uk/2015/11/19/real_icann_lobbying_expenses/
[305]

http://edition.cnn.com/US/9706/26/cda.overturned.hfr/index.html?eref=site search elsewhere. Rather than issuing top-down demands, many governments preferred to encourage web firms to regulate themselves. The governments set up partnerships and forums where companies such as Facebook and Google agreed to do things like making their services child-friendly, helping the copyright industry and bolstering the authorities' fight against so-called "online radicalisation".

However, governments that have no love for free speech – and that don't like their citizens using the internet to expose corruption and organise dissent – want to take a more heavy-handed approach to governing the internet. And they've repeatedly tried to organise global forums where they can exert stronger influence over internet regulation at the international level. This, researcher Ben Wagner has argued, is why "multi-stakeholder" organisations such as ICANN really exist – to stop other forums springing up and giving authoritarian countries a bigger say in global internet governance.[306] Not that the establishment of other forums hasn't been attempted. In 2005, Tunisia and others set up the World Summit on the Information Society (WSIS), an event that was designed to let governments come together and reach compromise positions on internet regulation. That aim failed, largely because the EU sided with the US over ICANN's supposed importance. The summit's main outcome was the creation of a non-influential annual talking shop called the Internet Governance Forum (IGF). In 2012, Russia, China and other countries – mainly from the developing world – tried to get control of the internet transferred to the International Telecommunications Union (ITU), a United Nations agency where they would have had much more influence.[307] They used the US's control of the DNS as one of their main arguments for getting more control for themselves.[308] They failed, as most of the world refused to sign the treaty they came up with, but the episode clearly demonstrated why it

---

[306] Ben Wagner (2016) – Global Free Expression: Governing The Boundaries Of Internet Content
[307] http://www.reuters.com/article/us-telecom-treaty-internet-idUSBRE8B800Q20121209
[308] https://readplaintext.com/heres-why-we-should-go-through-with-the-iana-transition-f07d36c42bb7#.8snqwum9w

was such a crucial public relations move for the US to give up its overt control over the internet's address book.

Will the dominance of largely powerless talking shops continue to maintain the status quo? As Ben Wagner wrote: "Multi-stakeholder institutions like the IGF and ICANN are increasingly becoming empty shells to justify a model with little international buy-in." The current situation might hold for a while, but the developing economies are not likely to stop trying to get more influence. After all, China has the most internet users of any country in the world – almost 700 million, versus 240 million in the US. India, with 340 million internet users, also outweighs the US. Brazil has over 120 million internet users, Russia has more than 100 million, and Nigeria has almost 90 million.[309] Developed countries may have relatively high percentages of their populace that use the internet, because of wealth and good infrastructure, but the developing world is catching up. It's not surprising that these countries' governments want more of a say in how the internet is governed.

In any case, the wind may be blowing in their direction. Europe in particular is starting to move away from *laissez-faire* regulation of online expression towards a system where tech firms face huge fines if they don't remove illegal information. The advantage of this self-regulatory approach was always that governments got to avoid having to come up with formal regulation that citizens might find overbearing and courts might find unconstitutional. The companies, meanwhile, got more leeway than they would under formal regulation, even if the arrangement created a kind of unofficial policing structure on platforms such as Facebook and Google – "quasi-public" spaces, as the activist Jillian York has called them.[310] Now that countries such as Germany, France and the UK are either enacting or threatening legislation that forces social media to remove hate speech and "fake news" from their platforms, this privatised policing structure is becoming formalised.

---

[309] http://data.worldbank.org/indicator/IT.NET.USER.P2
[310] https://opennet.net/policing-content-quasi-public-sphere

All this is encouraging news for more authoritarian countries – to an extent, it validates their approach to regulating the internet. But even if democratic countries are on the edge of censorship's slippery slope, there's a way to go before they risk replicating the injustices seen in some parts of the world.

The Right to Internet Access

Authoritarian governments have never been put off trying to enforce their laws in their own countries, just because they can't get the rest of the world to play along. Even if they lack influence over the big social networks and other online platforms, they can still get to the firms providing internet connections on their own soil. In many countries these telecommunications companies are still state-controlled monopolies, making it particularly easy to tell them what to do.

In some cases, that means telling them to just stop people from being able to access the internet at all. The digital rights group Access Now counted 61 internet shutdowns around the world during the first three quarters of 2017, up from 55 during 2016 and 20 during the whole of 2015.[311] The Brookings Institution, a US think tank, estimated that shutdowns of internet access and specific services cost the countries in which they occurred at least $2.4 billion in gross domestic product, over the latter half of 2015 and the first half of 2016.[312]

Governments cut off internet services for a variety of reasons. Wholesale shutdowns seem to be particularly popular in Africa and the Middle East. In 2016 alone, Gabon,[313] Uganda,[314] Burundi,[315] and

---

[311] https://www.accessnow.org/keepiton/

[312] https://www.brookings.edu/research/internet-shutdowns-cost-countries-2-4-billion-last-year/

[313] http://qz.com/771996/gabon-is-the-latest-african-country-to-shut-down-its-internet-as-election-protests-grow/

[314] https://advox.globalvoices.org/2016/05/11/social-media-blocked-in-uganda-ahead-of-president-musevenis-inauguration/

[315] http://extensia-ltd.com/burundi-access-urges-action-on-burundis-internet-shut-down/

Gambia[316] entirely blocked social media or internet access because of elections – the governments did not want opposition activists to be able to coordinate protests. In Algeria, the authorities ordered internet service providers to block access to social media during school exam time, in order to stop pupils sharing questions and cheating.[317] The authorities in Iraq took things a step further by blocking internet access across the whole country for three-hour periods during its school exams.[318]

To put it mildly, this again demonstrates how regulators struggle to effectively enforce rules in the online context without going overboard. Yes, the authorities in Iraq managed to achieve the online equivalent of banning kids from whispering answers to one another, but at the same time they shut down all elements of the economy that required the internet to do their work. That's rather excessive. Similarly, regimes trying to stymie protests by cutting communications are doing what they intended – clamping down on free expression – but they're also affecting millions of people who are just trying to get on with their day.

This raises an interesting question: should people have the right to internet access?

All rights are not created equal. For example, under the International Covenant on Civil and Political Rights (ICCPR), which entered into force across much of the world in 1976, some rights are absolute. These include the right to life, freedom from torture, freedom from slavery, and freedom of thought and religion. Some rights can be overridden under extraordinary circumstances – as discussed earlier, free expression can trump privacy, or vice versa – but generally the ICCPR lays out rights that countries have pledged to protect. Then there's the ICCPR's companion treaty, the International Covenant on Economic, Social and Cultural Rights (ICESCR), which is supposed to protect labour rights and the rights to health, education and an adequate

---

[316] http://www.bbc.com/news/world-africa-38157127
[317] http://fortune.com/2016/06/20/algeria-facebook-twitter-exams/
[318] https://www.theguardian.com/technology/2016/may/18/iraq-shuts-down-internet-to-stop-pupils-cheating-in-exams

149

standard of living. Many of these are more aspirational rights: things that countries will try to do as best they can.

Where might internet access fall into this scheme of things? We can take some guidance from a non-binding resolution that came out of the United Nations' Human Rights Council in 2016, partly addressing the issue of countries deliberately cutting off people's internet access.[319] The resolution noted that the internet was becoming particularly important for freedom of expression (for which, it added, online privacy is needed). It also pointed out that access to information on the internet is "an important tool to facilitate the promotion of the right to education" and an "enabler for development". Russia and China tried to push amendments that would have removed the resolution's wording about free expression and taking a "human rights based approach" to providing internet access, but they failed.[320]

Internet access is not a luxury – it has become an integral part of modern existence and is crucial to upholding certain more established human rights. If you cut off internet access, you stamp all over those rights. When Gabon and Gambia blocked access at election time, the whole point was to interfere with free expression. When Iraq cut off the internet at exam time, it violated the right to work for people who need the internet to do their jobs.

The online layer coexists with the offline layer, and essential rights span both the virtual and physical worlds. So can their abuses. When countries roll out internet access in certain areas but not others, the inconsistency tends to mirror the existing political exclusion of certain ethnic groups. European researchers found in 2016 that less powerful ethnic groups around the world had only 60 percent of the internet access of more powerful groups.[321] Discrimination in providing internet access is really just part of wider societal discrimination.

---

[319] https://www.article19.org/data/files/Internet_Statement_Adopted.pdf
[320] https://www.article19.org/resources.php/resource/38429/en/unhrc:-significant-resolution-reaffirming-human-rights-online-adopted
[321] http://phys.org/news/2016-09-ethnic-groups-internet-access.html

In late 2016 and early 2017, English-speaking parts of Cameroon were wracked by protests over perceived discrimination by the African country's French-speaking majority. Sick of being forced to use French in schools and courts, people went on strike and took to the streets, clashing with police. In mid-January, the Cameroonian telecommunications authority issued a statement warning people against using social media to spread what it called false news.[322] "As much as social media contribute to the development of digital economy, which is so dear to the President of the Republic, and to economic, social and cultural development in general, the malicious use of social media with an aim to misinform and distort reality, is likely to create psychosis in the public opinion and to disrupt social cohesion," the ministry said.

Days later, the internet went down in Cameroon's English-speaking regions, in the south-west and north-west of the country. And it stayed down for three months. The government gave no explanation, and there were no apparent technical faults.[323] Unlike the Syrian outage five years earlier, this was no mistake. It was a concerted effort to punish people that the government thought were potential law-breakers, which happened to be the occupants of entire regions. To go online, people from those areas had to go to the nearest French-speaking towns, where some people set up "internet refugee camps" to help their neighbours.[324] After it restored connectivity, the government promised the international community that it wouldn't do it again. But in October

322

https://www.minpostel.gov.cm/index.php?option=com_content&view=articl e&id=591%3Adeclaration-by-the-minister-of-posts-and-telecommunications-within-the-framework-of-the-awareness-campaign-for-a-responsible-use-of-social-media-in-cameroon&catid=49%3Aactualites&Itemid=27&lang=en
[323] http://www.bbc.com/news/world-africa-38895541
[324] https://qz.com/942879/an-internet-shutdown-in-cameroon-has-forced-startups-to-create-an-internet-refugee-camp-in-bonako-village/

2017, it cut off the internet in English-speaking regions again, to counteract protests.[325]

Some countries have already decided that internet access is a right in itself. In 2001, Greece amended its constitution to say that "all persons have the right to participate in the Information Society" – a bureaucratic term that means online life.[326] Finland said in 2010 that every citizen must have access to connection speeds of at least one megabit per second.[327] Like access to post and phone services, the government made broadband a legal right.

France, meanwhile, effectively established internet access as a right by first heading in the opposite direction. In 2009, the French government introduced a law called HADOPI, which was supposed to modernise copyright enforcement. The law included a so-called "three-strikes" rule – someone could be legally disconnected from the internet for up to one year if they were caught three times illegally downloading copyright-protected films or songs. The first couple of times, they would receive warning letters, then they would be cut off. The final decision on disconnection would come from a new organisation called the HADOPI council.

France's Constitutional Council told the government to redraft the law. In its ruling, France's highest court referred back to the country's 1789 Declaration of the Rights of Man and of the Citizen – the ancestor of documents such as the ICCPR treaty. The court pointed out that this centuries-old document entrenched the right to free expression. It said: "In the current state of the means of communication and given the generalised development of public online communication services and the importance of the latter for the participation in democracy and the

---

[325] https://qz.com/1091516/cameroon-internet-shut-down-as-southern-cameroons-ambazonia-protests-grow-in-bamenda-buea/
[326] https://www.diplomacy.edu/blog/right-access-internet-countries-and-laws-proclaim-it
[327] http://www.bbc.com/news/10461048

expression of ideas and opinions, this right implies freedom to access such services."[328]

Although the ruling declared internet access to be a human right, that wasn't the end of the story.[329] The court also noted that copyright is a form of the right to property, which is also protected under the 1789 declaration. If one right is going to be prioritised over the other, that's a matter that needs to be taken seriously. The law created a new council that would decide whether or not to cut off people's internet access, and the constitutional court decided that this body would have been too powerful for something that wasn't actually a court of law. The Constitutional Council also didn't like the fact that there would be a presumption of guilt, leaving it up to the accused to prove that they didn't illegally download the film or album in question. When the government came back with a revised law addressing these concerns, the council said the new version was constitutionally acceptable.[330] "No constitutional rule... precludes an administrative authority from participating in the enforcement of the penalty of suspension of access to the internet," it said. Again, this was about balancing rights, and the French court decided that the right to property could trump the right to free expression and, by extension, the right to internet access.

But in the end, the HADOPI law turned out to be a failure. It had been introduced by conservative president Nicolas Sarkozy (who is, pertinently, married to musician Carla Bruni), and the subsequent administration of François Hollande was much less keen on the idea. A 2012 report showed that the HADOPI council sent out 1.15 million first warning letters and over 100,000 second warning letters, but ultimately took only 14 people to court for infringing a third time.[331] In the mere

---

[328] http://www.conseil-constitutionnel.fr/conseil-constitutionnel/root/bank_mm/anglais/2009_580dc.pdf

[329] http://www.foxnews.com/story/2009/06/12/top-french-court-declares-internet-access-basic-human-right.html

[330] http://www.conseil-constitutionnel.fr/conseil-constitutionnel/root/bank_mm/anglais/en2009_590dc.pdf

[331] http://arstechnica.com/tech-policy/2012/09/french-anti-piracy-agency-hadopi-only-sued-14-people-in-20-months/

four cases that made it to trial, the defendants were only charged with failing to properly secure their internet connections – nobody tried to prove that they themselves committed the infringement. This lesser charge only carried a maximum internet suspension of one month.[332] Culture minister Aurélie Filippetti suggested that, at a cost of €12 million a year, the scheme wasn't worth it.[333] In 2013, French communications minister Fleur Pellerin said: "Today, it's not possible to cut off internet access… It's something like cutting off water."[334]

Starved of funding, HADOPI was effectively gutted. The right to internet access won out after all.

***

Lawmakers and regulators have a deeply unenviable task when it comes to regulating the internet. In societies that respect rights, different rights need to be thoughtfully balanced to ensure fairness. At the same time, technical realities limit the options for fully enforcing the law, making it easy to go overboard. The only way to stop French people seeing certain Google results really is to make Google scrub those results around the world. When Canada's Supreme Court in 2017 wanted to make sure people couldn't use Google to find a law-breaking company's website, it also ordered Google to censor those results on a global basis.[335] Unless Google does what these courts and regulators say, French and Canadian laws won't be perfectly enforced. But going down this route means eroding freedom of expression and information for all of us, country by country, ruling by ruling, complaint by complaint.

---

[332] https://papers.ssrn.com/sol3/papers.cfm?abstract_id=2322516
[333] https://gigaom.com/2012/08/03/france-will-cut-funding-to-its-piracy-police/
[334] http://www.nytimes.com/2013/06/03/technology/03iht-piracy03.html
[335] https://arstechnica.com/tech-policy/2017/06/canadas-supreme-court-orders-google-to-alter-search-results-worldwide/

If we're going to have balanced laws in the online context, we will need to accept that they may sometimes be imperfectly enforced. If Google removes a link to outdated information about a French person for those who use the search engine in France, then the "right to be forgotten" is doing its job: stopping unwelcome information from showing up all the time, when someone searches for the subject's name. Is it really worth trying to apply this law in Omaha just to stymie the few determined information-seekers who might hide their real location in order to access Google's US version? If it proves impossible to eradicate hate speech from Facebook without forcing the company to automatically censor what its algorithms think is illegal, do we attempt perfect enforcement and deal a massive blow to free expression? Some laws will survive imperfect enforcement, but where it's necessary to maintain people's rights, and it renders a law pointless, then maybe it's time to rethink the law.

We also need to have a good long think about who it is we want enforcing our laws. The problem with leaving enforcement to the big internet platforms like Google and Facebook is that, while they no doubt try to achieve a just outcome, they're not actual courts. They're businesses that are concerned about the bottom line, and that will invest as few resources as possible in fulfilling their role as the new internet police. Especially when threatened with fines if they don't quickly delete illegal posts, they have every incentive to lean towards deletion every time they face a tough call. They shouldn't even have this role in the first place. Our societies are just going to have to deal with the fact that the internet has encouraged people to express themselves more, as is their right, and if we want to police this flood of information then some form of public body is going to have to be involved, with a lot of investment. If that sounds too expensive, then the law needs to be relaxed.

The most fundamental property of the internet is the way it makes it easy to share information. Fighting this property means employing censorship and surveillance and, for perfect enforcement, cutting off people's internet access. Those of us living in democracies should tell our politicians that we don't want to go down this route. Meanwhile, countries should not be trying to foist their own censorship laws on other countries. It's one thing to claim jurisdiction over a company operating in your territory, and quite another to then tell that company what it can and can't do in other territories.

However, those lobbying for the free flow of information have always had a powerful adversary. If we look at the original motivations behind blocking websites and cutting off people's internet access, they usually have something to do with copyright enforcement. The holders of intellectual property rights are extremely influential around the world. And where intellectual property is concerned, the internet poses an existential threat.

CHAPTER 7: DIGITAL PROPERTY

In 1987, the Japanese video-game company Konami ported an arcade game called *Double Dribble* to the Nintendo Entertainment System (NES), a popular game console of the time. There was a glitch in the game – any 3-point jump shot taken from one of the top corners of the court would successfully go in. In 2009, a YouTube user called "sw1tched" uploaded a video of this bug in action.

Fast forward seven years, and the Fox TV show *Family Guy* used sw1tched's clip in an episode entitled "Run, Chris, Run", in a scene where Peter Griffin is repeatedly exploiting the glitch. Soon after the episode aired, the original clip disappeared from YouTube. Fox had sent YouTube a copyright takedown notice forcing the video platform to remove the clip, because it appeared to have been taken from *Family Guy* – never mind that the reverse was actually true.

Back in 2007, lawsuits from entertainment companies led YouTube to introduce a system that would automatically scan its videos for clips matching copyrighted footage.[336] The system, since named Content ID, lets rights-holders demand the clips' deletion. If you see unauthorised clips of TV shows and movies on YouTube that are zoomed in on part of the picture, or running slightly too fast or too slowly, it's because the uploader is trying to fool Content ID. In this case of the *Double Dribble* clip, Content ID led Fox to automatically issue a takedown notice under the US's 1998 Digital Millennium Copyright Act, or DMCA. When the studio realised its mistake, it let YouTube restore the clip.[337]

Few industries wield as much influence on the internet as the entertainment industry. Movie studios, publishing houses, record labels and artists themselves have long benefited from a monopoly on the rights to publishing and making money from the books, movies, music and other artworks that they create. With the advent of new

---

[336] https://www.wsj.com/articles/SB118161295626932114
[337] https://torrentfreak.com/fox-stole-a-game-clip-used-it-in-family-guy-dmcad-the-original-160520/

technologies, their traditional intellectual property rights are under threat, and they've not been shy about fighting back. However, it's a fight that increasingly threatens regular people's rights, even if they're not copying and sharing anything unlawfully.

Crackdowns

The DMCA strongly encourages online services such as YouTube to take down the copyright-infringing stuff that their users upload. Copyright holders can file DMCA takedown requests with these "user-generated content" platforms, as Fox did in the *Double Dribble* case. If the platforms respond quickly, they aren't held liable for the copyright infringement. The person who uploaded the content is supposed to get a chance to appeal against its removal, but this happens relatively rarely, because the uploader might then get sued for copyright infringement and have to pay up to $150,000 per infringement if they lose the case.[338] Challenging rights-holders is a risky business.

This is a system that has been repeatedly abused and misused. The *Double Dribble* episode is a frivolous example, but people regularly use DMCA notices to try to silence others. When an American organisation called Right Wing Watch used clips of a conservative politician called Gordon Klingenschmitt to criticise him, Klingenschmitt filed notices claiming his copyright had been violated. After three of his DMCA notices, YouTube automatically removed Right Wing Watch's account. Right Wing Watch claimed they had to threaten to take Klingenschmitt to court, with support from free-speech activists, before he stopped harassing the group.[339] Similarly, AIDS denialists used the DMCA to remove the videos of a video blogger called Myles Power, who criticised them by referencing clips of their

---

[338] https://www.techdirt.com/articles/20160330/01583234053/dmcas-notice-takedown-procedure-is-total-mess-mainly-because-bogus-automated-takedowns.shtml

[339] http://www.rightwingwatch.org/post/our-youtube-page-has-been-restored-and-klingenschmitt-has-been-warned-to-cease-and-desist/

propaganda movie, *House of Numbers*.[340] Using copyrighted clips in this way – for satire or commentary – is supposed to be allowed under what's known as a "fair use" exemption, but takedown systems are easily abused.

The US's DMCA has led to internet censorship that affects people around the world – it's worth noting that while both Myles Power and the producers of *House of Numbers* are based in the UK, the big online platforms are based in the US, so the DMCA applies. Takedowns aren't limited to the US, though – it doesn't matter where you as the user are; if you're using a service that falls under the DMCA's reach, such as Google or YouTube or Facebook, then US law will limit what you can upload or view. According to Google's takedown statistics, between March 2011 and November 2016 the company had to remove almost two billion links from its results lists, affecting almost a million websites.[341] Google approved 91.3 percent of the takedown requests it received and rejected just 2.1 percent (the rest were duplicates or invalid addresses).

The situation could conceivably be worse. In 2011, US legislators introduced bills called the Protect IP Act (PIPA, in the Senate) and the Stop Online Piracy Act (SOPA, in the House of Representatives). These pieces of legislation were designed to tackle the issue of copyright-infringing websites that are hosted outside US jurisdiction. SOPA and PIPA would have effectively made offending websites disappear – not just in the US, with British-style blocking orders, but everywhere. Rights-holders would have been able to demand that the sites be removed from the domain name system (DNS), the internet's address book. The sites would have still been technically available, as someone could find them via their numerical IP addresses, but their familiar names would have become useless across the globe. What's more, payment processors and advertising networks would have also been forced to cut their ties with the sites in question, removing their ability to make money.

---

[340] https://mylespower.co.uk/2014/02/09/the-dmca-situation/
[341] https://www.google.com/transparencyreport/removals/copyright/

The main problem, apart from the proposals being extremely heavy-handed, was that these mechanisms would not have required a court to decide whether or not a site should be disappeared. An organisation like the Motion Picture Association of America (MPAA) would only have had to file a notice. And what's more, if the site in question wasn't actually infringing copyright, it wouldn't be able to sue whoever ordered its takedown. The system was ripe for abuse. "The laws have been put together to allow an industry body to ask the government to turn off a website and the government can make people turn off the site without trial," said web inventor Tim Berners-Lee at a Florida tech conference.[342] "There are times when that could be very powerful and damaging, like before an election."

"If you're in America then you should go and call somebody or send an email to protest against these bills because they have not been put together to respect human rights as is appropriate in a democratic country," Berners-Lee told the audience at the event.[343] The protests were intense. On 28 January, 2012, a variety of major websites blacked out their services to draw attention to the bills' censorship threat – Wikipedia, Craigslist, Reddit and Tumblr all took part. When people in the US visited Google, they saw a blacked-out logo. Users of the Firefox browser found its default start page blacked out. People marched across US cities. And it worked. SOPA and PIPA were frozen partway through the legislative process, and they never thawed out.[344] That wasn't the end of the story, though.

Harsher copyright laws keep popping up as part of international trade agreements. Around the same time as SOPA and PIPA were being drafted, countries around the world were signing a treaty called the Anti-Counterfeiting Trade Agreement (ACTA). Formulated by the US and Japan and largely intended to fight the spread of knock-off

---

[342] http://www.v3.co.uk/v3-uk/news/2139758/web-inventor-tim-berners-lee-slams-sopa-pipa-legislation

[343] http://www.smh.com.au/it-pro/business-it/father-of-the-web-backs-sopa-protests-20120119-1q7rm.html

[344] http://www.huffingtonpost.com/2012/01/16/wikipedia-blackout-jimmy-wales-sopa_n_1208947.html?ref=technology

merchandise, the deal would have also ensured that courts across the world follow the UK model of blocking copyright-infringing websites. It would also have made it illegal to strip the anti-copying mechanisms from files and programs, a practice known as "cracking" software. The US also pushed for ACTA to include a three-strikes internet disconnection rule, in the style of France's doomed HADOPI law – the EU successfully pushed back on that one, though, as well as a rule that would have required internet service providers to spy on their customers' activities.[345]

But even with those elements out of the picture, ACTA infuriated many people, partly because of how secretively it was negotiated – people only found out about draft versions through leaks. There were huge protests against ACTA's signing in Poland, both on the streets and on the internet, where activists defaced government websites. The Polish government eventually reversed its position on ACTA, declining to ratify the treaty and advising other EU governments to do the same. Ultimately, the European Parliament roundly rejected the treaty.[346] To date, only one signatory has ratified it: Japan. Because ACTA would only come into effect after six signatories ratified it, the deal was dead.

Then came another contentious trade deal, the Trans-Pacific Partnership (TPP), which was negotiated – again under great secrecy – between the US, Japan, Australia, New Zealand, Peru, Vietnam, New Zealand, Chile, Malaysia, Singapore, Canada, Mexico and Brunei. TPP would have introduced harsh criminal penalties for copyright infringement, even if it was just casual file-sharing rather than a commercial-scale operation. It would have extended copyright terms to at least 70 years after an author's death. Again, it would have outlawed cracking across all those countries. TPP died in November 2016, not because of these copyright measures, but because the anti-globalist

---

[345] https://www.theguardian.com/commentisfree/2012/feb/03/act-acta-democracy-free-speech
[346] http://www.digitaltrends.com/web/european-parliament-crushes-acta-in-biggest-ever-legislative-defeat/

Donald Trump won the US presidential election.[347] The treaty was revived almost a year later by the rest of the countries, under the new name of the Comprehensive and Progressive Agreement for Trans-Pacific Partnership (CPTPP), but – apparently thanks to Canada – the stuff about copyright term extensions and cracking was taken out.[348]

Apart from attempts to harshen copyright enforcement through new legislation and international agreements, the aggression of some in the rights-holder industry has led to the deeply unpleasant phenomenon of "copyright trolling". Anti-piracy groups monitor file-sharing sites to identify their users, then employ law firms to write to them, accusing them of illegally downloading copyrighted material.[349] The letters threaten the recipients with lawsuits, unless they pay a fee to make the problem go away. Pornography companies are particularly keen on taking this extortionate route because most people would rather pay a fee of a few hundred bucks than go to court over their use of such material.

Why does the issue of copyright enforcement keep coming back again and again, with such dangerous implications? Because, while computers and the internet provide huge opportunities for musicians, film-makers and other creators to share their works, they also tend to remove creators' traditional revenue streams. As the threat comes from the same mechanisms that give people use to exercise their free expression rights, this is a power clash that's going to continue for a while yet. The result will affect us all.

Copy of a Copy

The idea of copyright first emerged in 16th-century England as a reaction to the development and rapid proliferation of the printing

---

[347] http://www.reuters.com/article/us-usa-trump-trade-canada-idUSKBN1582P3
[348] http://www.michaelgeist.ca/2017/11/rethinking-ip-in-the-tpp/
[349] https://www.techdirt.com/articles/20160907/09342735459/when-isps-become-anti-troll-advocates-bahnhof-turns-ip-tables-copyright-troll.shtml

press. Printing made it easy to churn out multiple copies of books, whereas before they had to be copied by hand – something that was traditionally done, slowly, by Catholic monks. Now ideas could spread quickly, outside of the Church's control. In 1557, Queen Mary granted a royal charter to the printers' guild, the Stationers' Company, and gave it a monopoly on producing books; anything produced by people outside the guild, which might offend the church or state, could be destroyed. This power was fortified in the Licensing Act of 1662 which, when it expired, was eventually replaced by the Copyright Act of 1710. Whereas the original copyright law was primarily a censorship tool, the Copyright Act (also known as the Statute of Anne) was explicitly aimed at protecting the rights of authors and, of course, their publishers.[350]

In the late 20th century, technology began to provide new ways to copy someone else's work. For small-scale copying, there was no longer any need to have expensive printing presses – photocopiers could instantly create a readable facsimile of any page. Cassette recorders gave regular people the ability to record what was played on the radio, or make copies of records, CDs and other cassettes, albeit with a little loss of quality. And then came personal computers and the internet.

Once something is in a digital format, it can be copied endlessly without losing any of its quality. What's more, it doesn't come with the constraints of physical media. You don't need a thousand blank tapes to copy an album a thousand times, and copying a book many times over doesn't mean making a major investment in paper and ink. Distribution of those copies is also no problem, as they can be hosted on a server somewhere (which costs very little) or just shared directly between people's computers using "peer-to-peer" technologies such as BitTorrent (which costs nothing). And because of the ease with which

---

[350]

http://scholarship.law.berkeley.edu/cgi/viewcontent.cgi?article=1856&context=btlj

digital files spread, once something is out there it can't be reined in again.

The internet doesn't just make copying and sharing easier; these concepts are integral to how the internet works. When you email someone, you're sending that person a copy of your message. When you visit a website, your web browser is automatically downloading a copy of that site into your computer's temporary memory, so that you can see it on your computer's screen. This last fact was central to a landmark EU case involving an online media monitoring service called Meltwater, which sent newsletters to public relations professionals including links to – and short extracts from – news articles they might want to see. News publishers successfully argued at the UK High Court and Court of Appeal that Meltwater's customers were breaking copyright if they didn't get licenses from the publishers of the articles. The logic here was that the customers were creating unlawful copies of the articles just by viewing them. However, the UK Supreme Court and the Court of Justice of the European Union then ruled that these were temporary copies that were legal under EU copyright law. The EU court said the copies were legal because they were "an integral and essential part of a technological process", which earned them an exemption under the 2001 Copyright Directive.[351]

There's considerable debate over how copyright laws should evolve to take account of current technology, while ensuring that people still get rewarded for creating new music, movies, books and other works. On one side, rights-holders argue that enforcement should be stepped up to dissuade people from doing what is, after all, so easy to do. Some artists, such as Metallica, have even targeted their fans for unlawfully downloading their creations. In 2000, after the band's incomplete recordings leaked and appeared on Napster, Metallica sued the file-

---

351

http://curia.europa.eu/juris/document/document.jsf;jsessionid=9ea7d2dc30
d583e92b09aecd4d259a04e4697cb19b72.e34KaxiLc3qMb40RchOSaxyKb3v0?
text=&docid=153302&pageIndex=0&doclang=EN&mode=lst&dir=&occ=first&
part=1&cid=352060

sharing service. As part of the suit, Metallica's lawyers drew up a list of hundreds of thousands of Napster users who had shared its music, and forced Napster to block them from accessing the service. Metallica also sued universities where students had shared its music. When universities agreed to block their students from using Napster, they were dropped from the suit.[352]

On the other side of the argument, digital rights activists say the laws should be relaxed to let people make the most of what sharing can offer. Indeed, a whole political movement – the Pirate Party – was formed around the issue of copyright reform a decade ago. The movement began in Sweden, but spread through much of Europe and around the world. Although it has also developed strong positions around issues such as governmental transparency and direct democracy, the Pirate Party maintains its focus on copyright, and has even had a degree of success in pushing its views. In 2014, the European Parliament put the Pirate Party's Julia Reda in charge of producing a review of existing copyright legislation. This was remarkable in itself, as Reda was the parliament's only Pirate. Her final report, as approved by the parliament, included progressive views, though as is the way with compromise-based parliamentary systems it was watered down to an extent.

For one thing, the report failed to mention an obscure but important concept called "freedom of panorama". Countries such as France make it illegal to photograph public works and post the pictures online – technically, you're not allowed to photograph the Eiffel Tower at night and show the shot to your Facebook friends. Reda wanted to recommend banning such laws across the EU, but others wanted them made mandatory, so in the end no-one got their way. However, the report did end up calling for reforms such as making it easier for museums to share their collections online. It also said researchers should be able to look for patterns in text and data without having to get a licence for copying the information into their databases.

---

[352] http://ultimateclassicrock.com/metallica-napster-lawsuit/

Reda's report, issued in 2015, was supposed to influence the European Commission's subsequent proposals for copyright reform. When these proposals finally came in late 2016, they did follow through on some of the parliament's recommendations. However, the Commission also called for some things that went completely in the opposite direction. The digital agenda commissioner, Günther Oettinger, proposed introducing ancillary copyright – the new right that would let news publishers charge Google for using snippets of article text – across the EU. He also suggested forcing web companies to actively monitor their platforms for potential copyright infringements. Full-scale monitoring would be expensive: YouTube spent $60 million developing its Content ID system for spotting illegal uploads.[353] Even if smaller platform operators buy such technology off-the-shelf, they would need to spend considerable time and money dealing with situations where the system incorrectly identifies something as infringing. This level of monitoring would also be very invasive, "requiring platforms to be constantly looking over users' shoulders", as the Internet Archive (a useful repository of old online content) noted in response to similar proposals in the US.[354] And in Europe, it would also conflict with an older law called the e-Commerce Directive that's supposed to protect online platforms from having to monitor everything their users do.

The overzealous online enforcement of copyright doesn't just interfere with people's rights to information and free expression; it requires mass surveillance to make sure people aren't sharing things they shouldn't. It's too easy to be heavy-handed in this area, and that's just taking into account today's media-related intellectual property violations. A looming revolution in manufacturing could make the situation a whole lot more complicated.

---

[353] http://www.theverge.com/2016/7/13/12165194/youtube-content-id-2-billion-paid
[354] https://blog.archive.org/2016/06/02/copyright-offices-proposed-notice-and-staydown-system-would-force-the-internet-archive-and-other-platforms-to-censor-the-web/

One development that will really test the old approaches to intellectual property is that of 3D printing, also known as additive manufacturing. This technology uses digital models as templates from which to "print" physical items. There are various techniques for doing this, including nozzles that slowly push out liquid plastic and build up the object layer-by-layer, and laser beams that gradually solidify metal powder into a coherent form. You can create a digital model for the printed product using a computer-aided design (CAD) program – the same sort of software that architects use to create virtual models of the buildings they're planning, and that animators use to create 3D characters.

3D printing is already heavily used in industries from aerospace to medicine to jewellery – it provides a relatively cheap way of prototyping new ideas, and there are certain designs you can't produce in any other way. Where traditional manufacturing techniques might produce parts that can be assembled into the finished product, 3D printing makes it easier to design something that comes in one piece. 3D printing also completely overturns the "economies of scale" that are associated with traditional manufacturing. The printers can make an infinite range of things and they can make each item differently, so, unlike with specialised manufacturing equipment, there's no reason to make lots of a certain thing in one session. This cuts down on waste. For example, Mercedes-Benz has started using the technology to produce spare parts for its trucks when customers need them, rather than making a bunch of parts at once and storing them at great expense until they're needed.[355]

But 3D printing isn't just for business; it's a consumer game, too. There are already many online services that let you upload your own design files or choose from those uploaded by others, then pay for the printing and receive the finished product in the mail. Retail and

---

[355] http://media.daimler.com/marsMediaSite/en/instance/ko/Mercedes-Benz-Trucks-uses-pioneering-future-technology-3D-pr.xhtml?oid=12788778

logistics outlets such as Staples and UPS are starting to provide 3D-printing services to the public, just as they provide photocopying and document-printing services. If the cost of capable printers falls to a sufficiently low level, and as the technology improves, we may start to see 3D printers in the homes of many regular people. They currently tend to be more for hobbyists and geeks, though hundreds of thousands of printers are already shipping each year. There are even 3D printers that are themselves made almost entirely from 3D-printed parts, which means someone with a printer can print most of another printer – again, something that can bring the cost down.[356]

The impact of all this could be huge. Not only would it be much easier for people to design and manufacture unique items for themselves, but 3D printing would also make it easier to copy things. If you need a simple part for a broken-down appliance, for example, it could be much quicker and cheaper to just print one for yourself, rather than finding, ordering and waiting for an official replacement. The manufacturer of the original item might even approve of this, though that could raise interesting liability questions if the home-made part breaks again, or if it ends up breaking something else in the appliance.

The replication of existing items could also be made easier by the proliferation of 3D scanners. For example, Intel has a depth-sensing camera technology called RealSense that's found today in webcams, but that could also be used in smartphones or virtual-reality goggles. The applications would include better face recognition if you're using the camera as a login mechanism, and better analysis of the room you're in, if you're trying to superimpose a virtual world onto that reality. But – particularly if the device is mobile – you could also use the camera to scan an item and create a digital model of it. Google, the company behind the Android mobile operating system, is working on a similar technology as part of a project called Tango, which has seen depth-sensing technology built into phones from Asus and Lenovo.[357] And

---

[356] http://reprap.org/
[357] https://arstechnica.com/gadgets/2016/12/google-tango-review-promising-google-tech-debuts-on-crappy-lenovo-hardware/

Apple has built similar potential functionality into the Face ID biometric security camera in its iPhone X.

Figurines are already proving to be popular items on 3D-printing sites. When Disney released a trailer for *Star Wars: The Force Awakens* long before it started selling merchandising for the film, a fan quickly created a printable 3D model for a Stormtrooper gun featured in the clip.[358] And some people are thinking beyond model guns. Although current consumer-grade 3D-printing plastics are less than ideal for such a heavy-duty item, and you need very expensive machinery to print things in metal, the files for actual 3D-printed guns are out there on the web and therefore impossible to effectively censor.[359] The first such weapon to achieve notoriety was the "Liberator" pistol, the files for which were published by an outfit called Defense Distributed.[360] The US State Department swiftly ordered the files' removal under arms trafficking laws, but they can still be found online.[361] Defense Distributed has also released files that allow people to print their own components for weapons such as the AR-15 rifle.

Is it possible to control the spread of digital models that can be easily made physical? Rights-holders will find it hard to sue individual users for possessing computer-aided design files of a patented item. Unlike with music or movies, the CAD file itself is not the copy of the protected product, which puts it into a grey area.[362] It's easier to put pressure on the websites that provide catalogues of files, such as Shapeways, which sometimes agree to take down designs. In 2013, the games company Square Enix told Shapeways to remove files that let

---

[358] http://www.wsj.com/articles/hollywoods-other-piracy-problem-3-d-printers-1437420799
[359] https://3dprint.com/139537/3d-printed-guns/
[360] https://defdist.org/
[361] https://thelede.blogs.nytimes.com/2013/05/10/printable-gun-instructions-spread-online-after-state-dept-orders-their-removal/
[362] https://theconversation.com/how-3d-printing-threatens-our-patent-system-52665

people print *Final Fantasy VII* characters. The company complied.[363] But there will always be other, easy ways to share these files. For example, The Pirate Bay, a service that's notorious for helping people share copyright-infringing digital media, hosts many designs for 3D-printed items.

Rights-holders could demand that 3D printers or the files come with digital rights management (DRM) technology built in, so they can't be used to copy protected items without authorisation. However, 3D printers can themselves be redesigned and made by amateurs. And think of the ease with which people "crack" popular games and other DRM-protected software – there's no reason to think they wouldn't do the same to 3D-printing files. This new technology will prove extremely difficult to control, though if the trend does start to seriously hurt manufacturers' and merchandisers' bottom lines, they will probably try to take action of some kind.

For the 3D-printing community, the safe bet seems to be to stick to designs that have been created on computers and licensed for free use under a scheme such as Creative Commons. This is an alternative to copyright (some call it "copyleft"), where the creator is happy for people to copy and even modify their creation under limited conditions. For example, they might want people to acknowledge their identity as the creator, and they might want to ban people from using their work to make money. A comparable licence, this time covering software rather than art and media, is the GNU General Public License (GPL) that allows people to use, distribute and modify programs for free. The Linux operating system "kernel", which is the core of Google's Android mobile operating system and of most of the software running servers around the world, is licensed under the GPL.

The more that these "open source" creations flourish, the less need there would be for anyone to replicate something that's protected under stricter terms, such as a design patent. 3D printing isn't mass production, so products can easily be designed for specialist needs. If a

---

[363] https://www.cnet.com/news/print-chop-how-copyright-killed-a-3d-printed-final-fantasy-fad/

freely available design is cooler and more useful to you, then why copy a heavily protected, mass-produced item?

However, the licensing of an item is really up to the creator, who is under no obligation to give away what they've made. And even if they do give it away under a Creative Commons licence, on the condition that people don't use the designs commercially, people sometimes break those terms by printing the designs and offering them for sale. When an eBay store was caught selling products that had been designed by members of the Thingiverse 3D-printing platform and offered under Creative Commons licenses, Thingiverse owner MakerBot responded angrily. "We see such violations as a direct attack on the very goal of Thingiverse and the Creative Commons framework," it thundered.[364] There will undoubtedly be an ongoing problem with people using 3D-printing technology to make unlawful copies of things. Thanks to the nature of the internet, this problem will be as difficult to stop through enforcement as music and movie "piracy" has been.

In the music and movie industries, though, the proportion of internet users who unlawfully share songs and films has dropped as the popularity of services such as Spotify and Netflix has grown.[365] Some people will always be "pirates" because they don't want to pay for anything at all – according to official UK figures published in 2016, around 14 percent of infringers say nothing could convince them to stop.[366] However, a lot of people just want easier ways to access what they want to listen to and watch.

The likes of Spotify and Netflix certainly offer ease of use. They represent part of a wider shift that's taking place thanks to modern technology. The concept of ownership is changing, though not always to the benefit of consumers.

---

[364] https://3dprint.com/121262/makerbot-responds-to-jpi/

[365] http://musically.com/2016/07/06/spotify-and-apple-music-effect-sees-uk-music-piracy-decline/

[366]

https://www.gov.uk/government/uploads/system/uploads/attachment_data/file/546223/OCI-tracker-6th-wave-March-May-2016.pdf

Once upon a time, when you bought something, you owned it and could generally do what you liked with it. If you bought a CD, for example, you could easily loan it to a friend or sell it on if you grew tired of it. If the record company stopped selling that CD, you could still keep your copy in your rack. If you bought the first edition of a new book, that item would be worth more than later paperback versions, with the potential to become collectible. Again, you were free to sell it one day, perhaps at a cosy profit.

This model is fading. If you pay a monthly fee to a streaming service like Netflix, for example, then you gain access to vast libraries of TV shows and cinema, but if you stop, then you can't watch them anymore. Buy a film on DVD and you can watch it forever, lend it to people or sell it on if you want to. With Spotify, if you don't pay then you can at least still access the music with added advertising – sort of an *à la carte* successor to radio – but if the label decides to withdraw it from Spotify's catalogues, then you don't get to listen to it anymore. This new mechanism can be used in an artistic way: when Kanye West unveiled *The Life of Pablo* in early 2016, he released the album as a work in progress, continuously replacing the versions that were available on streaming services as he tweaked the tracks.[367] But the shift from ownership to access has pretty radical implications for what it means to be a consumer these days.

Of course, you can also buy digital copies of books, music and movies over the internet. In theory, you should then be able to hang onto them for as long as you like. In practise, things may not always work out that way. In 2009, Amazon provided an interesting reading of George Orwell's *1984* and *Animal Farm*, novels that deal with themes of control and thought manipulation. When a company uploaded the novels to Amazon's Kindle e-book store without having the rights to do so, Amazon remotely deleted the copies that people had bought for

---

[367] http://consequenceofsound.net/2016/03/kanye-west-updates-12-tracks-on-the-life-of-pablo-album-available-everywhere-on-friday/

their e-readers.[368] A reader might have been halfway through *1984*, only to see it suddenly vanish. When it was called out over the incident, Amazon apologised and said it wouldn't react to these circumstances in the same way again. However, it said it would still remotely erase e-books if a court told it to do so.[369] In the old days, a product recall did not involve the seller barging into the customer's home and seizing the product in question.

The central issue is that, when you click "buy" and download digital media, you're not buying a copy of the album or movie itself. Instead, you're buying a license to download and use the media. The control over that product remains in the hands of the seller. That's why the seller can censor or change the item after the fact, so long as they also control the consumption device, like Amazon controls the Kindle.

It's also why the buyer does not get to sell the product on to other people. At least, that's what the terms and conditions say. Amazon, for example, tells those who buy music through its service: "We grant you a non-exclusive, non-transferable right to use Purchased Music, Subscription Content, Matched Music, and any additional Music Content we provide you access to through the Services only for your personal, non-commercial purposes, subject to the Agreement. Except as set forth in the preceding sentence, you may not redistribute, transmit, assign, sell, broadcast, rent, share, lend, modify, adapt, edit, license or otherwise transfer, or use Purchased Music or Subscription Content."[370]

That doesn't only mean that the buyer can't resell the music album or movie that they've bought – it also means they can't leave their library of legally acquired media to their heirs when they die, as is common with physical books and albums. As such a collection may represent a

---

[368] https://www.theguardian.com/technology/2009/jul/17/amazon-kindle-1984
[369]

http://www.pcworld.com/article/172953/amazon_kindle_1984_lawsuit.html
[370]

https://www.amazon.com/gp/help/customer/display.html?nodeId=2013800 10#content great deal of investment when accumulated over years, this rather undermines the concept of property rights.

Courts are starting to see the injustice in this approach. In Europe at least, people may gradually start getting the same rights when they buy virtual goods as when they buy something tangible that they can hold in their hands. The central concept here is that of "exhaustion" or, as it's known in the US, the "first sale doctrine". According to this longstanding principle, people and companies have the right to control the sale of what they produce. However, once they've sold it, that right expires. This means the buyer can then sell the goods on to someone else, without the permission of the original producer.

In 2012, the Court of Justice of the European Union issued a landmark ruling in a case involving Oracle, the US-based business software giant, and a German software reseller called UsedSoft.[371] Oracle, in common with most software firms, sold licenses to its business customers that allowed only them and no-one else to download the product, in this case database software. UsedSoft would buy Oracle licences from businesses that no longer needed them, then sell them on to other businesses. Oracle sued UsedSoft for breaking the resale restrictions in its licence terms. The case ended up at the EU's highest court, which decided that UsedSoft did, after all, have the right to resell those licenses.

There were certain conditions attached to the ruling, though. Crucially, the court said Oracle could do whatever was technically feasible to make sure that the person selling the license wasn't still using the software afterwards. The court also said it wasn't acceptable for a business to buy a bundle of Oracle licences, getting a bulk discount on the price, and then sell some of them on while still using the others. But the ruling did nonetheless establish that the original vendor of downloadable software can't stop the resale of their product, even if their terms and conditions claim that they can.

371

http://curia.europa.eu/juris/document/document.jsf?docid=124564&doclang=EN

Slowly, the impact of the UsedSoft decision is being felt in other areas, notably that of book publishing. The important thing here is to make sure that people don't sell something while keeping a copy that they continue to use. Because digital files are endlessly replicable, that's a real challenge, though not an impossible one – you can put a digital watermark on a file that proves it's the original.

In 2014, a Dutch company called Tom Kabinet opened a secondhand e-book store, using the UsedSoft ruling as its legal justification. The country's publishers tried to shut the store down. They repeatedly failed, but they did get an appeals court to place a restriction on Tom Kabinet: the court said the site could only continue operating if it made sure that all the books in its store had been legally bought in the first place. Tom Kabinet couldn't prove this, so it had to scrub all the books from its virtual shelves and start again. But it had at least successfully defended the principle that e-books should be treated the same as physical books. Then, in late 2016, the European Court of Justice ruled that Dutch public libraries could legally buy and then lend out e-books to their patrons, just as they can with physical books.[372] The publishers don't like this equivalence at all. As Martijn David, the secretary-general of the Dutch Publishers' Association, complained: "If you're going to start reselling digital goods, who would be the fool who buys the original book? A secondhand car is not new... A secondhand digital file [is] like a car which runs forever."[373] The Tom Kabinet case was referred up to the Court of Justice in mid-2017.[374]

Publishers have had more favourable rulings outside the Netherlands. German courts decided that e-books can't be resold, as the

---

[372] https://copyrightandtechnology.com/2016/11/20/dutch-public-libraries-and-the-one-copy-one-user-rule/

[373] http://arstechnica.co.uk/tech-policy/2016/05/reselling-digital-goods-europe-e-books-software/

[374] http://www.internationallawoffice.com/Newsletters/Intellectual-Property/Netherlands/AKD/District-court-refers-questions-on-sale-of-second-hand-e-books-to-ECJ

UsedSoft ruling does not apply to them, only to computer programs.[375] The US's biggest ruling on this subject, so far, rejected the ability to resell downloaded items. A company called Redigi wanted to make it possible for people to resell the MP3s that they bought over iTunes, but in 2013 it lost a case brought against it by the music industry. Redigi's software did check that the music files were legally bought. It even held the files in cloud storage, in an attempt to make sure that the original owner's copy was deleted when they sold it to someone else. However, a New York district court decided that uploading the file to the cloud constituted a copyright infringement in itself.[376] Interestingly, Amazon has filed a patent for a secondhand e-book marketplace that would allow it to do the same thing as Tom Kabinet, but hasn't made any announcement about actually launching such a platform.[377]

Even in the US, there's been a very limited move towards recognising people's property rights in a world of digital assets. In the state of Delaware, legislators passed a bill in 2014 that said the heirs of a deceased person should be able to get their digital content licenses as part of the estate, along with the usernames and passwords needed to access the content, unless the person had specifically asked for those login details not to be transferred to their heirs.[378] However, the law stops short of overriding the terms and conditions attached to the accounts, putting the situation into something of a grey area, with updated inheritance laws on one side and outdated transfer restrictions on the other.[379]

Ultimately, why shouldn't people have the same rights with digital goods as they have with physical things? The shift to digital versions of

---

[375] http://the-digital-reader.com/2014/08/28/used-ebooks-now-illegal-germany/

[376] https://www.eff.org/files/redigi_order.pdf

[377] https://www.wired.com/2013/02/amazon-used-e-book-patent/all/

[378] http://www.dehousedems.com/press/rep-scotts-first-nation-digital-assets-bill-becomes-law

[379] http://www.slate.com/blogs/future_tense/2014/08/22/digital_assets_and_death_who_owns_music_video_e_books_after_you_die.html

physical products should not diminish people's resale and inheritance rights if there's no good reason for doing so. And the same should apply to the practice of "reverse engineering", or taking something apart to figure out how it works. You've always had the ability to reverse-engineer the physical things you buy. Apart from being fun, it's a useful way to learn new skills, find flaws and figure out how to make a better product. If it's yours, you can break it – but, increasingly, not if it's in digital form.

One reason that open-source software is so successful, particularly on mobile phones and servers, is that geeks can look into the code to check that it's truly secure from attack and free of bugs, and can even change the code if they see problems or want it to do new things. However, software developers use several legal justifications for stopping people from doing this to their proprietary software. For example, it's typical for them to forbid such activities in their terms and conditions for downloading the product. As reverse engineering generally involves making a copy of the software you want to take apart, it might also lead to copyright infringement. The same Digital Millennium Copyright Act that aims to scrub copyright-infringing material from the internet also bans anyone from bypassing the protection measures built into software. This ban on cracking prevents not just copying, but also reverse engineering. Like similar laws around the world, the DMCA is an implementation of the World Intellectual Property Organization's Copyright Treaty of 1996, which demanded anti-circumvention laws from all its signatories. The DMCA does provide exceptions to allow reverse engineering, but they come with a lot of conditions – for example, reverse engineering may only be allowed if the company that makes the product gives its permission, and people may only be allowed to examine a product's code in order to create an interoperable product.[380]

Fortunately for security researchers trying to reverse-engineer software in order to find vulnerabilities that hackers might try to exploit, the Library of Congress passed a new DMCA exception in

---

[380] https://www.eff.org/issues/coders/reverse-engineering-faq

2015 that specifically allowed this in the name of "good-faith security research".[381] But again, terms and conditions (known in the trade as "end-user license agreements") can override these rights, making life hard for security researchers and stopping other companies from creating useful accessories or add-ons.

Sometimes, these agreements stop customers from doing essential repair work. American farmers have had a long-running fight with the tractor manufacturer John Deere, whose products are these days as full of software as any modern vehicles. In 2016, John Deere forced its customers to sign an agreement in which they promised not to have their tractors repaired by anyone other than a dealership or repair shop that's been authorised by the company. The tractors' software enforces this policy. "You want to replace a transmission and you take it to an independent mechanic – he can put in the new transmission but the tractor can't drive out of the shop," farmer Kevin Kenney told *Wired* magazine.[382] "Deere charges $230, plus $130 an hour for a technician to drive out and plug a connector into their USB port to authorise the part." To get around this limitation, which can be a big hassle if your farm is out in the middle of nowhere, many farmers have turned to cracked versions of John Deere's software that reportedly come from hackers out in Eastern Europe.

In 2015, when the US Copyright Office was considering various new proposals for exemptions to the DMCA law, General Motors submitted comments in which it said it was wrong to "conflate ownership of a vehicle with ownership of the underlying computer software in a vehicle".[383] In other words, when you buy a car, it's not really all yours to do with as you will.

381
https://community.rapid7.com/community/infosec/blog/2015/10/28/new-dmca-exemption-is-a-positive-step-for-security-researchers
[382] https://motherboard.vice.com/en_us/article/why-american-farmers-are-hacking-their-tractors-with-ukrainian-firmware
[383] https://copyright.gov/1201/2015/comments-032715/class%2021/General_Motors_Class21_1201_2014.pdf

Thanks to the rise of software and internet-based services, companies have gained extraordinary control over the products they sell, long after the sale has taken place. Meanwhile, the consumer's power has been drastically reduced, making them dependant on ongoing support from the product's supplier. Without that support, once-useful products can become hunks of useless plastic.

Bricked

In 2016, Google's Nest, a company that specializes in home automation, remotely shut down the products of a company called Revolv, which it had bought not long before. Revolv made a "smart hub" through which lights, door locks and alarms could connect to one another and the internet – the hub would let you do things like scheduling the automatic brewing of a pot of coffee for when you wake up.[384] Nest had only bought Revolv for the company's talent, not for its existing products. But instead of simply discontinuing those products, or saying it would no longer support them with security updates, Nest just stopped them from working.

To be fair, it's good to avoid a situation where you stop supporting a product with security updates, because withdrawing that support leaves the devices and their owners vulnerable. The security of internet-of-things devices is generally terrible anyway, and many of these products can be hijacked and used for cyberattacks. However, this was a product that customers had only owned for a couple of years, and it was suddenly entirely unusable. To quote one unhappy customer: "On May 15th, my house will stop working. My landscape lighting will stop turning on and off, my security lights will stop reacting to motion, and my home-made vacation burglar deterrent will stop working. This is a

---

[384] http://www.recode.net/2014/2/10/11623260/a-quest-for-high-tech-smartphone-controlled-coffee

conscious intentional decision by Google/Nest."[385] Eventually, following a predictable outcry, Nest provided refunds.[386]

The core problem here was that Revolv's hub, in common with many things sold today, was the combination of a product and a service. When the service stopped working, the product became useless and worthless. This is not something we're used to yet. When your non-internet-connected possessions go out of warranty, they may still function as well as they did when you bought them, years ago. That's a good thing. Even operating systems keep working after they are no longer supported. It may not be a bright idea to keep using that old copy of Windows XP, due to its many unpatched security holes, but it probably will still function even though Microsoft has washed its hands of it.

The "bricking" of Revolv's hub was not a one-off occurrence in the internet-of-things world, and its abandonment is partly down to the fact that this is still a very young market. Companies within this market are still trying out a variety of different technologies for getting all these "smart" things to talk to one another. In Revolv's case, the hub contained a bunch of transmitters and receivers for idiosyncratic wireless technologies such as Zigbee, whereas Nest's product line used the more familiar Wi-Fi and Bluetooth standards. Most people buying internet-of-things products at this nascent stage are taking a gamble on the products' long-term viability – and well-publicised stories such as that of Revolv's shutdown may have scared a lot of people away from the market for now.[387]

However, there is a way to avoid leaving customers in the lurch if you decide to discontinue and stop supporting a product like this: openly publish the software code for the product and its accompanying service, so that people can continue to maintain it and keep the device

[385] https://arlogilbert.com/the-time-that-tony-fadell-sold-me-a-container-of-hummus-cb0941c762c1#.l1x28f98r

[386] https://www.slashgear.com/nest-is-now-offering-full-refunds-to-revolve-hub-owners-14436384/

[387] http://www.ntca.org/november-december-2016/how-to-fix-the-smart-home-market/all-pages.html

functioning for a while longer. That ongoing maintenance won't necessarily happen – there have to be enough users to make such a project worthwhile, and enough knowledgeable people who care to do the maintenance – but creating the option is an act of good faith.

There used to be a startup in London called Berg Cloud, which made a cute internet-connected printer called Little Printer. The device was designed to do things like automatically printing out posts from Twitter. In 2014, Berg Cloud shut it down. But, rather than leaving customers with useless Little Printers, the company opened up the device's code to see "if the community would like to take it on".[388] And indeed, some customers did decide to take it on, keeping those Little Printers viable for years longer.[389]

The hybrid product-plus-services business model gives a lot of power to the company behind the device, as they effectively continue to control it even after they've sold it. The model allows the companies to pull in all kinds of data from their users that can both improve their products and form a saleable asset. It's only right that those companies should also recognise the ethical responsibility that comes along with the package they're selling.

***

We're in the middle of a major shift away from straightforward products and towards services, or product-plus-service bundles. Increasingly, you don't just buy a physical item that does a certain thing and will always do that thing – you pay for access to a service, whether through a browser or an app or a physical product that needs ongoing support from some remote "cloud" service provider to offer its full functionality. You don't buy CDs; you access a streaming music service. You don't buy a simple step-counter; you buy a wearable device that acts as an interface to an internet-based fitness-monitoring

---

[388] http://littleprinterblog.tumblr.com/post/97047976103/the-future-of-little-printer
[389] https://github.com/genmon/sirius/issues/8

service. You don't buy a home security camera that merely records to tape; you buy one that relies on a cloud service to analyse and store images and send them to your smartphone.

This shift comes with major implications for what we think of as consumers' property rights. In some cases, particularly where the product's supplier retains too much control over the product after you buy it, the new model is overly weighted towards the interests of the seller. This unjust rebalancing particularly stings where the new model *feels* the same as the old one, for example if you buy a piece of software as a download rather than a boxed copy – there's no good reason why you should be able to resell the boxed copy but not the download. If you buy an ebook, you should get the same rights to resell it or leave it to your heirs as you do with a paperback. And if you buy anything, you should have the right to tinker with or fix it to your heart's content.

However, some new models aren't unjust; they're simply different. If you choose to consume new music through a streaming service rather than by buying it, of course you don't retain full access to the streaming service's full catalogue if the company goes bust. It's basically just rental, paid for either by subscription or by watching or listening to ads, and your lack of control over the product is balanced by your ability to access almost any piece of music you can think of, at any time. It's not like you were able to access such a broad catalogue before streaming services came about, at least not unless you were extremely wealthy and had a lot of room in which to store all those albums.

But what about the creators of albums and movies and other artistic products, whose business has been upended by the internet? Property rights include consumers' ability to use and transfer the things they buy, but they also include creators' ability to make money off their creations. Making money off record sales was a fairly straightforward way to go about things, even if the industry has always been plagued by middlemen siphoning off more than they should. The internet's inherent encouragement of copying caused massive change by making it simpler for people to use file-sharing services than to go down to the record store and buy what they were after (if, indeed, their local record store stocked it). Streaming has again changed the scene, by giving people an even easier route to music than file-sharing provided. And indeed, record industry figures show that the industry is starting to recover after losing more than a third of its value between 2000 and 2015.[390]

Although a turnaround may be underway, the industry is still desperately trying to close what it calls the "value gap" – a perceived imbalance between the arts industries and tech titans such as YouTube, which make money by placing ads next to the videos people upload to the platform. Those videos often included copyrighted music and, although YouTube has built systems to give record labels an easy way to get their share of the ad money, the industry wants more. They want web platforms to lose their legal protections against liability for copyright infringement, they want the platforms to institute ever-more-invasive surveillance mechanisms to ensure people aren't sharing things without permission, and they want a bigger cut of the ad revenue. On the other side, the tech firms argue that the ad-based revenue model is just different to retail – it's a longer game, and people are unlikely to make as much money off their music unless it's hugely popular.

To be frank, it's very difficult to tell who's "right" or "wrong" in this debate. The tech firms may be incredibly powerful, but so is the copyright lobby – movie, music and publishing rights-holders are very good at persuading politicians that their national cultures depend on money flowing to these industries as it did before the internet. However these two sides stack up, it's vital that the solutions to their arguments don't involve more surveillance, or cutting people off from the internet. Property rights should be enforced, but doing so shouldn't override the general public's rights to privacy and free expression. Ultimately, the solution has to lie in making it easier to spend money on the culture you enjoy.

The internet certainly hasn't been all bad for creativity. If you're a musician or writer or budding filmmaker, it's easier than ever before to reach people through online services – and not just through the big

---

[390] http://www.ifpi.org/news/The-value-gap-the-missing-beat-at-the-heart-of-our-industry

platforms. Sure, it may be harder to make as much money as you might once have, if you hit the big time. That's no small concern – a million plays of your song on Spotify could net you as little as $5,000.[391] A healthy balance between creators and platforms is yet to be struck. But, if you're building your own niche, you no longer need to convince some big record company or publisher or movie studio that it's worthwhile before getting your works out there. And if that niche is what gets you going as a reader, listener or viewer, you've never had it so good.

The development of our connected world may have caused massive arguments over the bottom line, but it's been good for artistic diversity. We should cherish that, because when it comes to other sectors of the economy, the internet has unfortunately had quite the opposite effect.

---

[391] http://www.digitalmusicnews.com/2016/05/26/band-1-million-spotify-streams-royalties/

CHAPTER 8: COMPETITION

In 2013, a small British mapping company called Streetmap sued Google for abusing its search monopoly. Six years earlier, the US giant had started embedding its own Google Maps service at the top of its search results, when users were looking for a location. Streetmap, which had been in the mapping business since the mid-1990s, quickly lost its users. If they were searching for a location, they were unlikely to even see Streetmap's link in Google's results. Previously, Google had offered search users a link to its mapping service, alongside links to a couple of key rivals. Now, it was only promoting itself. The smaller company was wound up in 2009, but, several years later, it was back for justice.

It lost. The UK's High Court ruled in Google's favour in 2016 and rejected Streetmap's appeal the following year.[392] In the first ruling, the judge noted that Streetmap's functionality had already been significantly behind Google's in 2007 – the British firm didn't have maps that you can drag around with your mouse or finger, not did it offer natural-language search, so the fact that Google destroyed it wasn't necessarily a result of the bigger company not playing fair.[393] When Google started embedding maps at the top of its results, the judge said, it wasn't likely to "appreciably" affect competition in the online mapping market. And even if it was, Google's refusal to let other providers in to the top slot was acceptable, because adding links to other services "would involve much greater complication for Google than may at first appear".

392

https://www.theregister.co.uk/2017/02/07/streetmap_loses_google_maps_appeal/

[393] http://www.bailii.org/ew/cases/EWHC/Ch/2016/253.html

"I'm so happy I fought the battle because at least I can walk away with my dignity," company founder Kate Sutton told The Register after her appeal failed.[394]

Streetmap's experience was by no means unique. In the online business world, the winner often takes all. Because of the internet's innate lack of borders, a company can quickly dominate all sorts of markets in all sorts of places. Particularly when a company operates the gate to people's online experience, there's a strong temptation to exploit that position to gather even more power.

And that doesn't just apply to the likes of Google and Facebook. Before we examine the effects of today's online monopolies, it's worth taking a quick look at the industry that underpins the internet, but feels it hasn't reaped enough benefits from it. When interpreting tech's ongoing power tussles and the struggle for a balanced online economy, it's important to understand how the telecommunications industry is trying to cash in by picking favourites, and helping selected web firms corner their markets.

Net Neutrality

Once upon a time, telecommunications firms had a fairly clear-cut role, and it was a powerful and lucrative one. If you wanted to phone someone over a great distance, you had to do so over the companies' interconnecting networks, and the companies got to set the terms. Some numbers, such as those overseas, were expensive to call and generally not available on a flat-rate basis. And, best of all for the telcos, a phone line was a phone line. Once they'd installed their networks, all they had to do was maintain them and watch the cash roll in.

Then everything changed: the internet appeared and became popular. At first, people had to call an internet service provider's phone number to allow their computer's modem to connect to the network.

394

https://www.theregister.co.uk/2017/02/20/streetmap_founder_kate_sutton _google_lawsuit/

This meant access was metered by time. But dial-up internet access gave way to much faster broadband access that operated on a flat-rate model. The telcos were still involved, but by this point they were just providing a commoditised connection rather than a crafted communications service. They started losing control over what happened on their networks.

There are two key elements of online activity that really sting the telecoms companies. The first is communications. On the desktop, tools such as Skype essentially became free replacements for the companies' lucrative voice services. On mobile, messaging apps such as WhatsApp and Facebook Messenger became more popular than operator-controlled text messaging, because they're free to use over any distance, and they offer more features. These services replace the telcos' traditional cash cows and starve them of revenue. The second particularly painful element of the online world, from the telcos' point of view, is video. Movies, TV shows and video clips use a lot of data, and video accounts for more than 80 percent of the traffic flowing around the internet.[395] As broadband speeds have improved and competition has forced data packages to grow in size, people have been uploading and consuming more and more video. New generations of fixed and mobile broadband technology keep appearing, to better support the video explosion. So the telcos have had to invest more and more in their networks, to ensure that everything keeps flowing smoothly. If they don't keep upgrading, their competitors will steal their customers.

Thanks to the twin issues of communications and video, the telcos have been denied a lot of their traditional revenue at the same time as being forced to spend vast amounts to nurture their networks. They're at risk of being what's known in the telecoms industry as a "dumb pipe" – the thing that delivers the smart stuff, and does only that. In recent years, this situation has led to a lot of consolidation in the telecoms

---

[395] https://www.cisco.com/c/en/us/solutions/collateral/service-provider/visual-networking-index-vni/complete-white-paper-c11-481360.html

industry, along with mega-mergers between infrastructure firms and the companies that provide content, particularly video. Telcos these days don't just do voice and internet; they also offer internet-based TV services as part of the package, and buying the producers of those TV shows – such as Comcast buying out NBC Universal in 2013 – is one way to sell more than mere connectivity.[396]

This is not how the telecommunications firms wanted things to play out. For a long time, their ideal scenario has involved being able to go to the companies pushing out all that network-clogging content, such as YouTube, and demand that they pay for the privilege of having their content reach the telcos' customers. As those customers also pay for their own connections, this is essentially a double-dipping ploy. It also clashes with what has turned out to be a very popular principle: net neutrality.

The phrase "network neutrality" was coined in 2003 by Columbia Law School professor Tim Wu.[397] According to the principle, internet service providers should not discriminate between different types of internet traffic, or different online services. They should make all traffic and services available to the user without favouring one over another, and without blocking any traffic or services or deliberately making them function badly. There are many good reasons to maintain net neutrality. The internet is a remarkable platform that allows businesses to spring up at very low cost – just think of all those new journalistic outfits that challenged the traditional media titans, or the companies that help people 3D-print things. The internet constantly enables new kinds of services. It developed as an organisationally flat, decentralised system that lets people connect in the same way, wherever they are, and people are rightfully used to this state of affairs. The internet is, in theory at least, egalitarian and meritocratic – a competition machine. In reality, of course, things aren't quite so simple: producing a polished product usually requires lots of investment. Popular, data-heavy video

[396] http://www.nytimes.com/2016/11/07/business/media/media-merger-success-comcast-and-nbcuniversal-say-yes.html
[397] https://papers.ssrn.com/sol3/papers.cfm?abstract_id=388863

services also work most smoothly when copies of the video are running from datacentres located close to the user; again, this costs money.

There are specific, limited occasions on which a temporary suspension of "neutrality" makes sense. For example, internet service providers may genuinely need to manage the traffic on their networks at times of high congestion, in order to make things run as well as possible for their customers. When capacity is extraordinarily constrained, a level of prioritisation can be necessary and acceptable. It doesn't really matter if there's a delay of a second or two in the sending of an email, but that sort of delay might cause real problems if you're streaming real-time video, so prioritising video over email is sensible at times. However, it's one thing to address technical realities, and quite another to favour certain services over others for commercial reasons.

What does net-neutrality abuse look like in practice? In 2008, Comcast admitted it was blocking or degrading the quality of peer-to-peer (P2P) services, where users connect directly to one another rather than routing their communications and file transfers through a centralised service provider.[398] P2P is best known as the technological foundation of file-sharing services such as BitTorrent, but at the time it was also used by internet voice providers such as Skype (after Microsoft bought Skype in 2011, it centralised how the service works). Threatened by internet rivals that were using P2P to undercut its phonecall prices, Comcast tried to use its position as an internet-access gatekeeper to stifle their newfangled technology. Its behaviour helped push the US's telecoms regulator, the Federal Communications Commission (FCC), to propose formal net neutrality rules a couple years later.[399]

The blocking of internet telephony was a recurring theme. Many European mobile providers blocked or degraded the likes of Skype, to either keep their networks flowing or protect their own voice revenues,

---

[398] http://arstechnica.com/uncategorized/2008/08/fcc-spanks-comcast-for-p2p-blocking-no-fine-full-disclosure/
[399] https://www.wired.com/2010/12/fcc-order/

depending on whom you believed.[400] Another popular net neutrality abuse was to stop people "tethering" – using their smartphones as Wi-Fi hotspots for laptops or tablets. Mobile operators wanted to sell separate data packages for those larger devices, so if they detected tethering they would block or slow down the data connection. In the US, this behaviour earned Verizon a slapdown from the FCC.[401]

However, net neutrality abuses don't just involve telecoms firms using unethical tactics to protect their existing revenue streams. Perhaps the most emotive threat has been the idea of the aforementioned double-dipping – charging content providers to reach the broadband customers, while also charging the customers for their internet connections. In the nightmare scenario, the most affordable connection packages would no longer give you the open internet, with all the competition and free information that comes with it. Instead, you might get a limited subset of services, chosen by your internet service provider on the basis of its commercial deals with the content providers, or other self-interest. If you wanted the full-fat internet, you'd have to pay more.

This would put a massive brake on competitive development, because large content providers would be able to pay broadband companies to have their services reach all consumers, while start-ups might not have the cash to do the same. It would also be bad for internet users who can't afford to access all the information that they previously got. The internet's all-you-can-eat buffet would turn into a restaurant with an *à-la-carte* menu, where you can maybe only afford the starter.

Net neutrality abuses were largely outlawed in the US and Europe in 2015 – but in crucially different ways. In the US, the FCC reclassified broadband providers as so-called "common carriers", meaning they had to act in the public interest and avoid discrimination in their charges

---

[400] https://www.euractiv.com/section/digital/news/eu-regulators-say-telecoms-block-skype/
[401] https://www.cnet.com/news/what-verizons-fcc-tethering-settlement-means-to-you-faq/

and services.[402] However, in 2017 the new US president, Donald Trump, appointed an anti-net-neutrality advocate and former Verizon lawyer, Ajit Pai, as the head of the agency.[403] A few months later, Pai started the process of reclassifying broadband providers back again, to effectively kill net neutrality in the country.[404] The European Union made a less easily reversible move with a full-on law that banned the blocking, throttling and discrimination of online content and services, to stop internet service providers from picking winners and losers.[405] The EU rules are flexible enough to let internet service providers run dedicated services that require special treatment, such as connectivity for health applications or internet-based TV. However, these services need to have their own chunk of the underlying infrastructure assigned to them. Broadband companies can't degrade the quality of their regular internet services, and services can't get special treatment if they could instead be happily running alongside everything else, as part of the regular internet service.

The EU's rules even cover a particularly controversial form of ad-blocking. Ad blockers are typically plugins for users' browsers, but an Israeli company called Shine developed a blocking tool that operators could deploy on their mobile networks. This tool examined the web traffic going to a user's phone by using an invasive surveillance technique called "deep packet inspection", in order to identify ads and automatically block them on the pages that users were viewing. The idea, at least in terms of marketing, was that the operators could offer this as a service to their customers, to make their web-surfing experience less annoying. However, the operators could also use it as a threat against Google and other content providers, in order to extract payments from them for allowing their ads through the blocking filter.

---

[402] http://arstechnica.com/tech-policy/2016/06/net-neutrality-and-title-ii-win-in-court-as-isps-lose-case-against-fcc/

[403] https://arstechnica.com/tech-policy/2017/01/fcc-chair-ajit-pai-wont-say-whether-hell-enforce-net-neutrality-rules/

[404] https://www.theregister.co.uk/2017/04/26/fcc_pai_kills_net_neutrality/

[405] https://www.euractiv.com/section/innovation-industry/news/europe-will-have-stronger-net-neutrality-rules-than-the-us-regulators-say/

While Shine's system was rolled out by the Caribbean mobile operator Digicel, its planned deployments in Europe hit a major roadblock. Ads are content too, even if people would rather avoid them. EU regulators confirmed that the new net neutrality rules meant operators "should not block, slow down, alter, restrict, interfere with, degrade or discriminate advertising" when providing an internet access service.[406] Even if you're annoying, you're still protected by the EU's net neutrality rules. However, that doesn't mean certain areas aren't grey.

Zero Rating

Are the threats to net neutrality vanquished in Europe? Not quite. There's an ongoing controversy over "zero rating", the popular practice where an operator gives its customers access to a particular service without charging for the data that the service uses. If your mobile operator gives you free Spotify access or free Twitter access, then that's zero rating. It violates the spirit of net neutrality, because it allows operators to pick favourites – they only give people free access to a service after striking a deal with the service's provider. While zero rating may be popular with customers, it's really bad for the chosen services' rivals, because customers are steered away from their offers. If you're getting Spotify for free, why would you even consider using an alternative music-streaming service that would take data out of your monthly allowance?

In the EU, zero rating is legally acceptable, but only just. The bloc's net neutrality law doesn't specifically mention the practice, even though it violates the law's stated principles. So, in their guidelines for interpreting the law, EU telecoms regulators said it's acceptable to offer zero-rated services, but not to keep providing access to them once a customer has hit their regular data limit for the month. This sucked the wind out of the operators' sails, because it meant they couldn't get away with offering low data limits at the same time as charging companies to

---

[406] http://fortune.com/2016/02/19/three-network-ad-blocking/

have their specific services bypass those limits. In order to keep their promises about Spotify and Twitter being free, the operators would have to make sure that their data limits were high enough that people don't go over them. Meanwhile, in the US, FCC chair Ajit Pai said the agency wouldn't pursue operators over the net-neutrality implications of their zero rating offers.[407]

One interesting thing about zero rating is that it's not just the telecoms companies that are pushing it. Facebook has been a particularly enthusiastic cheerleader with a scheme called Free Basics, which is part of its "Internet.org" programme for extending internet access around the world. With Free Basics, Facebook gets operators to agree to zero-rate a special app that provides access to a limited set of services, ranging from Facebook and Wikipedia to public information and local services for jobs. The operators do this for free, because Free Basics is supposed to be used by people who've never shelled out for a mobile data subscription before. The operators hope that, once these people have gotten a taste of what's out there, they'll become regular mobile internet subscribers.

Sounds great, right? In many ways, it is. Getting online means getting access to more information. It means being able to interact with people over great distances, who might share common interests. It can mean being able to participate in economic activity more fully. "Who could possibly be against this?" asked Facebook CEO Mark Zuckerberg in a *Times of India* opinion piece.[408] A lot of people, as it turned out. The problem is that Free Basics, like all zero-rating schemes, flagrantly violates net neutrality.[409] The people who use it will become accustomed to using the services that are in the package, all of which are Facebook-approved. If they don't end up paying to access the full-fat internet, they will stay within Facebook's walled garden. At the very

---

[407] http://fortune.com/2017/02/03/trump-fcc-zero-rating-att-verizon/
[408] http://blogs.timesofindia.indiatimes.com/toi-edit-page/free-basics-protects-net-neutrality/
[409] https://bibhas.in/blog/free-basics-by-facebook-is-a-nightmare-on-the-internet/

least, the system is likely to entrench the phenomenon of people, particularly in emerging markets, thinking that Facebook *is* the internet.[410]

That can have serious consequences when you consider that Facebook is plagued with misinformation. As *The New York Times* noted, Facebook offers Free Basics in the Philippines, where president Rodrigo Duterte was conducting a bloody, officially-sanctioned war on drug dealers and users. Duterte's spokesman shared a photograph on Facebook that, he falsely claimed, was of a local girl who had been raped and murdered by a drug dealer.[411] The photo was used to support the massacres of alleged drug dealers and their families. The picture actually came from Brazil, not the Philippines, but those who only received their information through Facebook may have had a tough time debunking the lie.

Then there's the privacy problem. With all of users' activity being funnelled through Facebook's portal, the company has the power to watch everything, in order to aid its profiling activities. This becomes particularly dangerous in countries with authoritarian governments that might want to co-opt this viewpoint by forcing Facebook to let them see what citizens are looking at. Facebook's centralised nature already creates this risk within the social network, but the risk is amplified when you start drawing other services into the same portal. If everything goes through one gate, that gate becomes the obvious place to spy on people and block them from seeing certain things.

In early 2016, the Indian telecommunications regulator caused a stir by banning zero rating, a move that was prompted by digital rights activists' complaints about Facebook and Free Basics.[412] "No service provider shall offer or charge discriminatory tariffs for data services on

---

[410] http://qz.com/333313/milliions-of-facebook-users-have-no-idea-theyre-using-the-internet/

[411] http://www.nytimes.com/2016/11/18/technology/fake-news-on-facebook-in-foreign-elections-thats-not-new.html

[412] http://indianexpress.com/article/technology/tech-news-technology/facebook-free-basics-india-shut-down/

the basis of content," the regulator declared.[413] Chile banned zero rating in 2014.[414] Slovenia and the Netherlands also banned the practice, although their firm stance was superseded by the EU's grey-area zero-rating rules.[415]

When India shut down Free Basics, the prominent Silicon Valley venture capitalist and Facebook board member Marc Andreesen, who once played a major role in the web's development with his seminal Mosaic browser, complained about the move on Twitter. "Denying world's poorest free partial internet connectivity when today they have none, for ideological reasons, strikes me as morally wrong," he said. Someone retorted that he sounded like someone justifying "internet colonialism," to which Andreessen unwisely replied: "Anti-colonialism has been economically catastrophic for the Indian people for decades. Why stop now?"[416]

The neo-colonialism charge was not without merit. Facebook and Google are both very keen on extending internet coverage through a combination of telco partnerships and their own technology – Facebook is building internet-beaming drones, and Google is developing a network of internet-relaying balloons that will drift around the world, pushing connectivity into hard-to-reach places. This expansion of infrastructure is good for their businesses. Under the capitalist system, they constantly need to grow, and that means developing new markets by getting more people online. However, it's worth keeping an eye on the deals these companies strike, to make sure they don't entrench Facebook and Google's own services in a way that makes it difficult for local companies to launch their own social networks or search engines.

---

[413] http://trai.gov.in/WriteReadData/PressRealease/Document/Press_Release_No_13%20.pdf

[414414] https://gigaom.com/2014/05/28/in-chile-mobile-carriers-can-no-longer-offer-free-twitter-facebook-and-whatsapp/

[415] https://chrismarsden.blogspot.de/2015/10/slovenia-and-netherlands-formal.html

[416] http://www.reuters.com/article/facebook-india-internet-freebasics-idUSKCN0VJ2J2

If the new structures are mainly designed to entrench the US tech giants' power, there's a valid comparison to be made with the colonial railroads that the British Empire built in India and many African countries.

What matters here is motivation and control over the result. Those railways, which were part of the colonialists' "civilising" mission, were really built in order to extract resources and make it easier to control the populace by sending officers out to trouble spots. Projects for expanding connectivity should be designed for local interests and run according to local needs and priorities, while providing opportunities for local entrepreneurs to build their own communications and e-commerce services. They shouldn't just be about making rich foreign companies even richer. The deals also have to stick to the stated aim. It turned out that most of the people using Facebook's "free" service in India had used the internet before. So, even if you might think the benefits of getting people online outweigh the risks of violating net neutrality, that's not actually what was happening here.[417]

If the aim is to get people online for the first time, there are other ways to do this – for example, free Wi-Fi hotspots, set up by local government and non-profit initiatives. This has been done in South African communities through Project Isizwe, an initiative that began in the capital, Tshwane.[418] People in poor areas can use their phones to log onto a portal called Tobetsa, which gives them 250 megabytes of free data each day. Like the Free Basics app, Tobetsa provides access to a set of services that give people information and tools for finding jobs and setting up businesses. It even lets them make free voice calls to one another, when they're connected to the network. But it doesn't keep them confined to a walled garden – they can use their daily 250 megabytes as they wish on the open internet. When they hit the limit,

---

[417] https://medium.com/@sumanthr/a-data-driven-argument-on-why-marc-andreessen-is-wrong-about-free-basics-c472184b9682#.s43ya7nsv
[418] http://www.projectisizwe.org/index.php/2016/06/28/project-isizwe-rolls-out-free-wi-fi-for-tshwane/

the Tobetsa services remain accessible – it's not proper net neutrality, but it's a lot closer than what Free Basics provides.

As it happens, Facebook is a backer of Project Isizwe and others like it. If a company like Facebook wants to help expand new markets, there are clearly ways to let it do so without giving it excessive control over the result. But it's certainly understandable that the firm wants to be able to dictate what happens on its platform. It wouldn't want someone else using the exposure to seize people's attention.

The Next Layer Up

The best metaphor for how tech companies become giants by exploiting their predecessors can be found in the tech field itself: "virtualisation", a concept where physical things are replaced by software representations that are much more flexible and efficient to use. For example, "virtual machines" are programs that simulate whole computers. They can do anything a physical PC or server can, but you can run lots of virtual machines on one physical computer, all at the same time. This has huge advantages, particularly if you have a task that would require a lot of computers to process information simultaneously. Because you can get a virtual machine running with the click of a mouse – as opposed to going to a shop and buying a whole new computer – you can quickly deploy many of them at once, and you can quickly shut them down when they're not needed.

In this scenario, the underlying physical hardware becomes less important than it was before. Yes, it still needs to be there, but there's much less need to have specialised physical computers that can do this or that thing. As long as they can run virtual machines, which can be tailored to specific tasks as needed, you can have extremely generic computers running underneath. This is roughly how the likes of Google and Facebook run their services – in datacentres filled with commodity hardware that's cheap to produce but very flexible in use. The real value lies in the virtual machines running on top of that hardware.[419] Rather like the telecoms companies becoming a generic foundation for the diverse internet services that run on top of their networks, all the fun is happening on the next layer up.

The history of tech is littered with this sort of phenomenon. Microsoft got its big break when, back in 1980, IBM gave the company the contract to provide an operating system for its highly successful personal computers.[420] Microsoft duly bought in an operating system that someone else had developed, then supplied it to IBM. But because the contract allowed Microsoft to offer the operating system to other PC manufacturers too, it was Microsoft rather than IBM that ended up controlling the PC market. Microsoft's biggest rival, Apple, always reserved its operating system for its own hardware, but, as the personal computing market exploded, Microsoft licensed its MS-DOS operating system to pretty much every manufacturer out there. That created a virtuous circle: developers wrote their programs for MS-DOS in order to reach the most users, and users bought PCs running MS-DOS in order to access the most programs. The operating system, rather than the computer itself, became the centre of attention and the platform for new ideas. With MS-DOS and its successor, Windows, Microsoft held the greatest source of power in the business.

That is, until the web browser came along in the early 1990s. Just as the operating system made the underlying hardware less relevant, the browser made the operating system less relevant. In a new layer of abstraction, this single program was the portal to a world of web services that would gradually draw users' attention from the other programs running on the operating system. So Microsoft, recognising the threat to its gatekeeper status, decided to use its operating system monopoly to establish a new monopoly in the browser market. It bundled its own browser, Internet Explorer, with Windows.

---

[419] http://arstechnica.com/information-technology/2013/07/how-facebook-is-killing-the-hardware-business-as-we-know-it/
[420] http://forwardthinking.pcmag.com/software/286148-the-rise-of-dos-how-microsoft-got-the-ibm-pc-os-contract

The core principle of antitrust or competition law is this: it's acceptable to develop a monopoly in any given market, because that's how markets sometimes work, but it's unacceptable to use that position of power to deliberately warp the market by stopping rivals from being able to build up their own business. If a monopoly power successfully blocks competition, then it doesn't need to innovate as much as it otherwise would, and the market won't develop as it should. The details of antitrust law differ around the world – for example, in the US you have to prove that the monopolist has actively harmed consumers,[421] while in the EU you only need to demonstrate unfair or anticompetitive practices.[422] But the principle remains the same.

In Microsoft's case, the company was trying to hamstring competitors such as Netscape and Opera by making Internet Explorer the easiest browser to use – it was already included with Windows. At the time, internet connections were slow and it took a long time to download a rival browser. And in any case, people tend to stick with the default applications and settings they're given.

In the US, Microsoft's attempt to build a new monopoly in the browser market formed part of a wider antitrust case that in 2000 led a judge to call for the company's breakup – Microsoft appealed and won a settlement avoiding that drastic outcome. In 2009, EU antitrust authorities forced Microsoft to introduce a "browser ballot" screen that would over the next five years appear in front of people who were firing up a copy of Windows for the first time. The screen allowed people to choose which browser they wanted to install, from a range of 12 browsers presented in random order, rather than starting with Internet Explorer by default.

Over the next five years, Internet Explorer's European desktop market share dropped from 45 percent to 18 percent.[423] Meanwhile, Google's Chrome browser shot up from 4 percent to 47 percent. To

---

[421] https://www.ftc.gov/news-events/blogs/competition-matters/2016/02/antitrust-violation-vs-injury-fact-distinction-makes

[422] http://eur-lex.europa.eu/legal-content/EN/ALL/?uri=CELEX:12008E102

[423] http://gs.statcounter.com/#desktop-browser-eu-monthly-200911-201411

what degree was the browser ballot screen responsible for this drastic reshuffling of the market? It's hard to say; other likely factors include better broadband speeds that enabled the faster downloading of alternative browsers, and the fact that Chrome was a well-marketed, user-friendly product that provided integration with Google's extremely popular web services. It's also worth noting that Mozilla's Firefox saw its European desktop browser market share fall from 41 percent to 26 percent over the same period – the fact that it had such a high starting point suggests that the European Commission's action came rather late in the game. However, it's likely that the EU settlement played at least some part in eroding Microsoft's position, particularly within Europe, in a way that helped Google entrench its position.

Now it's Google's turn to feel the heat of antitrust regulation. In recent years, regulators – particularly in Europe – have been trying to tackle the firm over the way it uses its multiple monopolies to stamp out competition. The UK's Streetmap may not have succeeded in its legal battles against Google within that country, but similar behaviour on Google's part has brought it much more trouble elsewhere.

In mid-2017, the European Commission fined Google €2.4 billion for using its search monopoly to damage rivals in the comparison-shopping space. Since 2008, when you search for a product using Google, the results are headed up by click-friendly pictures of the product that will lead you to various retailers' offers. This is Google's own comparison-shopping service, and it treats it completely differently to rival services. Google's service automatically appears at the top of its results, while the others are subject to the standard search algorithm, which shunts them off to page four on average. As Google's search market share in Europe is above 90 percent, this behaviour has essentially made it impossible for anyone to set up a comparison shopping service and expect people to find it.[424]

On top of that, the EU regulators have charged Google with setting unfair terms for the Google-powered search box that other websites can use to let visitors search their sites. Like Google's main search service,

---

[424] https://www.statista.com/chart/4694/googles-dominance-in-europe/

these boxes return results that include ads. Google has a clearly dominant share of over 80 percent in this market, and the regulators accused it of using this position to ban site publishers from running ads from rival ad networks, and demand that they give premium placement to the ads coming from Google's network.

And then there's Android. Google's operating system runs on more than 85 percent of the smartphones in the world, and the company has used this monopolistic position to try to stymie the rivals to its services, in particular Google Search, Gmail and Google Maps. This has already been established in Russia, where a local company called Yandex provides alternatives to all these services. Yandex successfully complained to the country's antitrust authorities that Google forced mobile manufacturers to make Google Search the default search engine on their Android phones' homescreens, and pressured them to preinstall the full suite of Google services if they wanted to preinstall even one of them, such as Google's app store – again, people rarely change the defaults on the products they buy, so preinstallations matter greatly. Google lost the case in 2015 and lost its appeal the following year.[425] And EU antitrust regulators launched a very similar Android case against Google in 2016.[426]

Abusive behaviour is usually pretty easy to identify once someone complains about it. At the risk of over-simplifying what has to be a painstaking legal process – the companies will usually fight back in court, so the case must be watertight – all the antitrust regulator has to do is carefully define the market in question, establish that the complained-about company has a dominant position, and confirm that it's abusing its position. Then the regulator gets to tell the company to cut it out, and perhaps pay a fine.

However, when it comes to algorithms, misbehaviour will become much harder to establish. In the Google comparison shopping case, the investigators' task was relatively straightforward – Google was

[425] https://techcrunch.com/2016/03/14/google-loses-android-antitrust-appeal-in-russia/
[426] http://europa.eu/rapid/press-release_IP-16-1492_en.htm

applying different algorithms to its rivals' services. But what if a company such as Google were to apply the same algorithm to all services, while tweaking the code to favour its own offerings? As with the issue of "fake news" rising to the top of the list, unless you can peek inside Google's search algorithms, you can never be quite sure how the system works.

Despite wanting Google to play more fairly, the EU's competition commissioner, Margrethe Vestager, has insisted that she doesn't want to change how the company's search algorithms work.[427] And Google, like most tech firms, definitely doesn't want anyone peering too closely at its crown jewels. When the French Senate proposed forcing it to open its algorithms for inspection so investigators could look for bias, the company argued that doing so would lead to the "gaming" of its results.[428] There is indeed a whole search engine optimisation industry devoted to figuring out how search algorithms work, precisely so they can boost the rankings of their clients, so that's not a small concern. According to Google, these algorithms are trade secrets, and if they leak out they could cause commercial damage.

But again, this algorithmic opacity will become more of a problem as we move into a world of virtual assistants and the way they present information. If you're asking a virtual assistant for a piece of information or a recommendation about a good local restaurant, you don't want a lengthy list of options. You ideally want one answer, or maybe a very small selection, depending on the question. The potential for anticompetitive abuse here is extremely high, if regulators can't get some view into the workings of the algorithm that's generating that magic answer. One regulatory solution may be to "sanitise" the information flowing into the algorithm, to ensure that all sources of information are treated fairly. If that isn't enough, then the company may have to let officials inspect its algorithm under secure conditions.

---

[427] http://europa.eu/rapid/press-release_STATEMENT-15-4785_en.htm

[428] http://uk.businessinsider.com/google-algorithm-search-secret-proposal-senate-2015-4?IR=T

There is another great uncertainty in the regulation of online monopolies: the fast pace of the tech industry's development. No regulator wants to set rules that actually hold back a market's development. Antitrust cases also take years to build, and monopolies can sometimes be broken without regulatory intervention – if the company in question is going to be overtaken by a competitor in a couple years' time, there's no point charging them with antitrust abuses. Today's big online monopolies are actually not that old, even though it may feel like they've been around forever. Google is only two decades old and Facebook, by far the leader in social networking with its various products (Facebook, Facebook Messenger, WhatsApp and Instagram), is barely a teenager. Might others overtake these companies in the same way that they dispatched competitors such as Yahoo and MySpace? In theory, this should be possible, but there's a big difference between the current online landscape and the one that existed when Google and Facebook gained their positions of dominance.

Quite simply, many more people are online now. When Google became the preeminent search engine in 2000, a mere two years after its incorporation, there were fewer than 400 million internet users.[429] When Facebook overtook MySpace in 2009, there were about 1.7 billion people online.[430] Today, there are around 3.7 billion people using the internet. To be sure, there are still a lot of people who are yet to come online, but we're now around the halfway mark in terms of the world's population. A relatively small proportion of those with internet access today remember the time before Google and Facebook were the go-to services in their fields. Those coming online for the first time now will probably be doing so on Google's Android phones, and they may primarily engage with the online world through Facebook.

---

[429] http://lowendmac.com/2013/the-rise-of-google-beating-yahoo-at-its-own-game/

[430] https://www.theguardian.com/commentisfree/cifamerica/2009/jun/23/facebook-myspace-social-networks

Old habits die hard. Once so many people use a particular service, it may prove difficult to get a significant proportion of them using an alternative. Even if new internet users have access to more than Facebook's walled garden, the company's social network is where their friends and family most likely already have profiles. It's where those links between people already exist. Facebook's services have become part of society's fabric in ways that its predecessors never achieved, because most people were just not online at the time. It will be extraordinarily difficult to dislodge Facebook from that position of power. Indeed, it may take some kind of new technological advance – perhaps beyond the smartphone – that lets a new player establish its own monopoly in some adjacent space and use that position to draw users' attention away from Facebook. But even then, the new player would have to find a way to compete with all the data Facebook has gathered on its users.

Competition regulators are starting to realise that data, as an asset, can become a monopolist's tool. "We do need to keep a close eye on whether companies control unique data, which no one else can get hold of, and can use it to shut their rivals out of the market," Vestager said in a 2016 speech.[431] Earlier that year, the German and French competition authorities issued a similar warning. They said in a joint report that "the collection of data may result in entry barriers when new entrants are unable either to collect the data or to buy access to the same kind of data, in terms of volume and/or variety, as established companies".[432] The regulators also noted that competitors might use the secrecy of their "data-crunching algorithms" to illegally collude with one another – advanced cartel behaviour, in other words.

One factor that might ease the way for a serious Facebook competitor is the EU's new General Data Protection Regulation, which

---

[431] https://ec.europa.eu/commission/2014-2019/vestager/announcements/making-data-work-us_en
[432]

http://www.bundeskartellamt.de/SharedDocs/Publikation/DE/Berichte/Big%20Data%20Papier.pdf?__blob=publicationFile&v=2

will come into effect in May 2018. This will force Facebook to let its users take their data with them if they switch to another social network. What's more, Facebook and all other companies holding their users' data will have to provide that information in a "structured and commonly used format", so that the rival service can easily import it.[433] In short, people should be able to take their profiles with them – a concept known as "data portability". The EU regulation is mainly seen as a privacy law, but this element of it may serve as a powerfully pro-competitive force.

We need antitrust regulations to work if our markets are going to stay free and fair, but the rapid evolution of technology means competition authorities are going to have to evolve their own methods to keep up. Perhaps tools outside the traditional antitrust realm, such as data-portability laws, might prove useful. It will take a lot to restore balance to an online landscape where power is currently over-concentrated to a scary degree, but it needs to be done. That concentration has a real impact, not only on consumer choice, but also on economic diversity. And with big, well-funded internet firms already displaying a worrying ability to take over markets at speed, we need all the diversity we can hang onto.

Straight Rivers

The internet makes all sorts of things more efficient. Online platforms flourish because they make it easier for service providers and consumers to connect directly (as with eBay and Uber), and because they make it possible to buy just about anything in one virtual place (Amazon and eBay again). From the consumer's point of view, the internet brings unprecedented convenience. And, where it cuts out the middleman, it can make things cheaper. However, when considering the economy and jobs, there's a case for saying the internet streamlines things too much.

---

[433] http://eur-lex.europa.eu/legal-content/EN/TXT/?uri=celex%3A52012PC0011

Rivers provide a useful ecological analogy here. Over the centuries, people have straightened rivers for a variety of reasons, including making it easier for large boats to travel down the river. The straighter the river, the faster it flows, and the wider it becomes. And the bigger the boat, the more efficient it becomes to transport people and goods down the waterway. Removing bends (known as meanders) from the river also reduces flooding along its path, which can be useful if the flooding affects towns. However, meanders also create wetlands – the habitat for all sorts of plants and animals, and an essential natural filter for fresh water. And as the water flows more quickly, there's more risk of flooding downstream. It may be more efficient to make a river run in a straight line, and useful for some people, but this engineering can be very destructive. In recent years, countries such as Japan[434] and Denmark[435] have been deliberately "re-meandering" certain rivers because they realised that the bends support life.

Much as straightened rivers reduce biodiversity, the internet can be harmful for economic diversity. Amazon provides an efficient service that gives you one place to buy a range of goods, without needing to visit lots of different stores. Uber offers an efficient app that means you don't need to look up the details for your local taxi service. But these services kill off small businesses by starving them of custom. The water may flow more quickly, but the wetlands go thirsty.

Obviously, this is a trend that pre-dates the internet – just look at retail giants like Walmart, which wiped out many local businesses by running hyper-efficient, centralised logistics operations and stocking a wide range of goods. But the internet allows Amazon to beat even the Walmarts of this world. Amazon's retail arm is essentially little more than an increasingly automated logistics operation with a website as its human-friendly customer interface. It doesn't need physical stores, with all the employees those require. It doesn't need to keep shelves stocked

---

[434] http://onlinelibrary.wiley.com/doi/10.1111/rec.12101/abstract

[435]

https://www.bfn.de/fileadmin/MDB/documents/themen/wasser/teil02_8_th odsen.pdf with stuff that might not sell, in order to maintain appearances. All it needs is logistics centres where it can store and pack goods, before sending them to customers. Its range is so broad that it's even hurting department stores.[436]

Spotify may provide the most efficient way to find and listen to music – even easier than "piracy" – but it replaces music stores and radio stations around the world with an operation that employs fewer than 2,000 people. WhatsApp, the messaging platform that's hammering the revenues of traditional telecoms firms by providing over a billion people with a free substitute for text messages and phonecalls, employed all of 55 people when Facebook bought it for $19 billion in 2014.

What's more, the globalised nature of these companies allows them to shuffle money around various locations in ways that let them drastically reduce their tax bills. For example, in 2014 Amazon's UK business recorded revenues of £5.3 billion, but it only paid £11.9 million in tax. How? It only recorded a profit in the country of £34.4 million for the year, largely thanks to its complex tax arrangements.[437] Amazon has a subsidiary in Luxembourg that runs its European businesses and pays royalties to a separate subsidiary for the privilege of using Amazon's brand and technology. This reduces the first subsidiary's taxable income in Europe, while the Luxembourg tax authorities allow the second subsidiary to avoid paying tax on those royalties, due to its structure. Long story short: Amazon pays very little tax relative to all the money that flows through it. How is a small, local retailer, which has to pay its taxes in full, supposed to compete with that?

The rivers are flowing faster, leaving less support for life along their banks. Yes, this is largely a continuation of the globalisation trend, with multinationals wiping out small businesses around the world. But the

---

[436] http://www.businessinsider.de/amazon-is-killing-department-stores-2016-5
[437] https://www.theguardian.com/technology/2015/jun/24/amazons-uk-business-paid-119m-tax-last-year

internet enables a steroidal version of globalisation, where power can concentrate at unprecedented speed while the powerful shirk the traditional responsibilities that go along with being a big economic player.

The newest breed of online giant doesn't even need to make the kinds of investments that Amazon makes. Platforms operating in the "gig" economy position themselves purely as the link between suppliers and consumers, albeit a link that sets the terms for all transactions. Uber is the best known example here, though similar companies operate in sectors from house-cleaning to food delivery. Uber doesn't view its drivers as employees. It would rather avoid giving them standard worker benefits such as paid holidays or sick pay, though a British court ruled in late 2016 that it must do so.[438] But at the same time, Uber sets the rates that its drivers must charge, and it tries to keep those rates low for its own competitive purposes.[439] It makes its drivers pay for their own insurance. The drivers also have to pay for their own cars, which Uber insists must be relatively new. And because they are not employees, the drivers have difficulty in unionising. In New York, Uber's drivers won the right to be represented by a union, the International Association of Machinists, but they still don't have any real bargaining power and can't influence the levels at which Uber sets its fares.[440]

This is essentially a clever form of super-charged employer power that draws its strength from denying "employer" status. Pushing back means coming up with equally fresh ideas. When couriers for the UberEats food delivery service wanted to protest against the platform's pay cuts, they came up against the fact that they didn't know one another. They devised an ingenious solution for organising a protest: those who wanted to spread the word used the UberEats app to make

---

[438] https://www.bloomberg.com/news/articles/2016-10-28/uber-loses-london-lawsuit-over-drivers-rights-law-firm-says
[439] https://www.theguardian.com/business/2016/oct/28/uber-driver-hails-landmark-court-ruling
[440] http://www.recode.net/2016/8/13/12466930/uber-drivers-union-tipping-option-petition-independent-drivers-guild

delivery orders. When the couriers came with their food, they told them about the resistance.[441]

Uber has also clashed with regulators across the world over its insistence that it's just an app provider, not a transportation company. In many places, classification as a limousine or taxi firm comes along with a variety of obligations, such as insisting that drivers have gone through formal training and that the cars are insured for commercial use. Many cities have also long regulated their numbers of taxi drivers by forcing them to pay significant license fees. While some of these requirements are genuinely in the interest of passenger safety and ensuring a good service, others are more protectionist in nature and are increasingly out-of-date, given developments in technology. For example, London cabbies traditionally have to pass a test called The Knowledge to ensure that they have an intimate understanding of the city's labyrinthine street layout. A well-functioning satnav system should provide a reasonable substitute. In 2014, the French government introduced a law that forbade private-hire car services from offering apps with maps that showed the location of their cars – a move that served no purpose other than to hobble the likes of Uber.[442] But even where the rules need changing, the fact remains that it's deeply unfair for one company to bypass them while its traditional rivals remain bogged down, unable to compete on even terms.

Two things have powered Uber's lightning-fast expansion: a vast amount of financing from Wall Street – so vast that Uber was able to lose an estimated $3 billion during 2016 alone and still keep going – and the fact that it is, technically speaking, merely an app.[443] When it opens up shop in a new city, all it needs to do is hire a few managers to handle things like engaging with local drivers and fending off local authorities. It can roll out so quickly that everyone else has to play

---

[441] https://www.ft.com/content/88fdc58e-754f-11e6-b60a-de4532d5ea35

[442] https://www.nytimes.com/2015/06/07/magazine/ubers-french-resistance.html

[443] https://www.bloomberg.com/news/articles/2016-12-20/uber-s-loss-exceeds-800-million-in-third-quarter-on-1-7-billion-in-net-revenue

catch-up. And because it takes a long time for cities to change their regulations to ensure a level playing field, Uber can safely bet that it will benefit from an unfair advantage for a significant amount of time – long enough for the locals to become used to the service it offers.

Uber claims it creates tens of thousands of jobs, and this may be true, but what kind of jobs? [444] Many of these people also have to have other jobs in order to earn a decent living. They form what economists and sociologists call the "precariat": a class of people with no job security, no prospects for advancement and few workers' rights. [445] It's a phenomenon that has long existed in service sectors such as the restaurant industry, but, thanks to technology, it's spreading to make life more precarious for more people. When there are few local jobs, in part thanks to the hyper-globalising force of the internet, what choice do you have but to hawk your services for a few hours on a platform such as Uber?

In any case, Uber ultimately wants to get rid of its drivers altogether. The company is developing fleets of self-driving cars that will benefit from the foothold Uber has already established in cities across the world. To be fair, this is partly a defensive move on Uber's part. Google and various automotive companies are also developing self-driving cars, and Uber recognises that these rivals might in future launch a ride-hailing service based on their automated fleets. "If we are not tied for first, then the person who is in first, or the entity that's in first, then rolls out a ride-sharing network that is far cheaper or far higher-quality than Uber's, then Uber is no longer a thing," Uber's CEO at the time, Travis Kalanick, said in a 2016 Business Insider interview. [446] However, Uber is positioning itself to benefit from the self-driving-car revolution

---

[444] https://www.bloomberg.com/view/articles/2016-06-03/uber-and-lyft-are-adding-jobs-not-just-stealing-them
[445] http://www.wpr.org/who-precariat-economist-says-new-class-workers-fighting-recognition-stability
[446] http://www.businessinsider.de/travis-kalanick-interview-on-self-driving-cars-future-driver-jobs-2016-8

through the labour of thousands of easily-dispensable non-employees.[447]

In this and other ways, there's a real risk that the new wave of automation – "artificial intelligence", if you want it to sound sexier – will be deeply harmful for competition in business and for wider economic equality.

Automation and Jobs

Politicians and policymakers are only starting to grapple with the question of how we're going to cope with an automated world where jobs for humans are increasingly scarce. A 2016 World Bank report said there was a risk of digitalisation leading to "harmful concentration in many sectors" – economist-speak for mega-corporations taking over markets – but it also warned that "quickly expanding automation, even of mid-level office jobs, could contribute to a hollowing out of labour markets and to rising inequality."[448]

Cashiers are giving way to automated checkout systems at local supermarket. Personal assistants are being made redundant by their smart mobile counterparts. Legal secretaries and paralegals are losing out to digital replacements such as "e-discovery" systems that automate the exchange of information during legal cases.[449] And truck drivers won't be needed in a world of self-driving fleets. It has always been the case that technological advances make certain roles unnecessary, particularly where savings are to be made. However, there's a growing feeling among experts that this current wave may be different. The issue is that computers have become much more capable in areas where we never thought they would – at least, not in our lifetime. Rewind a decade and self-driving cars were widely seen as unfeasible. Not so

---

[447] https://newsroom.uber.com/pittsburgh-self-driving-uber/
[448]

http://documents.worldbank.org/curated/en/896971468194972881/pdf/102
725-PUB-Replacement-PUBLIC.pdf
[449] https://www.ft.com/content/c8ef3f62-ea9c-11e5-888e-2eadd5fbc4a4

now. Google, Uber and every car-maker out there are now developing their variants. Reliable automated vehicles are likely to become technically feasible around 2020, and this is because their central computers can increasingly think and react like a human driver can. The machine-learning research field, which makes this possible, is advancing at a dizzying rate.

Computers are no longer just being told what to do – they are being shown, so they can learn and mimic. Rethink Robotics' Baxter and Sawyer general-purpose robots, which cost less than €26,000, are trained by physically guiding their arms to perform tasks such as moving and packaging things, machining metals, and tending to other machines. Once they know how to do the job, they do so at minimal operational cost, certainly when compared with human counterparts that would need to be paid and given time off. A Rethink Robotics case study, about an increasingly automated sewing company that uses its Baxter robot, says it all: "Henderson Sewing now boasts more than 70 types of sewn products that are being created using automation. In 2015, Henderson Sewing had created a variety of mostly autonomous sewing systems, but still needed human labour to load and unload parts, and transfer materials between machines. It was this type of low-skilled, repetitive job that was hard to fill, but seemingly impossible to automate. After seeing Rethink Robotics' Baxter at a trade show, Frank Henderson knew his vision could be realised and purchased two of the robots."[450]

The scale of the potential shift was made clear in a seminal 2013 study by Carl Benedikt Frey and Michael Osborne of the University of Oxford's Oxford Martin School.[451] They created a model to predict how many jobs were at high risk of automation within the next decade or two, and they first used this model to analyse the US employment

---

[450] http://www.rethinkrobotics.com/wp-content/uploads/2017/03/Case_Study_Henderson_Sewing-Aug-16.pdf
[451]

http://www.oxfordmartin.ox.ac.uk/downloads/academic/The_Future_of_Employment.pdf

landscape. The result? Forty-seven percent of American workers may lose their jobs to robots or computer programs in the coming years. The two also worked with the Deloitte consultancy in 2014 to calculate that 35 percent of UK jobs are at similar risk. ING-DiBa, a German bank, used the model to come up with a much higher 59-percent figure for that country. According to Osborne, almost half of the counter clerks, personal assistants, secretaries and travel agents in the UK have lost their jobs since 2001. Even writers are not immune. In 2016, Associated Press started using automated systems to churn out its coverage of minor-league baseball games. The news operations had already been using similar technology to produce financial earnings reports for a couple years.[452] Where readers are just interested in scores and other mundane details, rather than deep analysis, why not replace human writers with automated systems?

Frey and Osborne's model doesn't factor in the societal pushback against automation that may take place. Importantly, it also doesn't take into account the creation of new jobs thanks to technology. In many cases, jobs that disappear are replaced. For example, the automotive industry long ago brought in robots to replace people on the production line, but this made it possible to produce more cars. In Germany, which has a major automotive industry, the increase in the number of car-making workplaces largely offset the reduction in jobs per workplace. Cars also contain more components these days, due to all the sensors and computers that are becoming standard, and this again means more jobs – they're no longer jobs for toolmakers and machine operators, but rather for information technology, electronics and data modelling specialists. Still, some people think artificial intelligence will develop to the point where machines can take over these jobs too.

There's also the uncomfortable fact that, particularly with workers who are already in the latter stages of their careers, it's not so simple to just retrain them with a completely different skillset. An experienced truck driver put out of work by the advent of self-driving trucks is

---

[452] https://www.poynter.org/2016/the-associated-press-will-use-automated-writing-to-cover-the-minor-leagues/419489/

probably not going to build a new career as a data scientist. If we do end up with vast numbers of people being put out of work by new technological developments, we're going to have to think about restructuring our economies. There's a tremendous risk of widening inequality, as the shrinking numbers of gainfully employed people hold an ever-expanding share of societal wealth, and more and more power accrues to those who own the machinery.

Those who are wary of new technology are sometimes sneeringly called "Luddites" – a term referring to wool-workers who revolted against the introduction of automation in the north of England in the early 19th century. The Luddites went around smashing the machinery in textile factories, and their violence became so extreme that many were hanged. But their problem wasn't so much the technology itself, which boosted production levels, as it was the economic inequality that came along with the change. Before the machines came, they were well-paid and had good working conditions. But when they became factory workers, their workload went up while their wages went down. The profits were going to the factory owners instead.[453] Technological change is always hard for some, but if the benefits of the new technology are not fairly shared, then it becomes catastrophic.

To avoid a full-blown crisis for our capitalist system – which, after all, needs people to be consumers with cash to spend – many are calling for the institution of an unconditional basic income, a flat rate of free money for all citizens. This is hardly a new idea, having been backed by figures as diverse as Martin Luther King and Milton Friedman, but it's become a hot issue again as people take notice of automation's threat.

Leaving aside the question of how a guaranteed minimum income would be funded when tech giants engage in massive tax avoidance, the concept might keep the system ticking over for a while. However, it would also create a massive underclass of people on the basic income, dominated by a small elite, and with no middle class to speak of. If our

---

[453] http://www.smithsonianmag.com/innovation/when-robots-take-jobs-remember-luddites-180961423/

future societies are going to avoid horrendous inequality, we will need political and economic systems that more evenly spread around the benefits of automation, and that recognise societal worth in more ways than the ability to out-earn other people.

***

The proper enforcement of competition rules and principles like net neutrality and data portability will go some way towards countering the excessive centralisation that's taking place in the online layer. However, regulation will not on its own strike the healthy balance we need to see emerging. What we ultimately need is a different, more decentralised approach to how online services work. And to find inspiration, we can look to the internet itself, as well as good old-fashioned email.

The internet is, technically speaking, a fairly decentralised system. There's no core hub through which all information flows, in the style of a network such as Facebook. Even if the internet were to break into pieces, those pieces could work just fine as separate mini-internets. It's a system that's designed for resilience, and it achieves this by being distributed and standardised. As long as those fragments can talk to one another using the same technical language, they can operate as a whole. Similarly, disparate email systems can all interoperate by using standard protocols – an email sent using Microsoft's Outlook will be perfectly readable by a Google Gmail user, and vice versa. Contrast this with the inability to communicate between closed-off messaging platforms such as, say, Facebook Messenger and WeChat. Those non-standardised platforms are designed to keep you within their proprietors' confines, whereas email is essentially a federated system that lets people use the email program they prefer to use, without foregoing common functionality. If an email service shuts down, it's usually very easy to take all your emails and switch to another provider.

If you're a Facebook user who's tired of the company's incessant profiling and tracking, and you'd prefer to set up a profile on a more privacy-friendly social network, you're free to do so. But if you have more than a handful of friends on Facebook, the move would be so inconvenient that it's effectively pointless – you can't take your profile with you, and good luck trying to convince all your friends to make the switch when each one of them is also heavily invested in Facebook. Because of this problem, there are no serious alternatives to Facebook. Even Google failed to make a serious impact in the social networking market with its Google+ service. Yes, there are group messaging services that attract enough of people's attention to be a worry for Facebook, such as Snapchat and WeChat, and Twitter's "microblogging" service is a social network of sorts, but none of these provides a replacement for Facebook's rich functionality and the personal histories that people have recorded into it. They're services on the side.

People have tried to fix this situation, more than once. In 2010, a social network called Diaspora launched with the aim of providing a more distributed, federated alternative to Facebook. Diaspora is a network of community hubs – "nodes" – that people can set up and run themselves. These nodes are interoperable, allowing communications across the network, but there's no central authority. This makes censorship more difficult. Everyone also retains full control over their own data, unlike with Facebook, where you allow the company to do what it likes with your words and photos. Diaspora is still going, but it's by no means a success, with active users likely numbering in the tens of thousands each month (exact figures are hard to find, due to the lack of a central Diaspora authority).[454] Facebook has close to two billion monthly active users and, once you're in that territory, collective inertia makes it very hard to tempt people across to rival services.

In 2017, Twitter users who were frustrated with the platform's abuse problem set up a rival called Mastodon. Again using freely available software, people can set up their own Mastodon networks that can be run according to their own cultures and social rules – rigorously child-friendly, perhaps, or gleefully profane – but that still allow people to communicate between the networks if they wish. This makes it possible for people to choose where they would feel most comfortable hanging

---

[454] https://the-federation.info/

out, while still being able to interact with friends and family who choose to reside elsewhere in the federation. It's a smart way of dealing with the abuse problem. However, while it's still too early to tell how Mastodon will pan out, history tells us it's unlikely to catch on in the mainstream.

If a similar idea *does* catch on at some point, though, the implications would be enormous. Social networks are already our virtual town squares. If they also become hubs for e-commerce – virtual high streets, if you will – then the diversity that comes with federation would allow many more small businesses to thrive. Imagine a network of communities, each of which with its own culture and rules, and with online services designed to serve that specific community.

The internet is made for niches. Imagine if we tried to encourage them again, rather than agglomerating everything into an environment that's dominated by a handful of well-funded titans. With such an approach, we could tackle the imbalances we see growing today in the online economy and in the fields of privacy and free expression. We could reintroduce choice and freedom where today we are increasingly corralled by mega-corporations and governments. It's by no means clear how we get from here to there, but having an idea of what "there" should look like is a good start.

CHAPTER 9: RETRIEVING CONTROL

It's hard to overstate the profundity of the changes that are emanating from our current technological revolution. They're affecting each of us as individuals, and all of us as societies. Power is shifting, in some cases being cannily grabbed by those who recognise what's underway, and in some cases just sloshing around without any grand plan. Whether or not there's method to this madness, though, our state of flux leaves us with the need for new settlements and resolutions.

One way or another, these will appear. The question is whether or not this future is balanced in a way that leaves us with enhanced personal autonomy and societal equality, or in a way that accepts an unprecedented concentration of power as the new status quo. It's not difficult to see the potential for dystopia, because we are frankly on its threshold: domination by a handful of global mega-corporations and the governments that can co-opt their mechanisms, all-pervasive tracking in both the online and offline layers of our existence; manipulation and discrimination enabled by boundless profiling and the insidious falsification of facts; the inability to organise meaningful protests; crushing, algorithmically-powered censorship; and a lack of control over our possessions, homes and cities. These scenarios are already bleeding into our reality and, where this sort of impact hasn't yet fully manifested, it may not take much to do so. Perhaps the widespread insecurity of our technologies will allow hackers to crash our cars, lock our doors and turn off our lights – cyberattacks that, if attributed to particular countries, lead governments to erect virtual borders and convince their scared citizens that the answer lies in more centralised control. Perhaps our online giants themselves will grow so powerful that they end up co-opting governments.

None of this is inevitable. Although we are potentially on the cusp of a terrible future, the fact that we are this far along our technological path also means we have an unprecedented ability to recognise the choices that we face. There are steps we can take now to achieve a better, fairer future. Some of these will have to be regulatory measures

219

and some will need to be personal. But if we are to make sure that technology works for us, rather than against us, we'll also require technological solutions.

Our Agents

Before examining the more immediate choices we face, let's jump forward a bit to consider the kind of technological development that might make it easier for us to trust our interactions with the connected world.

Algorithms already play a major role in our world as behind-the-scenes mechanisms that answer search queries, negotiate financial transactions and filter information on social networks, to name but a few of their myriad applications. However, technologists are giving these algorithms faces through the creation of what we today call virtual assistants and bots. These "characters" are evolving through machine-learning techniques. They converse with us in order to become better at imitating us, feeding on an endless diet of the data we produce in our online lives. Marketing departments sometimes call them artificial intelligences, and perhaps they will one day earn that name, but either way they provide a human-esque interface that connects us with a world of ones and zeroes.

The problem is, these proto-AIs don't really work for us. They're masks on the centralised systems with which we, as people, are interacting – cloud-based search engines and calendaring programs and e-commerce infrastructures. Essentially, they're virtual customer service agents that we carry around with us, but that remain entirely under the control of the organisations that deploy them. They are there to do precisely the opposite of representing us.

For now, this makes sense. The technology is immature. The systems behind the masks need to learn in a centralised way. They need to constantly draw in data from many sources, so they can aggregate that data to look for patterns and improve their methods for self-evolution. This requires an immense amount of data-processing power and storage, all of which consumes an immense amount of energy.

"The cloud" – that suitably hazy metaphor for other people's computers – provides the right model for these tasks, at this time. The smartphone in your pocket may be millions of times more powerful than the computers that put people on the moon half a century ago, but it can't begin to rival the might of Google or Facebook's datacentres.[455] The cloud is simply the most economical way both to process our requests and to use them as training material.

However, our processors are becoming ever more energy-efficient and the cost of storage continues to fall. Scientists are also making significant advances in the development of technologies that harvest energy from light, or our own motion, and that store it in flexible batteries – even in threads.[456] It's entirely possible that we'll end up with smart clothing that powers our portable computing devices or even, through the development of flexible electronics, that contains them. And at some point, AI technology will have developed to the point where it no longer needs to be tethered to a datacentre in order to meaningfully interact with and serve us.

Imagine a personal virtual agent that exists to represent you in your interactions with technology and those who lie behind it. There are many ways in which this could rebalance the power relationships that are emerging today and help you assert your rights.

Let's take the example of shopping. Today, vast online profiling systems track your activities in order to figure out what you like, in order to sell this information to advertisers. Your online movements, and increasingly your offline movements too, then trigger the appearance of the resulting ads and promotions in front of you, whether on webpages or by sending a notification to your phone as you pass a physical store. Now imagine that your agent is the one profiling you, not some remote, shadowy system. Because it's your constant companion, it knows you and your tastes very well. So let's say you tell

---

[455] http://www.zmescience.com/research/technology/smartphone-power-compared-to-apollo-432/

[456] http://www.latimes.com/science/sciencenow/la-sci-sn-fabric-captures-energy-20161026-snap-story.html

your agent to be on the lookout for a new smart jacket. Your agent knows your size and your favourite colours and textures. As you pass a clothing store, your agent briefly links up with the store's stock-management systems to see if there's something in there that it thinks you might like. It makes a suggestion to you, and you can then choose to go in and have a look, or to keep walking. Whether you buy the jacket or not, the episode improves your agent's understanding of you, so that it can make better suggestions in the future.

Crucially, at no point in this process is some external system profiling you, nor does the store have to learn anything about you. That's not to say you can't choose to tell the store something about you or your decision, in order to help the retailer make better decisions about the clothes it stocks – something that may ultimately benefit you as a consumer. But you would be in complete control of the information you broadcast, if indeed you choose to share any such information at all.

There's a lot more that your agent could do on your behalf, too. Right now, it's extremely unlikely that you read the full terms and conditions when you sign up to some new service or download a new app. Those terms are written by the service provider's lawyers to cover the company's back in court, which is fair enough, but they're not intelligible to most people. And even if they're written in simplified language, few of us have the time or inclination to go through them. This essentially means we're regularly agreeing to contracts that may not be in our best interests, giving far too much power in the relationship to the company that drew them up. What if our agents, which are entirely programmed to act in our interests, could go through these terms on our behalf and warn us when someone's trying to exploit us?

What if our agents perform fact-checks on our behalf? Every day, we wade through a flood of information on social media and on news sites. The internet gives us the theoretical ability to check the veracity of every assertion we encounter, but doing so requires time and a certain degree of media literacy. Under regulatory pressure, platforms such as Facebook and Google are increasingly working to weed out or suppress misinformation, but they have their own imperatives – sensationalistic information is a drug that keeps us coming back for more. Your virtual agent could do the job for you, motivated exclusively by a desire to protect you from lies. Today it's becoming ever easier to doctor media in a way that puts fake words in the mouth of major politicians.[457] Your agent could analyse audio, pictures and videos for you, to warn you if it detects signs of deliberate manipulation that might be imperceptible to all but the best-trained human eye. It could even be used to filter out online abuse in a fine-grained way that takes account of your immediate instructions. Perhaps you're only in the mood for upbeat interactions; perhaps you're up for a fight. Your agent could show you what you'd prefer to see, obviating the need to rely on some external platform's one-size-fits-all filtering mechanisms.

All this comes down to trust. If, in an interaction between you and another party, a virtual assistant works for you rather than the other party, you have much more reason to trust it. However, that means you need to know you can trust it and, for that reason, this sort of agent would have to be open-source. It must be possible to inspect its code, to check that it hasn't been tampered with. The clearest analogy here is that of encryption algorithms. Security experts do not trust encryption algorithms that aren't open source, because they can't see how they work, so they can't be sure that there isn't something hidden in there that subverts or otherwise undermines the algorithm's integrity. Trusted agents would need to be auditable and verifiable, either by certified bodies or perhaps even by other agents. There would also need to be a regulatory element to this scenario. For one thing, an organisation dealing with citizens and consumers would have to be legally obliged to accept their agents as their representatives. It would also make sense to outlaw the subversion of people's agents.

457

http://www.npr.org/sections/alltechconsidered/2017/07/14/537154304/computer-scientists-demonstrate-the-potential-for-faking-video

There are a lot of details missing from this picture, and a lot of technological development would be required to make the model work. But the core elements are here today, and they're going to be used one way or another. Why not use them to help fix the future?

Laying Down the Law

As for the more immediate future, here are a few things for policymakers to consider.

-   **Data control and ownership** is fundamental to ensuring balance in the online layer. Online, we are our data. It represents us. Therefore, our data needs to be protected and we need to retain control over it. The EU's General Data Protection Regulation isn't perfect, but it's currently the best law of its kind, and other countries would do well to take inspiration from it (indeed, they have to provide equivalent protections in their own laws if they want to maintain a free, legal flow of data between their companies and users in the EU). This means making sure that nobody processes people's personal data without their consent (outside of special circumstances), that people can take their data with them between rival services, and that people can tell service providers to delete their data (unless there's a public interest in denying the request). Personal data must be securely stored and, if there's a breach, the people who are affected need to be told about it. People also have to be able to resist being profiled against their will. Personal data should be anonymised or pseudonymised wherever possible, to reduce the risks to people. Privacy needs to be built into technological products and services from the very start, not tacked on as an afterthought. And all this needs to be backed up with the threat of serious fines, otherwise companies won't have any incentive to comply. At a municipal level, the development of "smart cities", festooned with sensors that track everything in order to improve city management and the allocation of resources, need to be designed in a way that leaves citizens in control of their data.

-        **Mass surveillance** is almost always unacceptable, with the only exceptions being temporary states of emergency. The key here is proportionality: mass surveillance is so damaging to our human rights, so chilling to our natural curiosity and sociability, and so corrosive of our trust in the world around us, that it cannot be the norm. It has no place in democratic societies. And we must be honest about what constitutes mass surveillance. It's not just something that happens when people are being actively watched all the time, either offline or online. If everyone's activities are being recorded so that investigators could retrospectively peruse them later – the phenomenon generally known as data retention – then that's also mass surveillance. Yes, mass surveillance may provide authorities with an easier route to targeted surveillance, by telling them who merits closer examination. But it's impossible to deploy without infringing on people's fundamental rights to privacy and free association. It's also just plain dangerous. Even if mass surveillance is rolled out by a government with the best intentions, the next government may have bad intentions, and the abuse of these tools may be too tempting for it to resist.

-        **Undermining security** is a betrayal of the citizens who rely on good security to keep them safe throughout their day-to-day lives. If state authorities deliberately hobble the security of communications services or the encryption algorithms that enable safe online banking and shopping, or if they find out about serious security flaws and don't try to help fix them, they are exposing their populace to criminals who are already getting increasingly powerful as more and more things get connected to the internet. Technological advances such as the internet of things have the potential to improve our lives, but not if we can't trust them. We rely on our authorities to help keep our environments trustworthy.

-        **Regulating expression on online platforms** is not necessarily objectionable in principle. It makes no sense to have diverging sets of rules for the online and offline layers of the same reality. If the law forbids someone from harassing someone on the street, it should stop them doing the same over social media. If it doesn't allow people to wave around Nazi symbols on physical paper, it stands to reason that

225

the same would apply in the realm of pixels. However, lawmakers and regulators have to accept that the nature of social media makes it very easy for people to express themselves, and that the mechanisms for stopping them can too easily be disproportionately heavy-handed. It is unfeasibly expensive to employ the numbers of human content moderators that are needed to handle platforms of the scale of Facebook or Twitter, so these companies are much more likely to try automated solutions. But algorithms are not yet good at determining context or truth, and there is a strong risk of them censoring content that should stay up because it's not actually illegal. There's also the added risk of censorship laws in democratic countries giving less democratic governments an excuse to follow suit, with fewer safeguards. Ultimately, it may make more sense to ease up censorship laws than to try and apply them in an online environment where they do more harm than good.

-    **Countries need to start talking to one another** about their online rules, particularly where those rules have a cross-border impact. It's not acceptable that we're heading towards a situation where multiple censorship regimes overlap and infringe on people's rights to see information that's perfectly legal where they're sitting. Again, this is a result of the internet's intrinsic nature making it hard to effectively enforce the law without getting disproportionately heavy-handed. Countries should not be trying to foist their national laws and norms on the citizens of other countries, even if that's the only way to perfectly enforce those laws and norms. If perfect enforcement goes too far and regulators can't live with imperfect enforcement, then they need to consider changing their rules.

-    **Where new business models are threatening older businesses**, the goal has to be to create balanced regulations that don't favour one set of interests over the other. Our technological upheavals are shaking up old orders, but that shouldn't lead regulators to try halting or turning back progress. When a company like Uber steamrolls into a market, it shouldn't be allowed to shirk the regulations that more traditional taxi companies need to stick to, but at the same time it shouldn't be shut down with absurd rules that, for example, make it

226

illegal to coordinate a transport service with apps. What's needed are new regulations that allow everyone to compete fairly. When media companies are losing advertising money to Google, the answer isn't to stop Google from providing an index for news articles. That's counterproductive and certainly not in the interests of news consumers. Instead, because the news industry is valuable to democratic societies, regulators should do everything in their power to help media organisations establish sustainable business models for the future.

-    **Competition regulators need to improve their methods** to deal with the monopolistic tendencies of online business. For one thing, they need to speed up their investigations to ensure that the solutions they come up with aren't already out of date by the time they try to enforce them. This may mean they need to be better funded, but technological development moves at speed, and it's essential that those trying to protect consumers and businesses can do the same. Antitrust authorities also need to start expanding the things they take into account when looking for illegal behaviour. In particular, they need to act on the way online monopolies hoard data and use it to disadvantage their rivals.

-    **People need to have the same rights with virtual goods** that they have with physical goods. Yes, new subscription models are popping up all over the place that fundamentally change the nature of consumption, but while it's still possible for people to pay money to download and keep a copy of a movie or game or e-book, in a way that's effectively the same as buying a physical copy, then they need to have the same rights. That means they need to be able to give or sell that item to somebody else, or leave it to their heirs. People also need to be able to tinker with the things they buy, regardless of whether they're purely physical or purely software-based, or some hybrid of the two. We've always had that right in the pre-digital world, and we need to be able to maintain it into the future. It's good for technical education and progress, and it allows us to maintain control of our possessions even if the company that sold them to us goes bust.

-    **Encourage innovation** wherever it arises, while constantly thinking about the consequences and how to manage them. Many

227

problems can't be solved by regulatory means alone, chief among them being the evolution of new business models for old, troubled industries. For example, journalists and artists are in trouble, and perhaps there needs to be a temporary role for artificial support – subsidies of some kind, as long as they're not used as leverage for favouring certain voices over others. But someone will come along with new business models that could help carry these vital industries into the future, as viable ongoing concerns. Lawmakers and regulators need to be ready to support those innovators in whatever way they can.

Building for Good

Which brings us to the innovators themselves.

- **Technologists have great power that may provide short-term gains** when abused. However, that's not a good long-term strategy. We're still in the relatively early days of the connected world, and there are still lots of people out there who remained dazzled by the novelty of new apps and services. It's still easy to sucker them into giving up too much data. Indeed, the industry's venture capital funding model encourages this, with over-collected data being many startups' biggest asset come sale time. But if this continues unabated, people's trust in technology will diminish. That could result in less or lower-quality data, as people either avoid signing up to new services, use them more sparingly, or deliberately seed them with false information in order to protect themselves. In the long term, it would hinder the growth of the tech industry, which means fewer tech jobs.

- **Regulation is coming**, whether tech firms like it or not, and the smart approach is to stay ahead of it. That means figuring out what regulators are trying to achieve, and making sure that business models aren't dependent on tactics that are likely to be banned. Again, there might be short-term gains to be had in exploiting what you can before the regulators catch up, but their methods will improve, particularly as public opinion gets behind them. As it increasingly will.

- **Technologists are citizens too**, so, given the immense potential for dystopia that lies just over the horizon, there should be every incentive for them to push back. Indeed, few groups of people are better qualified to try steering us all towards a brighter, more balanced future. That may mean working on more decentralised alternatives to today's platforms, both on a nuts-and-bolts level and in dreaming up the business models that could make these platforms fly. It may mean lobbying against state attempts to co-opt our increasingly powerful technologies. It may mean coming up with new tools with which ordinary people can protect themselves and each other in the online environment. And while we're on the subject of protection...

- **Stop connecting everything to the internet** for no good reason, unless you can absolutely ensure that it will remain safe from hackers and those launching cyberattacks. The vulnerability of our data is a big deal, but it pales in comparison with the dangers posed by connected but poorly secured cars, home automation systems and other things that can be hijacked to spy on, maim or kill us. No company wants to be the one that let that happen.

- **Be aware that widely-used information services** can and will be abused by forces who want to spread falsehoods and divide people. Even if countering these efforts runs against the services' general ethos of showing people what they want to see, it must be done for the good of society, and it must be done in a transparent way.

Up To You

Finally, and perhaps most importantly, we come to the majority of us who are neither technologists nor lawmakers. Here's a short list of things you can do right now, to fight back against those who want to take power away from you:

- **Always consider the implications** of those gadgets you're connecting to the internet, and the personal information you're feeding into those apps. Is there a good reason, apart from novelty, for doing so? Can you get the data out again? Do you know where it will be shared around? Do you know when the camera and microphone are on? What promises are the companies behind these goods and services making, and what questions are they leaving unanswered? If their customers don't ask these questions, companies have little incentive to pay much attention to their fundamental rights.

-    **Demand security** from anyone who's taking your money or making money off your data. We're used to our computers getting regular security updates to keep us safe, but the same can't be said for many smartphones, tablets and other new kinds of internet-connected device. Remember that attackers have really good motivations to keep looking for exploitable flaws. If the companies selling connected devices don't offer regular updates, strongly consider an upgrade or a switch to a rival device. Receiving security updates for the core operating system is more important than installing antivirus software, which may in itself be insecure. Android phones are particularly problematic in this regard, because the companies selling them typically only issue security updates for two years at most before leaving them exposed to criminals, and even then they tend not to issue updates very frequently. Apple is much better, updating its iPhones and iPads until they can't take it anymore due to the age of the hardware. However, there are certain Android manufacturers that promise to keep their phones up-to-date, including Nokia and Google itself.

-    **Consider your "threat model"**, which is security-speak for working out who might be after you, and taking suitable countermeasures. Very few of us are likely to be targeted by state intelligence agencies, for example, but we all might fall into the sights of criminals. Apart from creating a need for regular security updates, this means you should use encrypted communications wherever possible, back up your data so it can't be held hostage by ransomware attacks, and remember to shut down your accounts with services you no longer use. You should encrypt your phones and hard drives, where possible. When you buy connected gadgets for the home, such as security cameras or even smart lighting systems, you should always change the default password to something else. You must also avoid using the same passwords across different services, because at some point some of those services will be hacked and the passwords may be stolen. The best idea is to use a password manager, which stores your passwords for various services and even generates new random passwords to help you change them every so often. Ideally, you should use a password manager that only saves your passwords on your own devices, rather than in the "cloud". When a service gives you the option of requiring a unique code from your phone to log in, alongside your password, then take it (this is called two-factor authentication). If, on the other hand, you do think you're likely to be targeted by spies or highly motivated criminals, who are perhaps after corporate secrets, then you need to step up to more serious methods. These might include using different phones or computers to access different accounts, cultivating pseudonyms and doing all your web browsing through obfuscating services such as Tor.

- **Consider other people's privacy** as well as your own. So much of what we do online affects other people. When we download an app and let it upload our address book so it can more easily link us with other users who we know, we're giving the app provider all our contacts' details, without asking their permission first. When we post photos to Facebook that include other people, we're submitting those people's faces to the social network's facial recognition systems. Doing this without permission means denying other people their chance to choose where on the privacy scale they'd prefer to be. If you have a friend who's trying to avoid a stalker, for example, you might be exposing them to risk by putting their information online.

- **Obfuscate** wherever you can, unless you actively want to share your accurate personal data with others. Your privacy is under attack by services that don't respect it and that want to exploit you. For example, internet service providers in the US are free to monitor what people do over their networks and sell that profiling information to advertisers. It's perfectly reasonable to take countermeasures, for example by using a virtual private network (VPN) or a service like Tor to hide what you're doing from your broadband provider. When a registration process asks you for personal information such as your name or birthday, think about whether you really need to give it these details. Perhaps a false name or birthdate would suffice.

- **Support pro-privacy services, and stop supporting those that don't support you.** This one is easier said than done. Google and Facebook are very difficult to avoid, and it's unlikely that market pressure will force them to improve their privacy practices anytime soon – if anyone's going to achieve that, it will probably be regulators. That said, new services do keep appearing that provide much of the same functionality. For example, there's a privacy-friendly search engine called DuckDuckGo that doesn't collect or store your search history. It's not quite as useful as Google Search, in that it isn't integrated with video and shopping and mapping services, but it does the job in most circumstances. And where it doesn't, there's nothing stopping you from visiting Google. Is there a viable alternative to Facebook right now? Sadly not. But if one comes along, be ready to give it the support it will need to thrive.

- **Demand more from your elected representatives**, and keep an eye out for every opportunity to do so. Some of technology's power-related problems may have political or regulatory answers. This certainly applies to issues such as surveillance, digital property rights and the economic effects of automation. These are societal problems, and that's what politicians are there to solve. In many cases, the answers will not be easy to find, nor to sell to a population that's fearful of change. If your elected representative isn't at least thinking about these issues, tell them to start doing so. These are the sorts of debates that will shape our societies – and soon, not in some distant future. The time to be having them is now.

ACKNOWLEDGEMENTS

There are a number of people without whom the writing of this book would not have been possible. Some are the thinkers you'll find cited throughout the book – I hope I have relayed their ideas accurately and well as I wove them into this guide.

But there are others who have been utterly invaluable in their direct assistance, support, feedback and guidance. So, in purely alphabetical order, I am eternally grateful to: Helen Mary Anderson Durowoju, Rupert Goodwins, Doreen Homann, Matthias Jugel, Megan Kerr, Matthäus Krzykowski, Gaby Meyer, Jonathan Mills, Jonathan Pegg, Miriam Shiell, Scot Stevenson and Ben Wagner.

INDEX

www.ingramcontent.com/pod-product-compliance
Lightning Source LLC
LaVergne TN
LVHW042332060326
832902LV00006B/127